APEC
AND LIBERALISATION
OF THE
CHINESE ECONOMY

APEC AND LIBERALISATION OF THE CHINESE ECONOMY

Peter Drysdale, Zhang Yunling
and Ligang Song (Editors)

Asia Pacific Press
at the Australian National University

© Australia–Japan Research Centre 2000
This work is copyright. Apart from those uses which may be permitted under the Copyright Act 1968 as amended, no part may be reproduced by any process without written permission from the publisher.

National Library of Australia Cataloguing-in-Publication entry

APEC and liberalisation of the Chinese economy.

Bibliography.
Includes index.
ISBN 0 7315 3641 X.

1. Asia Pacific Economic Cooperation (Organization). 2. Free trade - China. 3. Tariff - China. 4. International trade. 5. China - Economic policy - 1976- . 6. China - Commercial policy. 7. China - Economic conditions - 1976- . I. Drysdale, Peter. II. Song, Ligang. III. Zhang, Yunling. IV. Australian National University. Asia Pacific School of Economics and Management.

382.951

Published by Asia Pacific Press at the Australian National University
http://www.asiapacificpress.com

Editor: Julia Minty
Pagesetting: Debra Grogan and Julia Minty
Cover design: Annie Di Nallo Design
Cover photograph of APEC leaders by David Scull, AFP/AAP Image. Reprinted with permission.
Cover photograph of President Bill Clinton and President Jiang Zemin by Greg Baker, AP/AAP. Reprinted with permission.
Printed in Australia by Paragon Printers, Canberra

CONTENTS

TABLES

FIGURES

ABBREVIATIONS

ABAC	APEC Business Advisory Council
ADB	Asian Development Bank
AFTA	ASEAN Free Trade Area
AIMS	APEC Impediments Management System
AMF	Asian Monetary Fund
APEC	Asia Pacific Economic Cooperation
ARF	ASEAN Regional Forum
ASEAN	Association of South East Asian Nations
ASEM	Asia–Europe Meeting
ASPAC	Asia and Pacific Council
AusAID	Australian Agency for International Development
BOT	build–operate–transfer
CAP	Collective Action Plan
CIF	Cost including freight
CCP	Chinese Communist Party
CIA	Central Intelligence Agency
CITIC	China International Trust and Investment Corporation
CNOOC	China National Offshore Oil Corporation
CSCAP	Council on Security Cooperation in Asia Pacific
CTI	Committee for Trade and Investment
EAEC	East Asian Economic Caucus
EAFTZ	East Asian Free Trade Zone
EAMF	East Asian Monetary Fund
EC	European Community
ecotech	economic and technical cooperation
EEC	European Economic Community
EPA	Economic Planning Agency
ESC	Sub-committee on Economic and Technical Cooperation
EU	European Union

EVSL	Early Voluntary Sectoral Liberalisation
FDC	Foundation for Development Cooperation
FDI	foreign direct investment
FFE	foreign funded enterprise
GATT	General Agreement on Tariffs and Trade
GDP	gross domestic product
GNP	gross national product
HRD	human resource development
IAP	Individual Action Plan
IMF	International Monetary Fund
IST	Industrial Science and Technology
ITA	Information Technology Agreement
JDA	Japan Defence Agency
JETRO	Japan External Trade Organisation
JEXIM	The Export–Import Bank of Japan
JNOC	Japan National Oil Corporation
JSDF	Japanese Self Defence Force
KEDO	Korean Peninsula Energy Development Organisation
LDP	Liberal Democratic Party
LTTA	Long Term Trade Agreement
MAPA	Manila Action Plan for APEC
MCEDSEA	Ministerial Conference on Economic Development in Southeast Asia
MFA	Multifibre Arrangement
MFN	most-favoured nation
MITI	Ministry of International Trade and Industry
MOFTEC	Ministry of Foreign Trade and Economic Cooperation of China
NAFTA	North American Free Trade Agreement
NATO	North Atlantic Treaty Organisation
NGOs	Non-governmental organisations
NIE	newly industrialising economy
NPT	Non-proliferation Treaty
OAA	Osaka Action Agenda
ODA	Overseas Development Assistance
OECD	Organisation for Economic Cooperation and Development
OECF	Overseas Economic Cooperation Fund
PAFTAD	Pacific Trade and Development Conference
PBEC	Pacific Basin Economic Council
PECC	Pacific Economic Cooperation Council
PEG	Partnership for Equitable Growth
PFP	'Partners for Progress'
PLA	People's Liberation Army

PMV	passenger motor vehicle
PRC	People's Republic of China
R&D	research and development
RCA	revealed comparative advantage
RFE	Russian Far East
RMB	renminbi
ROC	Republic of China
SDF	Self Defence Force
SEATO	Southeast Asia Treaty Organisation
SEZ	Special Economic Zone
Sinopec	China Petrochemical Corporation
SITC	Standard International Trade Classification
SLOC	sea lines of communication
SME	small and medium enterprises
SOE	state-owned enterprise
SOM	APEC Senior Officials Meetings
SSB	State Statistical Bureau
TC	trade competitiveness index
TCF	textile, clothing and footwear
TILF	trade and investment liberalisation and facilitation
TMD	theatre missile defence
UK	United Kingdom
UN	United Nations
UNIDO	United Nations Industrial Development Organisation
UR	Uruguay Round
US	United States
USSR	Union of Soviet Socialist Republics
WTO	World Trade Organization

SYMBOLS

.. not available

na not applicable

- zero

CONTRIBUTORS

Chen Luzhi served as Deputy Director and Director of the UN Secretariat in New York, Ambassador to Denmark and Iceland, and as Executive Vice-Chairman of the China National Committee for Pacific Economic Cooperation. He has also served as an adviser to the Foreign Affairs Committee of China National People's Congress and as a member of China National People's Consultative Conference.

Chen Chunlai is with the Chinese Economics Research Centre in the School of Economics at the University of Adelaide.

Peter Drysdale is Professor of Economics and Executive Director of the Australia–Japan Research Centre (AJRC) in the Asia Pacific School of Economics and Management at the Australian National University. He is responsible for an Australia-wide research program on economic relations with Japan and the Asia Pacific, involving research cooperation with economists in economies throughout the Asia Pacific region.

Andrew Elek is a Research Associate at the Australia–Japan Research Centre in the Asia Pacific School of Economics and Management at the Australian National University. He was formerly in Australia's Department of Foreign Affairs and Trade, responsible for APEC, and with the World Bank in Washington, DC.

Christopher Findlay is one of the region's leading experts on international trade, Chinese economic reform, Asia Pacific economy and regional economic cooperation. He is Professor of Economics in the Asia Pacific School of Economics and Management at the Australian National University and Director of Graduate Studies in Infrastructure Management in the National Centre for Development Studies.

Ross Garnaut was Australian Ambassador to the People's Republic of China (1985–88) and principal economic adviser to Australian Prime Minister R.J.L. Hawke (1983–85). He is Professor of Economics in the Economics Division, Research School of Pacific and Asian Studies of the Australian National University.

Yiping Huang is a Fellow in Economics and has been Director of the China Economy Program at the Australian National University. He was formerly a Policy Analyst with the then Research Center for Rural Development of the State Council in Beijing.

Kali Kalirajan is a Senior Fellow in the Australia South Asia Research Centre, Asia Pacific School of Economics and Management at the Australian National University.

Li Kai is Deputy Director General and Senior Economist with the China Economic Information Network, State Information Center, Beijing.

Hadi Soesastro is Executive Director of the Centre for Strategic and International Studies in Jakarta and an Adjunct Professor at the Australian National University. He has been a member of APEC's Eminent Persons Group. Since November 1999 he has been a Member of the National Economic Council of the Republic of Indonesia.

Ligang Song is Director of the China Economy and Business Program and a Fellow at the Australia–Japan Research Centre in Asia Pacific School of Economics and Management and the Research School of Pacific and Asian Studies at the Australian National University.

Sun Xuegong is a Senior Fellow with the Institute of Economics, State Planning Commission, Beijing.

Yongzheng Yang is a Senior Lecturer at the National Centre for Development Studies in the Asia Pacific School of Economics and Management at the Australian National University.

Zhang Jianjun has served in the Chinese Ministry of Foreign Affairs as Chairman of the Committee on Projects of International Jute Organisation (IJO) and as Director of the APEC and ASEM Division of DITEA. He is now a Senior Associate at PriceWaterhouseCoopers in the United Kingdom.

Zhang Yunling, Professor of International Economics, is Director of the Institute of Asia Pacific Studies, and Director of the APEC Policy Research Center at the Chinese Academy of Social Science (CASS), Beijing. He has also served as Chairman of the Department of Asia Pacific Studies, Graduate School, CASS, Executive Vice President, Chinese Association of Asia Pacific Studies, and as a member of the China Standing Committee for the Pacific Economic Cooperation Council (PECC), CSCAP and member of the Panel of Independent Experts for APEC. The State Council of China honoured him as a national outstanding expert in 1992.

Zhao Jianglin is a Research Fellow with the Institute of Asia Pacific Studies and APEC Policy Research Centre, Chinese Academy of Social Sciences, Beijing.

Zhou Xiaobing is a Senior Research Fellow with the Institute of Asia Pacific Studies and APEC Policy Research Centre, Chinese Academy of Social Sciences, Beijing.

NA

PREFACE

In 2001 China will host the APEC Summit and Ministerial Meetings in Shanghai. APEC has become an important forum through which China has been able to demonstrate its willingness and commitment to integration into the international economy since it joined in 1991. APEC has been all the more important to China because it is not yet a member of the WTO or the OECD. APEC's regional base and global objectives closely match China's strategic interests in the international economy. The meetings in Shanghai will provide an opportunity for China to entrench and extend these interests through APEC.

This book assembles papers that were produced under a three year collaborative research program on 'China and APEC' undertaken by the Australia–Japan Research Centre, in the Asia Pacific School of Economics and Management at The Australian National University and the APEC Policy Research Center, in the Chinese Academy of Social Sciences. The project was funded under the Australian government's aid agency, AusAID's, Australia–China Institutional Links Project. We are grateful to AusAID for support of this work.

We are also grateful to the authors of the papers included in this collection for their cooperation in putting the volume together and especially to Maree Tait, Julia Minty, Debra Grogan, Jacky Lipsham and Annie Di Nallo at Asia Pacific Press for efficient assistance in its timely production.

The work on this project and the papers in the volume provide a base for developing ideas that could be helpful to the policy agenda for APEC 2001. More importantly they build on the strong foundations of cooperation that have been laid over the last twenty years between The Australian National University and the Chinese Academy of Social Sciences in working together on these issues.

Peter Drysdale, Zhang Yunling and Ligang Song
Canberra and Beijing, April 2000

Introduction

CHINA'S INTERESTS IN APEC

ROSS GARNAUT, LIGANG SONG AND PETER DRYSDALE

China's integration into the international economy since 1978 has presented an immense challenge for domestic and international economic policy, both in China and in its trading partners. China is so large that its trading interests and influence are global. But its interests and influence are disproportionately powerful in its immediate Western Pacific and Asia Pacific neighbourhoods. The evolution of China's economic relationships with its Asia Pacific partners, in which APEC came to play a significant role in the 1990s, is thus a central part of the story of China's rapidly growing and changing interaction with the global economy.

China's economic strategy and pattern of economic development was inward looking and isolated from the new currents of internationally-oriented growth that began to reshape the East Asian economies in the 1950s and 1960s. Sustained, internationally-oriented growth in Japan, Hong Kong, Singapore, Taiwan and Korea, and its beginnings in several of the ASEAN countries, was at first unconnected to Maoist China's emphasis on 'self-reliance', focus on capital-intensive development, and perception of foreign trade as an occasionally unfortunate necessity. The success of its East Asian neighbours and China's leaders' recognition of the adverse long-term strategic implications of economic under-performance were important influences on China's initially tentative steps towards greater contact with the international economy through the 1970s.

From the time of the Chinese Communist Party's commitment to reform and opening to the outside world in December 1978, the international orientation of Chinese economic strategy and policy was unequivocal. Expanding foreign trade was an integral part of development strategy. Loans from OECD governments and capital markets, development assistance from OECD governments and direct foreign investments from and into the OECD economies were allowed, and grew rapidly. Growth in output, trade and foreign investment was on average stronger than in any other substantial economy, with China emerging by the late 1990s as by far the world's largest trading economy and recipient of direct foreign investment amongst developing economies.

There was no blueprint for the new economic policy from 1978. Internationally-oriented reform became a practical matter of observing what others were doing, experimenting with reform within China, and quickly deepening and widening the application of reforms that contributed positively to Chinese development. Interaction with Asia Pacific neighbours, especially in the Pacific Economic Cooperation Council (PECC) from the mid-1980s and APEC from the early 1990s, became an influential source of ideas, examples, and encouragement to political commitment.

There were always doubts about the open strategies in China. These had mainly ideological origins at first, as the strategy of internationally-oriented growth relying heavily on markets, associated with senior leader Deng Xiaoping, struggled with older Maoist commitments to self reliance. The success of the new policies in delivering economic growth, rising living standards and international *gravitas* became the decisive influences in the contest of ideologies.

By the early 1990s, the doubts about and resistances to China's deepening integration into the international economy were no longer mainly ideological, and were more familiar to people from other places, including the advanced capitalist economies of the West. There were familiar anxieties about the effects of structural change on employment and income distribution, and about the reliability of access to international markets.

China's size made the latter concerns acute. The internationalisation of the Chinese economy might be expected eventually to force larger structural change in the rest of the world than had been the case with Japanese growth in the 1960s or the newly industrialising economies in the 1970s and 1980s, and these developments had prompted important protectionist responses in the United States and Europe. Would not the reactions to China's internationally-oriented growth be even larger and more damaging, leaving China vulnerable to the political decisions of other countries? Concerns along these lines were reinforced by the increasing overlay of concerns about China's increasing strategic weight in American discussion of trade policy through the 1990s.

China's participation in the discussion of Asia Pacific economic cooperation was therefore a source of ideas and reassurance on policy, of practical examples of its implementation, and potentially of insurance against damage from foreign political responses to the expansion of China's economic relations with the rest of the world. The higher echelons of the Chinese political system focused on the emerging discussion of Asia Pacific economic cooperation through the academic exchanges between the Australian National University and the Chinese Academy of Social Sciences from 1979. China, with Chinese Taipei, was invited to the plenary session of the first PECC (then Pacific Community) conference at the Australian National University in 1980. China became a full member of the PECC in 1986 under a formula that allowed full membership by Taiwan as Chinese Taipei. Australian and Chinese officials were engaged in discussion of Chinese participation in the first APEC meeting when the declaration of martial law on 19 May, 1989 and the tragedy of 4 June, disrupted China's official relations with the international community. A formula within which APEC officials met as economies and not countries allowed full membership by China and Chinese Taipei from 1991, in time for China's participation in APEC leaders' meetings from their inauguration in 1993.

China's participation in APEC since 1991 has proceeded against a backdrop of continual effort to enter the General Agreement on Tariffs and Trade (GATT) and the World Trade Organization (WTO). APEC has been supportive of these efforts, and in the meantime has provided an alternative avenue for some aspects of China's official interaction with major trade partners on international economic issues.

China's President Jiang Zemin participated in the 1994 Bogor APEC leaders' meeting, which generated the understanding on free and open trade and investment by 2010 (for developed countries) and 2020 (for developing economies). In 1995 (in Osaka) and 1996 (in Manila), China chose the APEC meetings for announcement of major new steps in trade and investment liberalisation, towards China's commitments in the Bogor Declaration. While the APEC commitments to free and open trade and investment were not a central focus of Chinese domestic discussion of trade liberalisation, they were taken seriously and respected. The APEC meetings, with their requirement of unilateral rather than reciprocal commitments, and their multilateral context, made it politically more palatable for the Chinese government to be able to announce liberalising steps, without domestic criticism for conceding to American power and bilateral pressure. The consistent support within APEC for deeper Chinese integration into the international economy, including through membership of the GATT/WTO, was helpful to Chinese leaders fighting domestic reaction to setbacks on entry into the WTO and recurring tension in relations with the United States. China shared in the general advantage to the Asia Pacific region of APEC discussions on the importance of resisting protectionist pressures to recovery from the Asian financial crisis.

Any really important policy development in a large country has many and complex causes. The extension and success of internationally-oriented policies in China through the 1990s also had many and complex causes. Would it have worked at all without APEC? Would it have worked as well?

All we can really say is that APEC provided helpful and significant support for reform and opening to the outside world. The subsequent chapters of this book explain in detail some of the ways in which APEC provided this support.

In Indonesia and the Philippines, at least, APEC was of greatest value to domestic policy reform in the years in which they hosted Leaders' meetings. They had the advantage of hosting APEC summits at times of rapid output, trade and investment expansion, and optimism about the future. Now in mid-

2000, it seems likely that China will enjoy favourable circumstances and opportunity when it hosts the 2001 APEC leaders' meeting in Shanghai. The careful contributions to this book will be helpful to defining China's and the world's continuing interests in APEC, and therefore in defining the 2001 opportunity.

In Chapter 1, Zhang Yunling reviews China's liberalisation program in the context of APEC and WTO, two important international vehicles for carrying the trade reform and liberalisation program forward. China's progress with economic liberalisation after embarking on reform in the late 1970s, sets the context for China's commitment to the APEC process. For China, APEC has the great virtue of flexibility in timing the implementation of liberalisation. Flexibility suits China's gradual approach to reform, liberalisation and the transition to an open market system. China's Individual Action Plan (IAP) provides the guideline for China's commitment to APEC trade and investment liberalisation. However, Zhang notes, the pressure for standardisation and revision of IAPs in APEC is intensifying because of the need to make their implementation more effective and comparable.

On the relationship between APEC and WTO, Zhang Yunling argues that China's agenda in APEC has been closely related to its agenda on accession to the WTO. China's strategy has been to press its claims for accession to the WTO through its commitment to liberalisation in APEC and, at the same time, to keep pace with APEC's 'WTO plus' initiatives even though China is not yet a member of the WTO. As he points out, the lengthy negotiations and pressure from contracting parties have in fact sped up the pace of liberalisation of the Chinese economy.

Peter Drysdale deals with the strategic relationship between the principle of open regionalism, APEC and China's international trade strategies in Chapter 2. He argues that the idea of open regionalism is deeply rooted in the history of the evolution of APEC based on an understanding among many East Asian economies of their stake in the strength and continuity of an open trading system. Such understanding is at the core of three key issues facing the regional economies. First, the trading interests of East Asian and Pacific economies extend beyond APEC. Second, trade discrimination involves the unnecessary cost of trade diversion, complicated in the Asia Pacific region by the likelihood of high associated political costs both within and outside the region. Third, there is the sheer impracticability of undertaking regional trade liberalisation via a conventional discriminatory free trade area of the kind sanctioned by the WTO in such a diverse region.

On the implications of participation in APEC and accession to the WTO, Drysdale argues that such international commitments underwrite China's credibility in respect of the continuity and reliability of policy behaviour. These international commitments serve to limit opportunistic behaviour and to reduce the likelihood of distortionary interventions in trade and other international transactions both by China and by China's trading partners. Equally important, they bind policy and the evolution of policy in a way that affects the behaviour of domestic and foreign firms operating in China.

Drysdale highlights the importance of linking China's trade liberalisation to its domestic reform program. He observes that China's trade policy strategy is inextricably linked with other aspects of reform, such as the management of the state enterprise sector and financial market reform and macroeconomic policy reform. He argues that policy leaders, both inside and outside China, have a very substantial interest in forcing the pace of change. Accession to the WTO would entrench these reforms and help to maintain their momentum and APEC has been a critical vehicle through which China could re-position and maintain the momentum of its claim to WTO membership.

Drysdale also identifies conflicting paradigms across the Pacific in the approach to open regionalism, resolving the 'free rider' problem and dealing with 'sensitive sectors'. He concludes that APEC provides a useful vehicle for active and continuing trade and investment liberalisation by China and among the Asia Pacific economies..

In Chapter 3, Zhang Jianjun provides a critical review of the functions of APEC. He argues that APEC has developed a number of unique features and decision-making processes that differentiate it from other international or regional forums, such as its non-formal processes, the diversity of member countries, emphasis on consensus and concerted unilateralism and top-down direction. These features have allowed APEC to make remarkable progress through both voluntary and unilateral actions as well as collective initiatives on trade and investment liberalisation and facilitation. Member countries have lowered their average tariff levels by almost half. Greater transparency on non-tariff measures has been enhanced through identification and removal exercises. Member countries have voluntarily included investment liberalisation in their IAPs. Progress has been made in liberalising service sectors, establishing customs procedures and dispute mediation, formulating competition policy, and protecting intellectual property rights.

Zhang also notes the weaknesses in APEC: its inability to deal with the regional economic crisis; lack of effective mechanisms for implementing policies; lack of tangible outcomes from its policy initiatives including economic and technical cooperation (ecotech) and the early voluntary sectoral liberalisation (EVSL) initiative and lack of focus. Despite these problems, China has taken a positive stand on APEC's trade and investment agenda, recognising its role in managing the trends of globalisation and an open international trading environment. While China is unlikely to obtain from APEC badly needed capital, technology and managerial skills, APEC can act as an important information source for China, a platform for policy discussion and a stimulant in pursuing more liberal international trade and investment policies.

Zhang argues that, to cope with changing circumstances, APEC must further consolidate its position on trade and investment, develop a more effective implementation mechanism, and find better ways to carry out its ecotech agenda. Its leaders should act together to produce more focused and results-oriented outcomes. He also argues that APEC should work more closely with the business community and broaden its outreach to involve a wider segment of the business sector. He believes that these are crucial elements in ensuring healthy and sustainable development from APEC's endeavours.

Christopher Findlay and Chen Chunlai discuss Australia's APEC agenda and its implications for Australia and China in Chapter 4. The discussion of Australia's APEC agenda centres on the main features of the IAP for Australia and its implications for the reduction of Australian tariffs. It also includes Australia's proposal for the EVSL and its implications for trade between China and Australia. The discussion underlines the role of government in reducing the costs of doing business between Australia and China. They point out that the commitments on tariff reductions by the Australian government extend so far only to the year 2005, rather than 2010, the target date for developed countries' liberalisation under the Bogor goals. There are exceptions in some sensitive sectors such as passenger motor vehicles (PMV) and textiles, clothing and footwear (TCF). In addition, there are 'pauses' in the schedules of tariff reductions between 2000 and 2005. According to Findlay and Chen, these pauses and the manner in which were decided may make it difficult, in the process of reviewing tariffs beyond 2005, to commit to further schedules of reductions.

On the implications for Australia-China bilateral trade, Findlay and Chen show that the structure of remaining Australian protection is highly biased against China. The average tariff rate faced by Chinese exporters to Australia is much higher than that faced by exporters from other APEC members. Therefore, the tariff reductions scheduled by 2005 in Australia will create scope for gains from trade between the two countries. But a higher degree of integration would have occurred sooner if Australia had maintained its earlier commitments to continuous and steady reductions in tariffs—on TCF products in particular. Thus, APEC commitments may serve to constrain tariff rate setting in Australia and be useful in realising the potential for growth that still exists in the bilateral relationship between Australia and China. In particular, the bias they identify in Australian trade policy against China suggests the gains from liberalisation will be quite substantial.

In discussing the shared objectives in APEC and the international economic system, Andrew Elek points out in Chapter 5 that Asia Pacific economies cannot expect to realise their potential for development in isolation from the rest of the world. That is why APEC has consistently sought to promote global, not just regional, objectives by pursuing open regionalism. APEC also needs to ensure that new arrangements do not create new sources of discrimination, thereby fragmenting, rather than integrating regional markets.

Elek sets out a conceptual framework for development cooperation within APEC. He emphasises that economic and technical cooperation (ecotech) among APEC governments needs to be conducted on the basis of mutual respect, including respect for diversity, autonomy, mutual benefit, genuine partnership and consensus-building. Cooperative activities need to promote a working partnership with the private sector and the community in general, to ensure that cooperation is consistent with market principles and the efficient allocation of resources. He also proposes thinking ahead in the development of a strategy for global action to deal with 'sensitive sectors' which are less likely to be opened up through unilateral, voluntary decisions by individual governments.

Elek highlights several issues that need to be considered in designing cooperative arrangements among APEC economies. They include trade in goods and services, harmonising administrative procedures, mutual recognition of standards, technical cooperation, transparency and non-discrimination. He suggests that Australia and China might work together in promoting ways of addressing these issues.

In Chapter 6 Yongzheng Yang and Yiping Huang raise the question: How important is APEC to China? Using a global general equilibrium model, they evaluate the impact of APEC trade liberalisation on the Chinese economy. They find that under a scenario of comprehensive APEC trade liberalisation, there is a positive impact on China's real GDP growth. The large expansion of domestic production reflects the extent of trade distortion in China. Their results show that, measured in terms of equivalent variation, the welfare gain to China is not as significant as the increase in domestic production suggests mainly due to a substantial decline in China's terms of trade. However, they emphasise that the large efficiency gain from trade liberalisation more than compensates for the loss through the terms of trade effect. Further decomposition of the allocative efficiency gain indicates that a big expansion of imports is largely responsible for the higher efficiency, although export expansion also contributes significantly. They conclude that it is China's own liberalisation that is most important in enhancing Chinese welfare through the APEC process.

Their results reveal that if agriculture is excluded from APEC trade liberalisation, the increase in China's GDP is only slightly lower, but the overall welfare gain to China is reduced by nearly one-third. Furthermore, not only is the efficiency gain smaller, but the adverse terms of trade effect is larger. APEC trade liberalisation without agriculture is therefore a less desirable option for China than comprehensive trade liberalisation. They also find that welfare benefits to China from global trade liberalisation are larger than the gains from both APEC liberalisation and unilateral trade liberalisation. These findings support their view that APEC and the WTO are mutually re-enforcing in facilitating Chinese trade liberalisation. APEC prepares China for the WTO and WTO accession pushes China to be proactive in the APEC process. Both APEC and WTO accession propel China's domestic reform.

Sun Xuegong deals with the relationship between APEC investment and trade liberalisation and China's structural reforms in Chapter 7. The benefits and challenges from trade and investment liberalisation focus on three areas: reform of the state-owned enterprises (SOEs); rationalisation of industrial organistion; and reform of the grain sector. He argues that SOE reform has lagged behind trade liberalisation and has become an increasing impediment to further liberalisation. Synchronising SOE reform and trade liberalisation will lead to smoother and less costly adjustment. Thus, speeding up SOE reform rather than slowing the pace of liberalisation appears to be the logical solution.

Inefficiences in the structure of Chinese industrial organisation mean that, even in areas of fundamental comparative advantage, liberalisation will entail considerable adjustment costs. One solution is to exploit increasing returns to scale through the rationalisation and merger of domestic firms. Sun observes that some mergers have been taking place in China in recent years. To complement structural policies, he argues that China needs to improve its legal system and strengthen the enforcement of competition policy.

Sun points out that it is only a matter of time before China loses its comparative advantage in the grain market and that adjustment in this sector is inevitable. The prospect is that China will eventually liberalise its grain sector and integrate into the world grain market. There are several aspects associated with structural adjustment in this area. China's grain production is still likely to grow as the sector becomes more open to import competition as productivity improves. The pace of grain trade liberalisation will clearly depend on the preparedness of China's trading partners to open their markets to China's labour-intensive exports, including more labour-intensive agricultural products. And the food security issue will need to be settled before China takes dramatic steps to liberalise the grain sector.

The next two chapters deal with the liberalisation of three key sectors in the Chinese economy. In Chapter 8, Li Kai analyses the costs of protection in the automobile and textile industries. Li quantifies the protective effects of taxes and fees on automobile and textile products. Using these data, he calculates the costs of trade protection in both sectors and the impact of lower tariffs on the national economy.

Li concludes that reduction of the current nominal tariffs will not have a significant influence on the Chinese economy because of the gap between nominal tariffs and tariff rates that are actually applied. This situation gives the Chinese government room to push tariff reduction and ease non-tariff measures. High levels of protection have actually hindered the inflow of advanced technology and slowed the development of the domestic automobile industry. In the case of textiles, Li argues that low tariffs and the importance of the processing trade means that there is little real protection of the domestic textile industry. Thus the textile sector is an early candidate for early sectoral liberalisation.

Sun discusses the international competitiveness of China's chemical sector in Chapter 9. His estimates show that the chemical sector in China still has weak competitiveness due to high input costs. In some cases the price of chemical products is as much as twice the international market price. Furthermore, the quality, variety and grade of chemical products in China are inferior to those of other countries. Low labour productivity compared with Japan and the United States and the social burdens of SOEs offset the Chinese industry's advantage in cheap labour costs.

Given the industry's weak competitive position, China's participation in early sectoral liberalisation of the trade in chemical products would inevitably involve big adjustment shocks. Sun's regression results show that the most affected sectors of the industry are those whose products are highly substitutable with products from overseas. The early liberalisation of the chemical industry would also have repercussions on other sectors of the national economy with links to it. However, there are some factors which may recommend liberalisation for the industry. The chemical industry cannot satisfy domestic demand for chemical products and there is evidence that the competitive position of some parts of the domestic industry has strengthened following substantial tariff reductions. Sun concludes that China should continue trade liberalisation in accordance with its IAP commitments. Trade policy measures should be directed to the twin objectives of satisfying domestic demand and improving the competitiveness of China's chemical sector.

Andrew Elek and Hadi Soesastro argue in Chapter 10 that ecotech is at the heart of the APEC process. While trade and investment issues remain important, it has become evident that economic cooperation needs to be a central feature of the APEC agenda to nurture a sense of community among member economies. At the heart of the issue is capacity-building in the Asia Pacific region. To accomplish this goal, they advocate an integrated view of the APEC process within which all cooperative activities are seen as ways to strengthen the capacity of Asia Pacific economies in reaching their full potential for sustainable economic growth.

Their recommendations for implementing ecotech focus on strengthening the economic policy framework in member economies. Technical cooperation should focus on a small number of well-defined priorities and APEC governments should be encouraged to include commitments to promote technical cooperation programs endorsed by APEC leaders as a significant part of their IAPs.

Chen Luzhi presents a Chinese view on how to promote ecotech in Chapter 11. Referring to the Manila Declaration of 1996, he stresses that the ecotech agenda needs to be goal-oriented, with explicit objectives, milestones and performance criteria. It also requires that the public sector create a suitable environment for private sector initiatives. Thus ecotech activities should combine government action, private sector projects and joint public-private activities and should draw on voluntary contributions commensurate with member economies' capabilities. They should also generate direct and broadly-shared benefits among member economies and aim to reduce economic disparities.

Since ecotech is now defined as action-oriented cooperation for development with explicit objectives, tasks, measures and results, its implementation needs to be based on an effective mechanism which suits the nature of APEC.

In Chapter 12, Zhou Xiaobing and Zhao Jianglin emphasise the importance of creating an environment which is conducive to economic and technical cooperation among APEC countries. They identify several problems in APEC economic and technical cooperation including a lack of real progress in facilitating technical cooperation; lack of action in implementing proposals; insufficient start-up capital; and lack of operating models for project implementation. The diversity of APEC's membership also exacerbates the difficulties of cooperation.

Zhou Xiaobing assesses the impact of capital inflows and technology transfer on the Chinese economy in Chapter 13. After reviewing trends in foreign capital inflows and technology transfers into China, he discusses the role of foreign-invested enterprises in the Chinese economy and the challenges caused by the massive inflow of foreign capital. Problems include lack of a valuation system for state assets, high concentration of foreign capital in certain industries, lack of enforcement of regulations (such as pollution controls), and lack of social insurance for local employees. Problems associated with technology transfer include difficulties in accessing frontier technologies and an inability to assimilate advanced technology due to the lack of R&D expenditure. He points out that the APEC framework can play an important role in promoting the transfer of technology to China and that APEC technological cooperation could help to resolve these problems.

The last two chapters of the book deal with trade and trade efficiency issues in the Asia Pacific economies. In Chapter 14, Zhou Xiaobing and Ligang Song provide preliminary evidence on how the trade performance of the East Asian economies has been related to changes exchange rates—particularly the major currencies such as the US dollar and Japanese yen. Their policy discussion highlights the relationship between structural adjustment in China and the other East Asian economies. Since the export structures of China and some of the

ASEAN economies are very similar, competition in third country markets is inevitable.

Export competition among the East Asian economies recommends continuous industrial upgrading and trade transformation. This strategy requires accumulation of physical and human capital and secure export markets. Hence, mutually re-inforcing liberalisation of trade among APEC economies assumes considerable importance to East Asian economies, heavily dependent as they are on intra-regional trade growth.

In the final chapter of the book, Peter Drysdale, Yiping Huang and Kali Kalirajan use a stochastic gravity model framework to evaluate the efficiency of China's bilateral trade. Trade efficiency indexes are calculated for each pair in a sample of 57 trading countries. An equation is estimated separately to examine the efficiency of China's bilateral trade.

The results reveal that average trade efficiency for China was not only lower than that of the other East Asian economies as a group but also below the average of the whole sample. There appears to be a huge potential for improving efficiency in China's trade and greatly expanding both exports and imports. Trade efficiency may be improved through appropriate trade reform. Increasing economic freedom, for example, including through lowering the level of trade taxes, would enhance trade efficiency. A freer economic environment in China's trade partners also promotes efficiency in trade with China, a point which underlines the importance of the APEC process to China's trade prospects, since China's most important economic partners are within the Asia Pacific region.

APEC AND THE CHINESE ECONOMY: STRATEGIC ISSUES

1

LIBERALISATION OF THE CHINESE ECONOMY: APEC, WTO AND TARIFF REDUCTIONS

ZHANG YUNLING

Significant progress has been made in the liberalisation of the Chinese economy since the late 1970s, a natural result of the reform and opening up of the economy. Gradual integration into the world market has promoted economic development. China's involvement in regional and international organisations is an integral part of this process.

THE PROGRESS OF CHINA'S ECONOMIC LIBERALISATION

REFORM OF FOREIGN TRADE

Since 1979, China's foreign trade system has undergone remarkable changes. In 1988, foreign trade companies began to apply the contract management responsibility system. In 1991, export subsidies were abolished and companies were made responsible for their own profits and losses. In 1994, with the merging of the official rate and market rate of the renminbi (RMB) at its core, a single, managed RMB floating rate system based on supply and demand of the market was established. From 1996, the RMB became convertible for the current account.

In 1994, mandatory plans on total import and export volumes, export earnings and import spending of foreign exchange, were relinquished and a system of guiding plans was introduced. A unified tax reimbursement system under central finance was gradually established. In accordance with the principles of efficiency, fairness and openness, favourable conditions were created for public bidding, auction and standardised allocation for the quotas on import and export commodities. Actions have been taken to deregulate export businesses gradually to increase competitiveness.

Significant progress has been made to increase policy transparency. The Ministry of Foreign Trade and Economic Cooperation of China (MOFTEC) has made public internal standardised documents. The General Office of the State Council issued a circular, 'Reaffirming Relevant Rules and Regulations Regarding the Promulgation of National Foreign Economic and Trade Laws, Rules, Regulations and Policies' in October 1993, which stipulated that only those economic and trade laws, rules, regulations, administrative guidance and policies that have been made public will be implemented. Since 1 October 1993, MOFTEC has openly published such policies. More importantly, in May 1994, the 'Foreign Trade Law' was passed.

Despite these advances, significant efforts must be made before China can build a truly efficient and transparent foreign trade management system. Challenges are now coming from internal competition brought about by foreign producers who sell an increasing proportion of their products within China. With respect to foreign direct investment (FDI), the distinction between domestic and foreign trade is becoming less clear.

LOWERING TARIFFS

The basic principles in setting China's import tariff rates are that tariff exemption or low tariffs should apply to the necessities that bear on the national economy and the livelihood of the people but cannot be produced domestically or whose production cannot meet demand, like grain (wheat, corn, rice), iron ore and most other mineral ores and raw materials; tariff rates for raw materials are generally lower than those for finished or manufactured products; tariff rates for components of machinery equipment which can be produced domestically or whose quality is sub-standard, are lower than tariffs on final products; and, very high tariffs are levied on manufactured products whose domestic production requires protection.

China has made great progress in lowering tariffs. In 1991, tariffs on 43 commodities were lowered. In April 1992, import adjustment tax levied on a group of important machinery and electronic products and chemical fibre was lifted (the import adjustment tax levied on colour TV sets and cars then was 100 per cent). On 1 October 1992, when a new commodity catalogue system of coordination was adopted in formulating customs rules, the tariff on 225 commodities was lowered.

By the end of 1992, the tariff on 3371 commodities had been lowered, thus decreasing the general level of China's tariffs by 7.3 per cent, to 39.9 per cent.

From 31 December 1993, the tariff rates on 2898 items were lowered, including certain domestically scarce raw materials and mechanical equipment, the supply of which could not meet the demand. Those rates were lowered by 8.8 per cent, thus decreasing the average tariff rate to 36.4 per cent.

From 1 January 1994, the tariff on sedan cars has been lowered from 220 per cent to 150 per cent, and 180 per cent to 110 per cent—depending on cylinder size—thus further reducing the general level of tariffs to 35.9 per cent.

From 1 April 1996, tariffs on 4994 items began to be lowered, accounting for 76.3 per cent of the total 6350 tariff items. In the Chinese Customs Import and Export Tariff Regulations, the establishment of tariff tax items was readjusted in line with the decision of the Customs Cooperation Council and in light of China's economic conditions. The average tariff rate fell from 35.9 per cent to 23 per cent as a result of the reduction. This represented a 35.9 per cent fall (Kong Fanchang 1996).

From October 1997, the tariff rate fell to 17 per cent. Just under 5000 items were affected by the cut.

China's tariffs are dual rates—a preferential and general tariff are set for each commodity. In addition, in the China Customs Import Tariff Regulations, within-quotas tariff rates and temporary tariff rates are stipulated for certain products.

Preferential tariffs apply to the importation of goods from countries which have mutually beneficial trade agreements with China. Currently, China has signed mutually beneficial trade agreements with 137 countries.

General tariffs apply to the importation of goods from countries that do not have agreements with China. However, under special circumstances and with

Figure 1.1   China's tariff reduction trend (per cent)

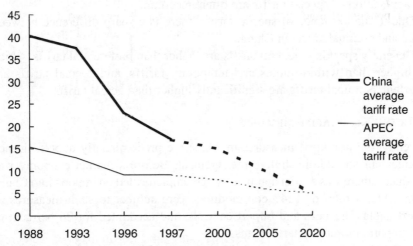

Note: Trend after 1998 does not include new members.

Source: *Manila Action Plan for APEC*, The Asia Foundation, 1996.

Table 1.1   Impact of 35.9% to 5% tariff reduction on the Chinese economy

1994	Real value	Simulation	Percentage change
GDP*	45005.8	44928.85	-0.17
Domestic demand	57059.45	57074.57	0.03
Import	12053.4	12145.72	0.76
Tariff revenue	330	46.31	-85.97
Labour	28084	28069	-0.05
GDP**	29350.51	29293.3	-0.19
Consumer index	156.6	156.24	-0.23

Note: GDP, 100 Million Yuan; Labor, 10,000; Consumer index, 1990=100.
*Current value; ** Constant value.

Source: APEC Policy Research Centre, 1997. *Trade Impediments in China*, Chinese Academy of Social Sciences:22B.

the approval of the Tariff Administration Office of the State Council, preferential tariffs may be applied to the importation of goods from such countries.

Temporary tariffs apply to the importation of part of the production equipment and raw materials.

Special tariffs refer to two categories. The first is the tariff reduction and exemption rendered by administrative authorities to certain special regions, units and individuals in their importation of certain products. The second is the reprisal and counter-reprisal tariffs implemented in international trade disputes. The size and application of special tariffs are often uncertain.

Due to the existence of special tariffs, there is a sharp difference between actual and nominal tariffs in China.

Generally speaking, general tariffs are higher than preferential tariffs, which are higher than within-quotas and temporary tariffs, and special tariffs are uncertain. Nominal tariffs are significantly higher than actual tariffs.

REDUCING NON-TARIFF MEASURES

Currently, the non-tariff measures in China are predominantly quotas, licence management and administrative management. Before a market economy was introduced, there was a strict approval system implemented on imports into China.

In 1992, a total of 1247 commodities were subject to such measures as import quotas, licences and import controls, and accounted for 20 per cent of total import commodity tariff items.

In 1993, the introduction of 'Management Measures of the Import of Machinery and Electronic Products' and the 'Quota Management of the Import of General Commodities', reduced quota and licence controls over many commodities, eliminating all stipulations for import substitute commodities and abolishing the temporary ban and licence control on the import of 34 production assembly lines.

In January 1994, import quotas, licences and administrative approval of 283 commodities—including steel and civil airplanes—were abolished. In June of that year, the import licences and quotas on a further 208 items were eliminated. A year later, quotas and licence controls on 367 goods were abolished. From July the range of import control on machinery and electronic products was further narrowed, reducing tax items from 196 to 160, and special product tax items from 190 to 119.

From April 1996, China further eliminated quotas, licences and other import controls on commodities of 176 tax items, accounting for 30 per cent of the total existing commodities under import license control. Currently, commodities under import control measures account for less than 5 per cent of total import tax items (Kong Fanchang 1996).

This represents 384 commodities of a total 6000 tariff items affected by non-tariff measures. China only implements unified control over 16 important export commodities such as oil, coal, cotton, grain, maize and tea, while management of other commodities has been decentralised. However, it is argued that China still has too many quotas and licences, and they should be gradually abolished.

As a result, China's foreign trade management system has undergone significant changes. These have included the separation of the functions of administration from those of management, reducing government intervention in enterprises' activities; abolishing mandatory plans regarding export quotas, the obtaining and use of foreign exchange, replacing them with guidance plans under which the state exerts influence on foreign economic activities and trade mainly through economic means such as tax revenue, credit and exchange rates. In the pursuit of transparency, batches of internal documents have been brought into the open and many of them scrapped. An increasing number of companies and enterprises have been granted the right to import and export independently.

However, permission to engage in foreign economic activities and trade needs to be further deregulated. Currently, firms must still gain government approval before they can engage in foreign trade. Few foreign-invested trade companies have been allowed in the foreign trade business. Pressure has been building from outside China to open this field quickly.

China has plans to identify and review all its non-tariff measures and to make public such measures as import quotas, licence and administrative measures, in order to enhance and guarantee the transparency of its non-tariff measures. Meanwhile, it has committed to take concrete steps to reduce gradually or relax its non-tariff measures to bring it in line with international practice. In the intermediate term—from 2001 to 2010—further cuts will be made.

A significant effort must be made for China to change from its familiar administrative tools to the rules and measures accepted and recognised internationally. For instance, China has not properly effected laws and regulations pertaining to anti-dumping, countervailing duty, or anti-monopoly. China must go beyond reducing non-tariff measures, to improving the management system to comply with the market system.

Companies and enterprises must also be quick to readjust and adapt to the new situation. Failure to respond quickly may see them pushed out of the market under intense competition. The commitment to reduce non-tariff measures must be made commensurate with the pace of the country's reform and opening up so as to avoid unnecessary losses from excessive pressures on the national economy.

LIBERALISING THE SERVICES SECTOR

Significant progress has also been made in liberalising China's services sector, widely considered to be the most protected field. Foreign banks and other financial institutions were permitted from the late 1970s, when the reforms began. An experimental step was made in 1982 when China permitted a Hong Kong bank to set up a branch in the Shenzhen Special Economic Zone (SEZ). From 1985, four other SEZs, as well as 13 coastal open cities were allowed to establish branches of foreign banks. A new step was taken in 1992 when China gave permission to a foreign insurance company to start business in Shanghai and Guangzhou. A joint venture was formed between China Construction Bank and Morgan Stanley in 1995. It was the first investment bank allowed to do business in China. Certain foreign banks are allowed to do RMB business in Pudong area, Shanghai, and in Shamen, Fujian Province. Further liberalisation in this area—such as of security and accounting businesses—continues.

The retail sector is also opening up. Foreign investors in production may sell a certain proportion of their products in China's domestic market according to the agreement. Hainan province and another 10 cities—including Shanghai, Beijing and Guangzhou—are open to a few foreign companies. However, the wholesale sector remains closed to foreign business.

Progress on liberalisation has been made in the transportation sector too. Joint ventures are encouraged in international ocean shipping. Coastal and inland navigation and highway transportation have been permitted limited joint ventures. Airlines are not yet open to foreign companies, but joint ventures may be formed in businesses like plane repairs and airport construction (non-military).

Public communication and specialised communications in China are still closed to foreign companies, although all kinds of investment in communication manufacturing are encouraged. Equipment for communication terminals is allowed to be sold in China under licence.

Despite these advances, the services sector remains weak in China. More time is needed before it can become competitive.

The pace of liberalisation of the Chinese economy is rapid, but further steps are necessary to make it more open and competitive. China has adapted to the world market and begun to follow internationally accepted trading rules. This has become an irreversible trend.

However, China's market-oriented economic system has yet to be perfected and its enterprises are in the process of transformation. China is very cautious in opening those sectors that are still under transformation and less competitive. For example, as a result of the East Asian financial crisis, China may draw the conclusion that it is dangerous to open the financial sector too quickly.

CHINA'S INVOLVEMENT IN APEC

China has taken a positive attitude and an active policy approach towards APEC activities. It is well understood that China's major economic relations and interests lie in the Asia Pacific region. The progress of APEC brings significant benefits to China. For example, according to a study done by the Economic Committee of APEC, China may gain as much as US$14.3 billion—the largest amount of all the APEC members—from the Manila Action Plan for APEC (APEC 1997).

CHINA'S INTEREST IN APEC

The major role of APEC is to provide a formal mechanism to integrate regional economies and create a more open and cooperative environment for long-term development and prosperity. APEC membership gives China an opportunity to work together with the economies of the Asia Pacific region. APEC is also an important forum where China can voice what it wants and what it opposes.

However, the major benefit for China is APEC's flexibility. China needs a gradual transition as it is a large developing country with very low per capita income, on the difficult road from a planned economic system to a market system. China needs time and room to reform, thus it wants APEC to move unilaterally and gradually. China rejects any efforts to make APEC a strong organisation with mandatory powers and insists that APEC should be an open and flexible forum.

Considering the great diversity of the region, APEC needs to take into account fully the differences in the stages of economic development and socio-political systems of its members in initiating and implementing actions. A flexible approach is essential in achieving this.

APEC has two aims: liberalisation and cooperation. Economic and technical cooperation are underlying features of APEC, strengthened by liberalisation and facilitation of trade and investment. They are strong mechanisms to make APEC economies integrated, interdependent and balanced. China has made continuous efforts to promote economic and technical cooperation in APEC.

APEC'S ROLE IN LIBERALISATION

The dynamics of the Chinese economy are based on an open system. Total imports and exports increased from US$20.6 billion in 1978 to US$340 billion in 1998. Following increasing integration of the Chinese economy the regional and world markets, it has become open. However, active steps must be taken to reduce tariffs, as well as non-tariff measures.

APEC has no mandate to force its members to reduce trade and investment barriers. Yet the forces of 'peer pressure' can encourage and facilitate them to do so. China's actions in APEC are not just a reflection of this pressure. China uses APEC as an arena to show its willingness and determination to reform

Table 1.2   APEC members gain from Manila Action Plan for APEC

Economies/Regions[1]	GDP	
	Percentage change	Amount[2] (US$billion, 1995)
Australia	0.4	1.8
Canada	0.4	2.0
Chile	4.9	3.3
China	2.1	14.3
Hong Kong, China	0.4	0.6
Indonesia	2.4	4.9
Japan	0.1	7.2
Korea	0.8	3.8
Malaysia	7.4	6.3
Mexico	0.7	1.7
New Zealand	1.3	0.8
Philippines	4.3	3.2
Singapore	1.5	1.2
Chinese Taipei	1.3	3.3
Thailand	3.1	5.2
USA	0.1	8.9
APEC total	0.4	68.5
Rest of world	0.0	2.4
World MAPA total	0.2	70.9

Notes: 1. Due to data constraints, Brunei Darussalam and Papua New Guinea could not be specified.
2. Amounts are based on the level of nominal GDP of the economies in 1995.

Source: APEC, 1997. *The Impact of Trade Liberalisation in APEC*, Economic Committee, APEC.

its economy and integrate itself into the regional and world economy. A significant step was taken in 1995 when President Jiang Zemin announced a 30 per cent tariff reduction on 4000 import items during the Osaka meeting, thus reducing China's average import tariff rate from 35.9 per cent to 23 per cent. A further reduction was announced in September 1997, before the APEC summit meeting in Vancouver, bringing the rate to 17 per cent. Since then, tariffs have been lowered on various goods voluntarily.

The IAP provides a general guideline for China to implement its commitment to the APEC process of trade and investment liberalisation. According to China's IAP submitted to the Manila meeting in 1996, the average tariff rate will be reduced to 15 per cent by 2000, 10 per cent by 2010 and 5 per cent by 2020.

China's tariff level by 2000 may be the highest among the 18 APEC members. China will certainly meet further pressures to speed up the reductions. There is a big gap between nominal and real implemented tariff levels, indicating strong potential for further reductions than those actually planned.

Within 5 years of accession to the WTO, China will gradually carry out the transition from the examination and approval system of foreign trade to the registration system of foreign trade to enterprises. In the long term—from 2012 to 2020—China will, in compliance with the timetable for non-tariff elimination, completely abolish all non-tariff measures that are inconsistent with the WTO agreement. The problem is there is a big gap between China, the United States and the European Union (EU) in the timetable for reducing non-tariff measures in the negotiation for China's entry to WTO. Due to the difficulties of reform and transition—especially for state-owned enterprises—China wants to have a longer transitional period, on which its counterparts from developed countries do not agree.

As mentioned above, the service sector is the most troublesome. China has planned to increase the number of operational branches established by foreign banks in 24 designated cities and also gradually allow more foreign insurance companies to establish operational branches in places beyond current trial cities during the period 1997–2000. There is to be further relaxation of restrictions on geographical coverage for access to banking business by foreign banks, insurance companies and security companies in the period 2001–10. For transportation, communications and retail and wholesale areas, no clear actions have been elaborated in the medium or long-term. It is obvious that action plans are still very difficult to establish at this early stage of service sector reform. The big challenge is for China to make quick changes once entering the WTO and join the Information and Telecommunication Agreement (ITA) in the near future.

The pressure for standardisation and revision of IAPs in APEC has become strong in order to make implementation more effective and comparable. The IAP process is not static but an ongoing process based on continuous revision. China has shown its positive attitude to this process. For example, in 1997, China committed to reduce its tariff rate to 10 per cent by 2005, rather than by 2010 as planned in its IAP presented in Manila in 1996. China will be eager to invite an independent reviewing group to evaluate its progress in implementing the agenda set up by APEC.

Early sectoral voluntary liberalisation is considered an important approach to facilitate the process of trade and investment liberalisation. However, due to the diversity of the APEC economies, it is difficult to reach consensus on how and when to liberalise the 15 sectors. China favours an approach which would start with the easy sectors, and opposes any effort by the United States to enforce early liberalisation.

APEC INVOLVEMENT AND WTO ENTRY

APEC plays an important role in facilitating China's economic liberalisation. In recent years, China's major tariff reduction measures have been announced at APEC meetings. However, China's actions are not solely APEC-related. They have close ties to China's entry into the WTO.

China began to request the resumption of its GATT membership in 1986. The failure of China's push into GATT made its entry into the WTO more difficult. Lots of working sessions on China's entry into the WTO have been conducted, but China has not yet been admitted entry.

China insists that it has already satisfied the necessary conditions of the WTO as a developing country, while the United States and some other countries argued that China was still far from meeting the basic requirements. The delay has been largely considered a political barrier made by the developed countries, especially by the United States. The debate between the major powers centres on 'entry first' versus 'change first'.

China has about one-fifth of the world's population, is the 10th largest trading nation, and has increasing influence on the world economy. China's accession to the WTO will not just benefit China itself, but also the international trading and economic system. For China, WTO membership will allow it to receive all the benefits of the GATT/WTO agreed market access results, and to export to other WTO members at the rates of duty and levels of commitments negotiated in past and future Rounds. Thus, China will be safeguarded from discriminatory treatment in trade. Equally important, as a member, China will be able to participate in the writing of rules and help to influence the evolution of the multilateral trading system in the next century. China's entry will strengthen the multilateral trading system and enhance the scope of the WTO. China's membership will create more opportunities in terms of access to the Chinese market.

The lengthy negotiations have forced China to revise its commitments again and again in order to meet the requirements of the WTO. This has in fact sped up the pace of liberalisation of the Chinese economy. Tariff reductions are one example. China originally only committed to lowering its average tariff rate to 35 per cent within 5 years of joining the WTO, but already the rate stands at 17 per cent, even without accession.

By mid-1999, China had finished bilateral negotiations with many WTO members, including Japan and Australia. This should help China's attempts to enter the WTO. Of course, the major concern is still approval of the settlement with the United States, as well as the settlement with the European Union.

It is true that China likes the APEC way since it is more flexible and unilateral in managing trade and investment liberalisation. However, there is obviously a relationship between China's WTO accession and its actions in APEC—what China has done within APEC has close relation to its entry into the WTO. In fact, the two cannot be separated. On the one hand, China has had to revise its commitments to the WTO continuously under the pressure of the working party for China's accession; on the other, it has to keep pace with APEC's 'WTO plus' initiatives, though it is not a member of the WTO. Strategically, China must limit its actions in APEC so as not to exceed its commitments for WTO accession; otherwise there will be pressures for it to commit more in later negotiations. However, this is very difficult to manage since the two are both ongoing processes. For example, the level of tariff reductions by China after the Osaka meeting was far beyond the earlier commitment made by China for its WTO entry. China stated in 1995 during the second Senior Official Meeting of APEC that it would implement the Uruguay Round (UR) agreements selectively though it was not yet a member of the WTO. In fact, the efforts made by APEC members should speed up the pace of implementing the UR agreement. China also committed to sign the ITA in the near future, likely before its entry into the WTO. It seems that APEC involvement and WTO entry are two forcible means for China to liberalise its economy further. Nevertheless, delay of China's WTO membership is not an ideal strategy to encourage China's reform and opening.

REFERENCES

APEC, 1996. *Manila Action Plan for APEC*, The Asia Foundation.

——, 1997. *The Impact of Trade Liberalisation in APEC*, Economic Committee, APEC.

APEC Policy Research Centre, *Trade Impediments in China*, 1997. Chinese Academy of Social Sciences:22B.

Chulsu Kim, 1997. Issues in the negotiations on China's accession to the WTO system, remarks, Lausanne, 20 September.

Jiao Feng Chao Rihui, 1996. *On China's Entry into WTO*, Development Study, October.

Kong Fanchang, 1996. *Survey on China's Tariff and Non-tariff Barriers*, APEC Policy Research Center (APRC), No. 2 (Chinese), Beijing:12.

Long Yongtu, 1997. 'The new measures on China's service sector liberalization', *International Business Daily,* 8 December.

State Statistical Bureau, 1993–97. *Statistical Yearbook of China*, China Statistical Publishing House, Beijing.

Zhang Yunling, 1996. *China and APEC*, APRC, No.2 (English), Beijing.

——, 1997. *Early Sectoral Liberalization in APEC: implications to China*, APRC, Beijing.

2

OPEN REGIONALISM, APEC AND CHINA'S INTERNATIONAL TRADE STRATEGIES

PETER DRYSDALE

While developments over the past few years have raised many questions about the immediate prospects for East Asia's economic growth, the force of East Asian industrialisation has already transformed the contours of world economic power and influence (Drysdale and Elek 1997). Japan was the leading edge of East Asian industrialisation and, in the postwar period, emerged to join the same league as the industrial economies of North America and Europe. The new role that East Asia began to assume more clearly in the 1980s was defined in a pluralist structure of economic power, encompassing the effective representation of broader Asia Pacific and global interests, as well as those of the United States and Europe (Funabashi 1995:Ch. 9).

Strong commitment to these regional and global goals has provided the stimulus for every major initiative for economic cooperation in the Asia Pacific region for more than thirty years, from the establishment of the Pacific Basin Economic Council (PBEC) and the Pacific Trade and Development (PAFTAD) Conference series, through to the foundation of the Pacific Economic Cooperation Council (PECC) and the APEC forums. In all of these initiatives Australia and Japan played a leading role, crucially engaging the ASEAN countries, winning the support of the United States in the PECC and later the APEC initiative (Drysdale 1988; Terada 1998) and later incorporating the interests of the Chinese economies (Drysdale 1997b). From 1999, China was also actively involved in dialogue with Australia on these issues.

The establishment of APEC was part of the response to the need for regional structures in the Asia Pacific, notable for their paucity compared with those in the Atlantic. Asia Pacific community-building was needed to cope with the realities of growing economic interdependence (APEC 1993), and to allow Asia Pacific governments to contribute to collective leadership to shape a new global order following the end of the Cold War (Funabashi 1995:Ch. 9; Drysdale 1991).

CENTRAL PRINCIPLES

At the core of the APEC philosophy is the idea of 'open regionalism' (Funabashi 1995:3). From its beginnings, APEC 'was not to be an economic bloc or legally bound free trade area like the European Community or the North American Free Trade Agreement (NAFTA)'. Rather, APEC 'sought to realise a vision of global free trade, driven by the liberalisation of the Asia Pacific region's dynamic economies' (Funabashi 1995:3). The objective of promoting economic consultation and cooperation among Asia Pacific governments was essentially a conservative one, to preserve the conditions needed to sustain the positive trends of rising prosperity and the productive integration of the region's economies (Garnaut 1996:Ch. 1).

Hence, APEC was born in 1989 out of deep concern among East Asian and Western Pacific economies about the fate of the global, multilateral trade regime and the slow progress of multilateral trade negotiations in the Uruguay Round through the 1980s.

The East Asian economies understood their stake in the strength and continuity of an open trading system, based upon the principle of non-discrimination in trade embedded in Article 1 of the GATT. This was why the idea of open regionalism came to define the approach to the development of APEC and Asia Pacific integration from its beginnings.

The idea of open regionalism is deeply rooted in the history of the evolution of APEC. The experience of discriminatory trade policies of the interwar period is seared into Japanese policy memory, and non-discrimination in trade policy stands out as the central guiding principle of Japan's postwar international trade diplomacy. Takeo Miki, one of the early advocates of Asia Pacific economic cooperation, declared that 'it would be an act of suicide on our part to create an exclusive and closed trading bloc in the Pacific area' (Miki 1968). A little over a decade later, the Ohira Study Group concluded that 'a regionalism that is open to the world, not one that is exclusive and closed, is the first characteristic of our concept a regional community...without a perspective for a global community has no possibility of development and prosperity' (Japan Pacific Cooperation Study Group 1980:19). These ideas were first given precision in English at the Pacific Community Seminar convened by Crawford at the initiative of Prime Ministers Ohira of Japan and Fraser of Australia at The Australian National University in September 1980 (Garnaut 1996:6). They became entrenched through the work of PECC after 1980 and were the intellectual foundation on which APEC was launched in Canberra in November 1989 (Crawford and Seow 1981; Drysdale, Elek and Soesastro 1998).

PRECEPT TO PRACTICE

APEC's agenda has evolved around the giving of substance to the idea of open regionalism. The APEC meetings in Seattle in 1993 elevated the process of cooperation to the highest level of government. At the initiative of US President Clinton, an APEC informal leaders meeting was held in conjunction with the established ministerial meetings. The leaders issued an Economic Vision Statement which contained three elements. The first was an affirmation of an open multilateral trading system and the determination of Asia Pacific leaders to take steps to produce the strongest possible outcome of the Uruguay Round (APEC 1993). The APEC leaders meeting the following year in Bogor (Indonesia) produced the Bogor Declaration of Common Resolve (APEC 1994), which set the goals of free and open trade and investment in the region by 2010 for developed members and 2020 for developing member economies. The commitment by leaders to achieve free and open trade by a certain date was an important milestone in APEC's development.

In spite of the principles set out in the Bogor Declaration, there remained some ambiguities about the modality for achieving the APEC goal of free and open trade and investment in the region. These arose in proposals, including those put forward by the APEC Eminent Persons Group (APEC Eminent Persons Group 1994), which amounted to advocacy of a process of negotiated liberalisation among APEC members along the lines of a conventional free trade area, whose benefits could be extended to non-member only on a mutually reciprocated basis and in a way that would eliminate the problem of 'free riding', either within APEC itself or by non-members, notably Europe.

The task of clarifying these issues rested with Japan—the chair of APEC in 1995.

APEC formally espoused open regionalism at its Osaka meetings in 1995 and the Osaka Action Agenda (APEC 1995) was premised on the voluntary nature of the APEC process, an essential corollary to the idea of open regionalism. Commitment to unilateral liberalisation of barriers to trade and investment by APEC members, in their own self interest, is a necessary condition of progress on the basis of open regionalism. Such commitments are not seen as concessions for exchange in a negotiating process, but their collective effect (concerted unilateral liberalisation) is mutually reinforcing of regional trade liberalisation, consistently with Article 1 of the WTO and without requiring an Article 24 style discriminatory agreement (Drysdale, Elek and Soesastro 1998).

Equally important, in the context of Asia Pacific community-building, is the sense of comfort that this modality provides to APEC member economies, by allowing flexibility in the implementation of liberalisation commitments not based on uniformly negotiated schedules. APEC's trade liberalisation and facilitation agenda is adopted and implemented by the decisions of individual governments. Each member's liberalisation program is entered into voluntarily, in accordance with common guidelines for APEC cooperation adopted by consensus within the APEC process. Unilateral efforts are reviewed and monitored within APEC. As agreed in Osaka, members' Individual Action Plans (IAPs) cover trade liberalisation and trade and investment facilitation measures. In addition, Collective Action Plans (CAPs) open the possibility of non-discriminatory sectoral liberalisation, in sectors of special interest to APEC members, an option that was taken up in the Vancouver APEC meetings of November 1997. In Manila, APEC members also laid the basis for adoption of the Information Technology Agreement at the WTO Ministerial Meetings in Singapore in late 1996 and subsequently (APEC 1996).

In brief, there are three reasons why the East Asian and other Western Pacific economies have eschewed discrimination in the approach in the approach to Asia Pacific regional cooperation (Garnaut 1996). First, the trading interests of East Asian and Pacific economies extend beyond APEC, including to Europe. A conventional free trade area strategy towards liberalisation would deter internationally oriented reform in the region's neighbouring developing economies and introduce tension into relations with neighbours and major partners outside the region. Second, trade discrimination involves the unnecessary cost of trade diversion, complicated in the Asia Pacific region by the likelihood of high associated political costs both within and outside the region (Garnaut and Drysdale 1994:Ch. 5). Third, there is the sheer impracticability of undertaking regional trade liberalisation via a conventional discriminatory free trade area of the kind sanctioned by the WTO in such a diverse region—the most likely outcome would be a 'dirty bloc', in which there would be backsliding into partial preferential liberalisation, with a picking and choosing of the sectors to be liberalised, at different times, by different players, in bilateral deals (Drysdale, Vines and House 1998:7).

APEC has already become more than just a loose community of like-minded economies encouraging each other in a process of unilateral trade and investment liberalisation. It is also a structure, an umbrella, under which trade, technical cooperation, (recently) financial cooperation and, to a lesser extent, political tensions within the Asia Pacific region are managed.

CHINA, WTO ACCESSION AND APEC

ACCESSION TO THE WTO

The elevation of China's status in world trade has accelerated over the last several years, as the reform process has deepened and has encouraged active Chinese trade diplomacy in both global and regional fora.

Yet China itself is still outside the important global institutions that govern the rules and arrangements of the multilateral trading system. China has no access through membership of the WTO to representation or redress over matters of trade cooperation and application of the rules of trade it embodies, or over matters of trade disputation. China's political weight in international affairs and the power of mutual interests in bilateral economic arrangements provide it with influence in dealings with its international trading partners—even the United States, as was seen most clearly in 1994. But the fact remains that China has a much less confident basis on which to proceed in such dealings than other nations of comparable importance in world trade (Drysdale and Song 2000).

This is the crux of the priority that attaches to China's membership of the WTO and the importance of APEC in Chinese trade policy strategies.

China's entry to the WTO will affect Chinese and international policy and enterprise or corporate behaviour in at least three important respects. It will affect the behaviour of China's major trading partners, such as the United States, Europe and Japan, in policy behaviour towards China. It will affect Chinese policy behaviour, in respect of trade, investment and other rules and practices, and the environment in which both domestic and foreign firms operate in China. And it will affect the behaviour of domestic as well as foreign enterprises in their activities within the Chinese market. These consequences are of considerable importance even if, as will be the case from time to time, disputes or difficulties arise in the application of WTO rules and protocols by, and towards, China on whatever final terms entry is negotiated.

There are two key points here.

The first is that an international commitment, such as that involved in accession to the WTO, underwrites credibility in respect of the continuity and reliability of policy behaviour (Itoh 1996:8). It serves to limit opportunistic behaviour (such as quarantining favoured sectors of the economy from international competition, treatment of foreign firms on a different basis from national firms, treatment of a particular country's goods on a discriminatory basis or inconsistently with accepted rules and principles) and to reduce the likelihood of distortionary interventions in trade and other international transactions—both by China and by China's trading partners. Violation of WTO rules after entry would, of course, undermine policy credibility but, while many such problems do and may arise, the experience of China's approach to the honouring of its international agreements and of the approach of most WTO members to the trade rules suggest that China's entry to the WTO would secure an important international commitment and assurance of policy credibility both ways round. In this context, China's impressive trade liberalisation over the past decade cannot be viewed independently of negotiation towards GATT/WTO accession nor guaranteed independently of eventual success in these negotiations.

The second is that the international commitment required of China by WTO entry will bind policy and the evolution of policy in a way that affects the behaviour of domestic and foreign firms operating in China. Commitment to agreed rules and schedules of liberalisation changes the corporate strategic environment in which enterprises plan and develop their activities. While such policy change may not be entirely impervious to domestic pressuring and influence-peddling, it is likely to be less susceptible to easy resistance, manipulation and reversal than policy change undertaken without external constraint. The way in which Japan's accession to the GATT after the Second World War shaped corporate behaviour and the political economy in the 1950s and 1960s in that country is a relevant example of this effect (Itoh 1996:9–14).

CHINA'S TRADE STRATEGY AND ECONOMIC REFORM

A commitment to WTO rules and to meeting the standards of trade policy behaviour already achieved by the major players within the WTO—inadequate though these standards sometimes appear—implies a further radical change in China's economic policy regime, the necessary next step in meeting the objectives of economic reform. Accession to the WTO, and meeting the critical international obligations it must entail, can vastly assist the management of the reform process in China. The gains from the significant liberalisation of trade that China will phase in—through more efficient allocation of resources and its impact on the productivity of resource use—will be large, but there will also be costs in the process of adjustment, and the political resistance to these adjustments is not trivial. The resistance to change has origins in ideology and in appeal to other East Asian policy models, as well as in the vested interests in the highly protected and inefficient state enterprise sector and in the inefficient rural sector (Lu 1994; Hai 1996). Connecting the next important round of liberalisation in the Chinese economy to the benefits of more reliable access to the international marketplace, delivered through WTO accession, assists with managing the politics of reform. The successful conclusion of the Uruguay Round in 1994 considerably enhanced the economic and political benefit of the accession bargain for China, since faithful implementation of the Round will result in substantial liberalisation of the Multifibre Arrangement (MFA) governing textiles trade, an area of key interest in Chinese trade growth.

China's ambition to enter the WTO is a central element in the world trade policy agenda at the beginning of the twenty first century. This element needs to be reviewed in the broader context of the relationship between trade strategy and economic reform.

China's trade and economic policies are already considerably more in line with WTO principles than when it first applied for membership in July 1986. China undertook substantial economic reform in the 1980s and the process of reform accelerated after 1989. Careful studies of the relationship between China's changing resource endowments and the structure of specialisation in the international economy provide strong evidence of the convergence between these patterns and what would be expected from market-determined outcomes

(Song 1993). The marketisation of the Chinese economy—even of its state enterprise sector—is confirmed in studies of the behaviour of Chinese enterprises in the course of reform. While the state enterprise sector enjoys considerable direct and indirect support and there remains an array of measures that are inconsistent with the letter as well as the spirit of the WTO, including direct controls and subsidies, the stage has been set for state enterprise reform in a definable period of time so as to meet the objectives and requirements for WTO membership. The draft protocol of accession of December 1994 addressed this issue. The trade law of May 1994 laid an appropriate basis for ensuring the necessary transparency and uniformity in trade policy and a retreat from administrative in favour of market measures in the management of trade. The tariff liberalisation announced at the APEC meetings in Osaka in November 1995 and carried forward in the APEC meetings at Manila in November 1996 represented not only a considerable step towards achievement of China's trade liberalisation commitments under the APEC Bogor Declaration but also a substantial forward commitment on meeting the terms of accession to the WTO. The service sector (including banking and transportation) remains sheltered, but this sector as well as trade in commodities and technology is being thrown open to market principles.

In 1988 China's unweighted average tariffs were 40.3 per cent (PECC 1996:8). In 1993 they had been reduced to 37.5 per cent and by 1996 they were down to 23.0 per cent. The tariff average is now 15 per cent. China has substantially and steadily reduced the number of goods subject to quotas and licensing: at present around 700 tariff line items remain subject to nontariff trade barriers (NTBs), 600 of which are scheduled for removal. Figure 2.1 describes the extensive tariff reduction to which China is committed on a voluntary basis under the APEC Individual Action Plans (IAPs), significantly ahead of the trend necessary to achieve free trade in 2020. China is also gradually opening up more sectors to direct foreign investment and progressively granting national treatment in foreign investment policy.

In practice, trade policy strategy is inextricably linked with other aspects of the reform, such as foreign exchange reform (already taken a long way through unification of the two-tiered exchange rate and with the target of full currency convertibility), state enterprise reform, financial market reform and macro-economic policy reform.

The liberalisation of trade policy associated with accession to the WTO in effect forces the pace of reform in other areas, especially in the management of the state enterprise sector, and financial and foreign-exchange markets. Policy leaders, both inside and outside China, have a very substantial interest in forcing the pace. Accession to the WTO would entrench these reforms and help to maintain their momentum.

The alternative would be a loss of momentum and serious misdirection of the process of reform and industrial transformation. One aspect is the potential for a shift towards costly 'import substitution' strategies fostered by the maintenance and extension of subsidies and state controls, and away from the thrust towards 'export orientation' or, more accurately, 'open market' strategies. Advancing the trade liberalisation agenda, through accession to the WTO, or by whatever means, promotes reform of the enterprise system through the positive effect of the export sector and enhanced market discipline on industrial activity.

In agriculture, the stakes are now set to become higher. China has switched from being an agriculture-taxing to an agriculture-subsidising industrialising economy (Drysdale 1997b). The burden of agricultural protection will become higher and higher and more difficult to unravel, unless the moment to negotiate a relatively open trade regime is taken soon.

Protectionist sentiment abroad and reactionary sentiment in China find common cause in focusing on strategies which eschew 'export-oriented' development and focus on 'self-sustaining' growth in a huge domestic market. Such thinking is based on incorrect understanding of the nature of industrialisation in East Asian economies. Chinese economic modernisation is not an independent event. In all the major East Asian economies, domestic market growth *as well as* openness to international market disciplines have been key elements in the development of dynamic comparative advantage and internationally competitive economies. The evolution of dynamic comparative advantage will differ in China from other East Asian economies because of the wider range in China's economic

Figure 2.1   China's tariff reductions

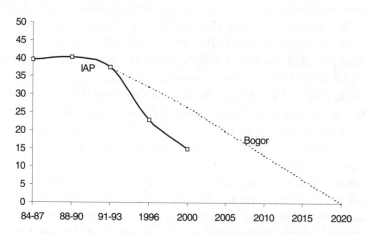

Source: PECC, 1996. *Perspectives on the Manila Action Plan for APEC*, Philippine Institute for Development Studies, Manila:13.

structure, the regional diversity of its resource endowments and a history of investment in capital-intensive industry. But China is far from reaching its full potential in the development of externally oriented activities and will continue to realise significant gains from growth through trade, investment and technology flows and integration into the international economy.

This perspective is critical in judgment about the appropriate strategies towards industrial transformation and industrial policy in China.

CHINA AND APEC

China's trade and other foreign economic relations are overwhelmingly concentrated in the Asia Pacific economy (Table 2.1).

The APEC group of economies includes all China's most important trading partners and accounts for over 54 per cent of its import and export trade if Hong Kong's trade is included while that of China and trade between the two economies is excluded from their total trade. Among them are the United States and Japan. While the relationship with the United States is not free of problems (the human rights issue, arms sales, intellectual property rights, illegal textile trans-shipments, the Taiwan issue, and market access for US products in China) and the relationship with Japan carries the burden of history, China shares more interests with the Asia Pacific economies than with other trading nations. Trade ties have grown strongly within the region—even around diplomatic barriers to trade, such as those affecting trade with Taiwan or, until recently, with Korea. The growing depth of trade and business ties between China and the United States has begun to constrain the more divisive elements in bilateral relations and to encourage a strategy of engagement over any inclinations towards confrontation. APEC economies enjoy directly and disproportionately the benefits of China's economic growth and are natural allies in international economic diplomacy (Garnaut and Drysdale 1994:Ch.1).

The pioneering efforts by the PECC, tensions in trans-Pacific trade relations, the slow progress of the Uruguay Round and the European movement towards a single market all contributed to the launching of the APEC process in 1989 (Elek 1995). The PRC, Taiwan and Hong Kong were invited to join the process at the second ministerial-level meeting in Singapore in 1990, and all three participated in the third meeting in Seoul in November 1991. The inauguration of the informal leaders' meeting in Seattle in November 1993 gave APEC new clout and direction in a way that was of special importance to China.

The APEC framework provides a useful vehicle for Chinese foreign economic diplomacy in four main ways.

First, APEC provides a valuable forum within which the three Chinese economies can find common cause in regional economic cooperation. Second, APEC's objectives and principles, which stress the desirability of liberalisation

Table 2.1 China's geographic trade structure, 1970–96 (per cent)

PARTNER	Import share					Export share						Total trade				
	1980	1985	1990	1994	1996	1970	1980	1985	1990	1994	1996	1980	1985	1990	1994	1996
Japan	15.1	15.8	11.6	15.3	18.1	27.6	25.7	29.6	15.4	18.6	16.6	21.0	24.0	13.8	17.4	17.1
Korea, Rep	0.1	0.1	1.6	3.1	4.4	0.6	2.0	1.6	3.2	5.3	6.5	1.1	1.0	2.6	4.6	5.8
Taiwan	0.5	0.4	1.2	2.0	2.1	3.0	4.0	4.1	7.2	10.1	9.5	2.5	2.6	4.7	7.3	6.9
ASEAN	7.8	8.8	6.2	6.1	6.4	4.7	6.7	4.9	6.9	7.8	9.2	7.2	6.5	6.6	7.2	8.2
East Asia	23.5	25.1	20.6	26.6	30.9	35.7	38.4	40.2	32.5	41.8	41.8	31.8	34.1	27.7	36.4	38.1
Australia	2.0	1.6	1.0	1.2	1.1	4.4	2.8	2.0	1.6	1.4	1.6	2.4	1.8	1.3	1.3	1.4
North America	19.4	28.0	16.3	20.9	20.1	11.8	18.4	11.7	11.1	10.1	10.5	18.9	18.3	13.2	13.9	13.8
New Zealand and PNG	0.3	0.3	0.1	0.2	0.2	0.2	0.6	0.4	0.2	0.3	0.3	0.5	0.4	0.2	0.3	0.3
APEC	45.5	55.3	38.3	49.4	52.7	52.2	60.6	54.6	45.5	53.8	54.6	53.9	54.9	42.6	52.2	54.0
Western Europe	24.4	15.6	14.5	14.1	14.4	25.5	16.4	16.1	14.3	13.8	13.4	20.0	15.9	14.4	13.9	13.8
Rest of the world	30.0	29.1	47.2	36.5	32.9	22.3	23.0	29.3	40.1	32.4	32.0	26.1	29.2	43.0	33.8	32.3
WORLD	100.0	100.0	100.0	100.0	100.0	100.0	100.0	100.0	100.0	100.0	100.0	100.0	100.0	100.0	100.0	100.0

Note: China here includes Hong Kong, net of China-Hong Kong trade.

Source: UN trade data, International Economic Databank, The Australian National University, Canberra.

in ways that are not to the detriment of other economies, reinforce China's claim to MFN treatment in the international trading system, especially by its APEC partners. Third, APEC's focus on the facilitation of trade and other international transactions, and the regional infrastructure to support it, provides encouragement to sub-regional integration on a basis consistent with the guiding principle of open regionalism. The avoidance of sheltered, discriminatory, sub-regional markets is important to China's ability to manage its integration within the Northeast Asian economies (notably Hong Kong, Taiwan, and Korea) and develop its relations with the ASEAN and Indochinese economies. Asymmetry in China's relations with its neighbours has the potential to bedevil them unless they are part of an open trade and economic system in the region. This aspect of China's sub-regional relationships is also relevant to its response to Malaysia's East Asian Economic Caucus (EAEC) idea. China's involvement in any tight arrangement linked to the East Asian economies (even including Japan) is likely to be fraught with economic and political difficulty because of both the perception and the reality of asymmetry in such sub-regional arrangements. China is already a big economy and a big power and will have more comfortable relationships with smaller economies and polities, the more open those relationships are. Hence finally and most importantly, APEC is of particular value to China in the pursuit and projection of interests in the global system. The APEC framework offers the opportunity for a constructive and cooperative partnership between China and its major partners in the Asia Pacific region—the United States and Japan—and a role in fostering peace, stability and prosperity on the world stage in ways helpful to China's own ambitions for reform and development.

China has indeed played a very positive role in developing the APEC agenda of trade and investment liberalisation, especially over the past five years, and in forging the link between its regional interests and the global agenda, consolidating the base for accession to the WTO through its initiatives at the Osaka and Manila APEC meetings. APEC, in turn, has been a critical vehicle through which China could re-position and maintain the momentum of its claim to WTO membership.

CONFLICTING PARADIGMS ACROSS THE PACIFIC

APEC has special potential to be helpful in trans-Pacific relations. The tendency of the United States to conduct aspects of its trade relations bilaterally, and to seek bilateral reciprocity in its trade negotiations, is well known. It is also understandable. For a hegemonic power—which the United States still is—there is a natural temptation to use muscle to force market opening (in the name of both self interest and the general good). APEC has been a useful forum in which tensions between the United States and Japan, resulting from such actions by the United States, can be diffused and calmed. The APEC Summit in Manila also provided a congenial setting for Presidential talks to set United States–China relations on a more productive course. APEC has established its worth in managing trans-Pacific tensions through its serving as a vehicle for China's liberalisation agenda and its support for China's entry into the WTO. It was also effectively directed to management of the regional financial crisis in Vancouver, at the same time keeping the trade liberalisation agenda on track.

Yet there are aspects of developments in United States trade diplomacy over the last decade and a half that are potentially less benign for the prospects of open regionalism in APEC. These developments were born of impatience with the process of multilateral negotiation, frustration in large bilateral relationships such as those with Japan and Europe, and the challenge of the Single Market initiative in the European Union.

These developments, and the impact of the East Asian crisis, have recently aroused Japanese interest in sub-regional discriminatory trade arrangements.

Whether or not the awakening of United States interest in preferential trade arrangements was (or Japanese interest is) largely tactical, regionalism took on a life of its own among US policy makers (Saxonhouse 1997:2) and it remains an active interest, for example in consideration of new 'fast track' negotiating authority for the US Administration (Bergsten 1997).

This is the US policy context in which APEC was launched. It is also the policy context, it is worth remembering, in which Prime Minister Mahathir first put forward the idea of an East Asian Economic Caucus as, among other things, a tactical defence against North American regionalism. Of more relevance here, it is also the policy context in which a number of Americans, both inside and outside government have been eager to maintain a preferential trading arrangement option for APEC (Saxonhouse 1997:4).

Bergsten (1997:12) suggests a modification of open regionalism which qualifies its essential (most-favoured nation) feature. In his scheme, APEC members would afford liberalisation only to those outsiders who offered similar liberalisation themselves. The requirement for reciprocal liberalisation has earned this approach the label 'reciprocitarianism'. The element of conditionality in Bergsten's formula means that the final choice of whether free trade or a free trade area was the endpoint of reform would be left until tariff reduction reached its final stages. Flamm and Lincoln (1997) echo Bergsten's critique of open regionalism, strictly defined, in a recent tract.

There are a number of vital objections to Bergsten's proposal (Drysdale, Vines and House 1998:19). Foremost, it is entirely infeasible in that there is no collective action mechanism by which this proposal could be carried through within the loose APEC grouping. Under Article 24 of the WTO, a formal agreement and an agreed timetable would be required for WTO approval. APEC has eschewed any moves in this direction.

APEC is not founded on an international agreement, nor does it possess any supra-national authority that would allow it to take collective action of the kind presumed in such calculations. There is no prospect that this will change, given the approach of Japan, East Asian and Western Pacific members to Asia Pacific economic cooperation.

Drysdale, Elek and Soesastro (1998) propose that a positive response to APEC's lead on trade liberalisation, in which the European Union commits itself to eliminating all border barriers to trade and investment by 2020, would resolve the 'free rider' problem, about which Bergsten worries, and set the stage for effective cooperation among both groups to achieve free and open trade and investment between them as well as within each region.

This relates to the question of whether voluntary cooperation will be adequate to dealing with 'sensitive' sectors. Will it be possible to achieve deep liberalisation of agricultural trade in Northeast Asia, for example, without the pressure of hard negotiations and reciprocated exchange of concessions? The answer to this question may well be 'no'. But, consistently with the objectives and character of Asia Pacific economic cooperation, it is possible to plan ahead and deal with the liberalisation of some sensitive sectors in which there is also substantial extra-APEC interest within the WTO, consistently with its main principles. This should begin a few years down the track, after the digestion of Uruguay Round commitments and before the APEC industrial country free-trade deadline in 2010. This strategy also presents a way of dealing with United States concern about European 'free riding', and offers the opportunity to lock Europe into liberalisation of border barriers comparable to that taking place within APEC.

Further, there is the question of whether the APEC formula can manage American lust for reciprocity, both from other APEC economies and from non-APEC members. Over the next few years or so, this is not a major problem. In practice, the United States will itself largely 'free ride' within APEC as the major effect on liberalisation and internationally oriented reform continues to be in East Asia and the Western Pacific (Garnaut 1996:Ch. 1). This is reflected in the United States minimalist Individual Action Plan presented at Manila. The United States can best liberalise its remaining border measures in the context of broader WTO negotiations or an APEC Round. In this context there has been recent talk of reviving the trans-Atlantic initiative in a different form.

These reservations do not, in any way, suggest that APEC is simply a holding operation. Quite the reverse. They underline the importance of APEC in providing a vehicle for active trade and investment liberalisation when this is an urgent priority for the industrialising economies of East Asia and other economies in the Western Pacific, rather than their holding back until the next comprehensive WTO round of negotiations delivers an opportunity for policy progress. These are all elements of the utmost importance to China's trade policy and reform strategies.

REFERENCES

APEC, 1993. *Economic Vision Statement,* Seattle, November.

——, 1994. *Bogor Declaration of Common Resolve,* Second APEC Economic Leaders Meeting, Bogor, November.

——, 1995. *Osaka Action Agenda: Implementation of the Bogor Declaration,* Third APEC Economic Leaders Meeting, Osaka, November.

——, 1996. *Manila Action Plan for APEC,* Ministerial-level meeting, Manila, November.

——, 1997. *Leaders Declaration,* Vancouver, 25 November.

APEC Eminent Persons Group (EM), 1994. *Achieving the APEC Vision: Second Report of the Eminent Persons Group,* Asia Pacific Economic Cooperation, Singapore.

Bergsten, C. Fred, 1997. 'Open Regionalism', *The World Economy,* 20(5):545–65.

Crawford, J.G. and Greg Seow (eds), 1981. *Pacific Economic Cooperation: Suggestions for Action,* Heinemann Asia, Petaling Jaya, for the Pacific Community Seminar.

Drysdale, Peter, 1988. *International Economic Pluralism: Economic Policy in East Asia and the Pacific,* Columbia University Press, New York, and Allen and Unwin, Sydney.

——, 1991. 'Open Regionalism: A Key to East Asia's Economic Future?', Pacific Economic Papers 197, Australia–Japan Research Centre, The Australian National University, Canberra.

——, 1997a. 'APEC and the WTO: Complementary or Competing?', Paper presented to the Institute of Southeast Asian Studies APEC Roundtable, Singapore, 6 August.

——, 1997b. 'The implications of China's Membership of the WTO for Industrial Transformation', Paper presented to a conference on Chinese Industrial Upgrade: International Transformation and International Cooperation, CASS, Beijing.

Drysdale, Peter and Andrew Elek, 1997. 'APEC: Community-building in East Asia and the Pacific', in Donald C. Hellman and Kenneth B. Pyle (eds), *From APEC to Xanadu,* The National Bureau of Asian Research, Seattle, and M.E. Sharpe, New York:37–49.

Drysdale, Peter, Andrew Elek and Hadi Soesastro, 1998. 'Open Regionalism:

The Nature of Asia Pacific Integration', in P. Drysdale and D. Vines (eds), *Europe, East Asia and APEC: a shared global agenda?,* Cambridge University Press, Cambridge, UK:103–36.

Drysdale, Peter and David Vines (eds), 1998. *Europe, East Asia and APEC: a shared global agenda?,* Cambridge University Press, Cambridge, UK.

Drysdale, Peter and Ross Garnaut, 1989. 'A Pacific Free Trade Area?' in Jeff J. Schott (ed.), *More Free Trade Areas?: Free Trade Areas and US Trade Policy,* Institute for International Economics, Washington, DC:217–54.

Drysdale, Peter and Ross Garnaut, 1994. 'Principles of Pacific Economic Integration', in Ross Garnaut and Peter Drysdale (eds), *Asia Pacific Regionalism: Readings in International Economic Relations,* HarperEducational, Sydney:48–61.

Drysdale, Peter and Ligang Song, (eds), 2000. *China's Entry to the WTO: Strategic Issues and Quantative Assessment*, Routledge, London.

Drysdale, Peter, David Vines and Brett House, 1998. 'Europe and East Asia: A Shared Global Agenda?' in P. Drysdale and D. Vines (eds), *Europe, East Asia and APEC: a shared global agenda?,* Cambridge University Press, Cambridge, UK:3–30.

Elek, Andrew, 1995. 'APEC Beyond Bogor', *Asian-Pacific Economic Literature,* 9(1):1–39, May.

Flamm, Kenneth and Edward Lincoln, 1997. 'Time to Reinvent APEC', *Policy Briefs,* No. 26, Brookings Institution, Washington, DC.

Funabashi, Yoichi, 1995, *Asia Pacific Fusion: Japan's Role in APEC,* Institute of International Economics, Washington, DC.

Garnaut, Ross and Peter Drysdale (eds), 1994. *Asia Pacific Regionalism: Readings in International Economic Relations,* HarperEducational, Sydney.

Garnaut, Ross, 1996. *Open Regionalism and Trade Liberalisation*, Institute of South East Asian Studies Singapore, and Allen and Unwin, Sydney.

Hai Wen, 1996. 'Agricultural Policy Adjustment in the Process of Trade Liberalisation', paper presented at a conference on China and the WTO: Issues and Impacts on China and East Asian and Pacific Economies, Tokyo 8-9 May 1996.

Itoh, Motoshige, 1996, 'A Few Theoretical Remarks on China's Entry to the WTO' paper presented to a conference on China and WTO: Issues and Impacts on China and the East Asian and Pacific Economies, Tokyo, 8-9 May 1996.

Japan Pacific Cooperation Study Group, 1980. *Report on the Pacific Basin Cooperation Concept*, Prime Minister's Office, Tokyo.

Lu, Weiguo, 1994. 'China's GATT Re-entry and the Liberalisation of its Wool

Textile Industry', paper presented to workshop on China and East Asian Trade Policy, The Australian National University, Canberra.

Miki, Takeo, 1968. 'Japan's Foreign Policy', speech delivered at the Australian National University, Canberra, 29 July.

Saxonhouse, Gary R., 1997. 'Regional Initiatives and US Trade Policy in Asia', *Asian–Pacific Economic Literature*, 11(2), November:1–4.

Song, Ligang, 1993. *Sources of International Comparative Advantage: Further Evidence*, PhD Dissertation, The Australian National University, Canberra.

Terada, Takashi, 1998. 'The Origins of Japan's APEC Policy: Foreign Minister Takeo Miki's Asia Pacific Policy and Current Implications, *The Pacific Review*, 11(3):337–65.

NOTE

This paper draws on work completed recently with Andrew Elek and Hadi Soesastro ('Open Regionalism: The Nature of Asia Pacific Integration', and David Vines and Brett House ('East Asia and Europe: A Shared Global Agenda?'). Many of the ideas and words are property shared with these colleagues. The argument in the paper is elaborated in Drysdale (1997a, 1997b). I am grateful to Ross Garnaut for his critical and helpful comments. I alone am responsible for the final shape of the argument.

3

THE FUNCTIONS OF APEC AND IMPLICATIONS FOR CHINA: A CRITICAL REVIEW

ZHANG JIANJUN

Asia Pacific Economic Cooperation (APEC) is experiencing a critical time in its short history. Founded in 1989, APEC includes all the major economies of the region and the most dynamic, fastest growing economies in the world and claims to be a major contributor to global prosperity and stability. Its 18 members had a combined GDP of over US$16 trillion in 1995, and 42 per cent of global trade. With the arrival of the new millenium, there are some key questions to ask. Ten years after its establishment, is APEC able to deliver? What are the factors behind its present situation? What will be APEC's future configuration and activities? How will China cope with APEC's trade and investment agenda? There are many questions that remain to be answered.

This chapter analyses APEC's evolving features and functions, and its achievements and pitfalls. It examines the significance of APEC to China, China's attitude towards APEC's trade and investment liberalisation process, and the interactions between China and APEC under the trend of increasing globalisation and economic interdependence. Finally, it underlines the key issues that need be addressed by APEC in the long term.

HISTORICAL REVIEW

Throughout the 1980s, the economies of the Asian members of APEC grew at rates substantially higher than those of Europe and North America. Partly created and accelerated by increasing foreign direct investment from Japan, Asia's trade and investment tends to be more concentrated within the region. With widespread anxiety about emerging regional trading arrangements elsewhere in the world, Asian economies—which are mostly export-oriented—considered setting-up their own arrangement in the event that regional arrangements elsewhere became inward-looking trading blocs.[1] Meanwhile, frustrated with the slow progress of the Uruguay Round negotiations of the General Agreement on Tariffs and Trade (GATT), the United States resorted to regionalism and promoted the establishment of the North American Free Trade Agreement (NAFTA). In 1993, it offered to host the first economic leaders' meeting of APEC, and thus created a new dimension of Asia Pacific cooperation. It was believed that the creation of APEC would serve to maintain an open international trading regime and reduce the growing number of trade disputes involving APEC members. Moreover, APEC would help enhance the process of economic integration and exchange of views among APEC members and promote a positive conclusion of the Uruguay Round negotiations of the GATT (Janow 1997:951).

The establishment of APEC has been described as 'like-minded people [meeting] together' to engage in trade and investment liberalisation and economic cooperation in Asia and the Pacific region. While not devoid of political content, it is safe to say that APEC has developed primarily in response to the growing interdependence among Asia Pacific economies (Janow 1997:991).

DISTINCTIVE FEATURES

Over the years, APEC has developed a number of unique features and decision-making processes that differenentiate it from any other international or regional forum. To start with, APEC is neither a formalised free-trade arrangement—such as NAFTA—nor anything like a European-style common market. Instead it has coined the unique term of 'open regionalism' to describe its approach to trade and economic issues (Janow 1997). In other words, APEC has committed to offer the liberalisation it has achieved to non-members on a non-discriminatory basis. This was designed to avoid the inherently preferential nature of free trade arrangements and the deleterious effect of the proliferation of such an arrangement on the newly formed World Trade Organization (WTO).

It was agreed that APEC would be a non-formal forum for consultations among high-level representatives of APEC economies on matters of common interest and concern. Therefore, it is not surprising to note that the economic leaders' meeting is usually prefixed with the word 'informal', and all rules and principles adopted by APEC are labeled as 'non-binding', such as 'Non-Binding Investment Principles' and 'Non-Binding Principles on Government Procurement'.

Diversity is an important feature of APEC, which now consists of 21 member economies with rich differences in terms of political system, cultural background, religious beliefs, and population size as well as level of economic development. This diversity can be interpreted as both a source of action and—more frequently—hindrance to quick decisions and actions.

Recognising the diverse interests and circumstances of its membership, APEC has developed new approaches to solving its problems, the 'APEC approach'. Thus far there is no clear definition of this term, but in practice people most often refer to it in the following circumstances.

- Consensus. Consensus constitutes the core element of APEC's decision-making process. This means every member has *de facto* veto power over any proposal. To date, this principle has been strictly adhered to over the course of APEC activities. During the deliberation of Early Voluntary Sectoral Liberalisation (EVSL), however, the term 'critical mass' or the (then) '18 minus X' formula was introduced. This means further sectoral liberalisation can proceed through a plurilateral agreement among a group of APEC economies if a 'critical mass' exists in its favour. This formula directly contradicts the principle of consensus and still remains controversial.
- Concerted unilateralism. This refers to the fact that with commonly agreed targets and principles each APEC country should take unilateral actions through voluntary steps. APEC's liberalisation program is supposed to be reflected in the Individual Action Plans (IAPs) and Collective Action Plans (CAPs). APEC is expected to strengthen liberalisation initiatives through a combination of multilateral, regional and unilateral actions.
- Top-down direction. This is another newly developed approach in response to the slow progress achieved thus far. Some significant issues like the EVSL and the Information Technology Agreement (ITA) were directly handed over to ministers and leaders who meet annually, instead of first spending time with the cautious working-level officials. This approach has proved to be a very powerful weapon, as justifications have to be made for the annual summit, and this method makes APEC more results-oriented.

SIGNIFICANT STEPS

APEC has come a long way since 1989. From the initial stage of exchanging views and project-based initiatives, it has been transformed into a forum of greater substance and higher purpose. At Blake Island in November 1993, when the leaders met for the first time for informal discussions, they envisioned a community of Asia Pacific economies in which the energy of diversity would be harnessed, the spirit of openness and partnership would be deepened and dynamic growth would be sustained through cooperative efforts (in Seattle 1993). In 1994 in Bogor, Indonesia, leaders translated the vision of an open trade system into the ambitious goal of free and open trade and investment in the Asia Pacific by 2010 for developed members and 2020 for developing members (in Bogor 1994). In Osaka in 1995, APEC leaders adopted a framework for achieving their goal—

the Osaka Action Agenda (OAA)—which establishes the three pillars of APEC activities: trade and investment liberalisation (TILF), business facilitation and economic and technical cooperation (ecotech). OAA also clearly spelled out the general principles for liberalisation and facilitation and essential elements for economic and technical cooperation (in Osaka 1995).

The Manila Action Plan for APEC (MAPA) adopted by economic leaders in 1996 includes the IAPs and CAPs and progress reports on the joint activities of all APEC economies in their endeavour to achieve the goal set out in Bogor. The leaders also outlined six priorities for economic and technical cooperation: developing human capital, fostering safe and efficient capital markets, strengthening economic infrastructure, harnessing technologies of the future, promoting environmentally sustainable growth, and encouraging the growth of small and medium-sized enterprises. At their Vancouver meeting in 1997, economic leaders reaffirmed their commitment to update their IAPs annually and adopted the 15 sectors for early sectoral liberalisation, with nine to be advanced throughout 1998 and implementation to occur in 1999.[2] They also encouraged more active participation of the business community, young people, women and civil society. Leaders endorsed 'The Blueprint for APEC Customs Modernisation' as a model for business facilitation as well as the 'Vancouver Framework for Enhanced Public-Private Partnership for Infrastructure Development'. Electronic commerce was discussed for the first time and instructions were made on the development of a work program (in Vancouver 1997).[3]

At their Kuala Lumpur meeting in 1998, APEC leaders committed to work together to pursue a cooperative growth strategy to end the financial crisis that had engulfed the region. They agreed to seek an EVSL agreement with non-APEC members at the WTO, and pledged to strengthen social safety nets, financial systems, trade and investment flows, the scientific and technological base, human resources development, economic infrastructure, and business and commercial links to provide a firm basis for sustained growth into the twenty-first century (Kuala Lumpur 1998). At the Auckland meeting in September 1999, leaders endorsed new APEC Principles to Enhance Competition and Regulatory Reform, further work on an APEC Food System, and agreed to give priority to trade facilitation in 2000. They also pledged to strengthen domestic financial markets and improve the international framework governing the flow of international trade and investment (in Auckland 1999).[4]

When assessing the progress of APEC, it must be recognised that APEC has made remarkable progress through members' voluntary and unilateral actions as well as collective initiatives on trade and investment liberalisation and facilitation. APEC members have lowered their average tariff levels by almost half from 15 to 9 per cent. Many developing members such as Chile, China, Thailand and the Philippines experienced a dramatic decline in their average tariff levels. Now 14 members have tariff levels below 15 per cent with the majority of these below 10 per cent. Three members have average tariff rates at close to zero (PECC 1996). Greater transparency on non-tariff measures has been enhanced through identification and removal exercises. With respect to investment, members commit to review their investment regimes for investment liberalisation and voluntarily include in their IAPs, wherever possible, the list of specific options to be developed by the Investment Expert Group. The annual investment symposium facilitates APEC's investment reform process and improvement of the investment environment in the APEC region. In terms of services, few APEC economies impose barriers on foreign providers of computer, telecommunication or tourism services (PECC 1995). Three sectors—education, distribution and business services—have been identified as priority sectors to compile a list of measures affecting trade in services. An APEC Directory on Professional Services, covering accountancy, architecture and engineering is under development. A list of existing databases containing statistical information on trade in services has been compiled, and trade in services arrangements within APEC have been reviewed.

In other areas such as customs procedures, intellectual property rights, dispute mediation, competition policy and deregulation, contact points were established, databases on government laws and regulations were set up, various training programs were conducted to enhance members' understanding, and commitments were made by members to further liberalise their domestic regimes and to facilitate business transactions. A set of non-binding principles on government procurement is under active discussion to be concluded one year in advance by 1999. Various working groups under ecotech have undertaken similar kinds of activities. In addition, the creation of a senior officials meeting, a 'Sub-committee on Economic and Technical Cooperation' (ESC) to coordinate and oversee APEC's ecotech activities will add new impetus to the implementation of the 1996 'Manila Declaration on an APEC Framework for Strengthening Economic Cooperation and Development'.

REGRETTABLE LOOPHOLES

While recognising the achievements of APEC, it must be said that APEC has failed to live up to all expectations. It is facing a reputation problem. Critics charge that 'APEC has policies aplenty, but few implemented'. Others describe APEC as a 'talk shop'. Checking the grand CAPs, it is easy to agree with the accusations: ten years after its founding, most APEC activities still remain at the stage of dialogue and information exchange. All the action plans look impressive, but there is nothing substantial. According to its work program, APEC was supposed to begin implementation in 1997. Concrete outcomes are yet to occur.

Except for its slow progress on trade and investment liberalisation and facilitation, APEC has yet to prove its value, *inter alia,* in the following areas.

APEC failed to act swiftly and responsively to the East Asian financial crisis that severely affected 12 of its 21 member economies. From 1997 throughout 1998, APEC, apart from rhetoric, undertook no serious concrete actions

APEC as the most powerful forum in the Asia Pacific region, could have played a much more significant role in taking collaborative action to alleviate the crisis and sending the right signals to the international community with respect to the region's economic stability and growth. The crisis is the Asia Pacific's own problem; it is too important for APEC to stand aloof.

Economic and technical cooperation has been recognised as one of the three pillars of APEC and should be given equal attention. But in reality, ecotech has been overshadowed by the trade and investment liberalisation and facilitation process. This has caused frustration and reduced interest in liberalisation among developing economies. In many cases, the first priority of the developing members is economic development, and to achieve that, they need infrastructure, technology and knowledge. But now there is growing concern that APEC's ecotech agenda is too business-biased and is looking increasingly like trade facilitation rather than economic cooperation among the governments. This is partly due to the reluctance of some developed members to offer contributions to the process.

While APEC's approach to ecotech differs from the traditional 'foreign aid' system, it does not exclude member governments from taking specific actions.[5] Actually, trade and investment liberalisation and ecotech are mutually and equally reinforcing. Ecotech provides APEC with a feature that distinguishes from the WTO, which only offers developing economies a delayed phrasing-in of obligations. A successful program on ecotech will help foster the confidence building among APEC members and enable the developing economies to benefit from market opening initiatives. As well, it is as important in building domestic political support for reform, or in some cases countering opposition for more liberal economic policies. Therefore it is not surprising that developing members hold high expectations of the newly formed ESC to address their concerns.

In economic and financial turmoil such as the crisis, many people start to doubt the benefits of globalisation and liberalisation. Some argue that the causes of the East Asian crisis were directly related to the free trade and investment policies of their governments, and thus call for policy changes. APEC needs to develop sound outreach strategies towards the community, to inform them about the benefits of liberalisation as well as associated adjustment costs. Only when this issue has been properly tackled can APEC make further progress towards liberalisation. In this juncture, the project on the impact of liberalisation undertaken by Australia is crucial in addressing these problems.

APEC's lack of tangible outcomes is causing angst among business people. On the one hand, this is partly due to insufficient communication with the business community, and on the other hand, it reflects APEC's failure to provide convincing outcomes in the short-term. In a sense, the EVSL process, which was supposed to be implemented in 1999, posed a great challenge for APEC to prove its worth and effectiveness. The end result was discouraging—after hot debate, EVSL implementation was transferred to the WTO.

FUNCTIONAL BARRIERS

It is appropriate to ask why APEC is not functioning as envisaged. There are a number of reasons, among which the following could be identified as the most important.

- Traumatic political and economic situation. APEC is now at a critical time and strong leadership is badly needed. However, the actual situation of APEC members is problematic. While East Asian countries—in particular Korea—have been struggling with the worst economic crisis of the 1990s, Japan is trapped in economic sluggishness. Prime Minister Obuchi proved the effectiveness of the government stimulus measures in its bid to save the ravaged financial system. President Clinton, running to the end of his term in his office, has been severely restrained by the Republican dominated Congress in any major initiatives. President Wahid of Indonesia is buried with ceaseless domestic unrest and massive economic problems. China has been locked in government restructuring, shrinking export and foreign investment, and an increasing rate of unemployment. Affected by Russian economic turbulence, Latin American countries are starting to experience economic slow-down. With APEC's steering team in such a poor shape, the Kuala Lumpur summit had difficulty in producing anything significant.

- Embedded structural problems. As revealed by the EVSL process, APEC has no implementation mechanism. None of its decisions are legally binding, which allows its members leeway in non-performance. Most of APEC's actions are carried out through unilateral and voluntary steps. There is no supra-national authority to administer or develop rules. With respect to the IAPs—the main channel for trade and investment liberalisation—the only existing mechanism is through voluntary peer review, which cannot guarantee faithful and effective enforcement and improvement of the IAPs. Moreover, APEC's decision-making process is primarily based on consensus. With such a diversity of membership, it is extremely difficult for members to reach unanimous views on substantive issues. This partly explains why 'critical mass' was introduced over the deliberations on sectoral liberalisation. Thus the APEC modality of voluntary measures, while both unique and popular among APEC members, has yet to demonstrate that it can produce meaningful results over time.

37

- Shaky foundations. The developing members look to APEC for economic cooperation while the developed members appear to be single-minded about market opening. Dominated by trade and investment agendas and frustrated with the slow progress on ecotech, the developing members are getting more suspicious of the developed members' commitment to carrying out the ecotech agenda. The two sides have not had sufficient time to build up the trust and understanding needed to advance the APEC agenda hand-in-hand.
- Lack of focus. There are 15 areas in APEC's TILF agenda, and 13 areas in the ecotech agenda.[6] Almost each area has its own expert group/ working group and work program. This adds up to a daunting amount of work. In addition, APEC has on its agenda an enormous number of other items such as EVSL, IAPs, CAPs, emergency preparedness, financial stability, electronic commerce, energy, environment and population, infrastructure, ABAC, women, youth and civil society, as well as reviews of the economic outlook. In fact APEC has evolved into a dinosaur that can be hardly controlled and made manageable.

RATIONALE FOR CHINA'S ADMISSION

China joined APEC in 1991. At that time it considered APEC as an 'informal, loose forum' that engaged in promoting dialogue and economic cooperation among its members. Being a non-member of the WTO or any other regional arrangement, China viewed APEC as an important venue for developing and deepening consultation and cooperation activities with the major trading partners in the region.

There are a number of important factors that determine China's stands on APEC. First of all, although APEC has not been a venue for ameliorating serious points of tension between individual members, it has provided a venue through which officials are able to cooperate in a constructive fashion on a broad range of work programs. APEC meetings also afford leaders and ministers the opportunity to convene separate bilateral meetings to discuss broader issues separate from the APEC agenda (Janow 1997).[7] This has proven extremely important in the post-Tiananmen period, when President Jiang Zemin had the chance to meet regularly with President Clinton and other APEC leaders to exchange views on matters of common interest and concern. Second, the Asia Pacific region, which is the foothold of China's open-door policy, plays a pivotal role in China's foreign economic and trade relations. In 1995, China's trade with APEC members reached US$206.2 billion, accounting for 73 per cent of China's total trade. Among China's major trade partners, all top five economies are APEC members. With respect to investment, 76 per cent of China's foreign direct investment was from APEC members. This trend has been reinforced in subsequent years with the deepening of regional economic integration.[8] Third, being a non-member of WTO, China for the first time participated on an equal footing in trade and investment policy deliberations. Meanwhile, China strives to use this platform to defend itself against US bilateral trade approaches towards China. The principle of non-discrimination, of which a compromise was reached at the last stage in Osaka, was considered a remarkable achievement. This constitutes an important leverage in underwriting China's most-favoured nation status.

AIMING HIGH

Recognising the irreversible trend of globalisation and the need to maintain an open international trading environment, China has taken a positive stand on APEC's trade and investment agenda. It considers APEC's overall direction as consistent with the spirit of the 15th Party Congress, national policy on reform and further opening up of the economy. Since its admission to APEC, China has reduced its average tariff level remarkably, from 40.3 per cent in 1992 to 17 per cent in 1998. It has made a commitment to reduce its average industrial tariffs to 10.8 per cent by 2005, the weighted average to 6.6 per cent, and to eliminate tariffs on 185 information technology products. Meanwhile, many non-tariff measures have been removed, allowing more foreign financial institutions to open branches in China; active participation of foreign firms in commercial retailing, power generation and oil and gas exploration has been encouraged; the investment regime has been streamlined to make it more business-friendly; and the intellectual property rights enforcement system and competition policy legislation have been strengthened.

Nevertheless, China is still at the early stages of reform. The government, headed by President Jiang Zemin and Premier Zhu Rongji, is facing great challenges at home. Tremendous efforts have had to be made to slash the bloated government bureaucracy, to stop the money hemorrhaging from state enterprises, to overhaul the antiquated financial system, and to resist rising pressure for a renminbi devaluation. Moreover, the government has to create in an expeditious fashion a social security net to protect the alarming number of workers laid off due to state-owned enterprise restructuring. At the same time, they have to guard against the traditional leftists who vehemently vow to steer China off its reform course. These problems restrain China from making more positive contributions towards APEC's liberalisation process. Nonetheless, since China has adopted an open-door policy as its state policy, it will continue to participate in APEC activities in a positive manner. This is a unique platform from which China can express its opinions on the world's new economic order. China has offered to host the APEC meeting in 2001. On past experience, the host government, regardless of its previous stance, is usually very cooperative and constructive in making its year at the helm of APEC a successful one.

INTERACTIONS WITH CHINA

Judging from the mechanism and functions of APEC, China is unlikely to obtain from APEC badly needed 'hardware' such as capital, technology and managerial skills. But APEC may act as an information source for China, a platform for policy discussion, and a stimulant for pursuing more liberal international trade and investment policies. In this context, APEC is valuable to China in providing 'software' to guide future economic development.

In reality, the impact of APEC is obvious. When drafting long-term plans for trade and investment, Chinese officials are increasingly conscious of President Jiang's commitment to APEC's goal of free and open trade and investment by the year 2020, and amend their plans accordingly. The ongoing APEC process is also exerting a direct influence on China's policy-making process. One example is in the area of government procurement, which is a new concept to China. Through hosting training programs and exchanging views with other member economies, China has gradually recognised the value of a sound government procurement system and has begun to initiate its own government procurement laws and practices in accordance with APEC's 'Non-Binding Principles on Government Procurement' and the practices in APEC member economies. Now a special task force has been established and relevant institutional work is underway. A draft law governing the operation of government procurement has entered into the second reading of China's legislative body, the Chinese People's Congress. None of these actions could have occurred without the impetus provided by APEC. Undoubtedly, efforts of this nature will help accelerate China's integration into the world economy.

In the past, China regarded APEC's trade and investment agenda as a non-binding, long-term process, and drafted its IAPs in that fashion. But this perception was strongly challenged with the rapid evolution of the EVSL process. China's domestic industries have begun to face pressure from foreign competition. Affected industries have vehemently called for prolongation of protection. This has presented the government with a dilemma. On the one hand, China—unlike small economies such as Hong Kong and Brunei—has, over the years, invested heavily in and developed a relatively complete industrial system covering all sectors of the economy. But to date most of those industries are known for overstaffing, obsolete equipment and technology, high costs and low efficiency, and are not competitive with their foreign counterparts. The government is not prepared to absorb the sunk cost and shoulder the social welfare expenses that would come with opening up the economy. On the other hand, it has realised that non-action is equally suicidal, as moribund industries are using precious resources each year. With its state enterprises undergoing reform, China therefore seeks a longer phasing-in period for EVSL proposals. While the outcomes remain to be seen, EVSL has indeed changed China's perceptions of APEC and forced it to amend its even-paced approach towards APEC's trade and investment agenda.

LOOKING AHEAD

APEC is now at a critical moment. In recent years, it has made remarkable progress in defining its goals and promoting its trade and investment agenda. Its firm commitment to free and open trade and investment has greatly improved the business climate in the Asia Pacific region. APEC's principles of WTO-consistency and non-discrimination have strengthened the international trading system and had a significant impact upon the development of regionalism. Its pioneering trade and investment agenda ensures APEC adds value to state-of-the-art issues. Through wide exchange of experience and information, APEC members have developed a growing sense of 'APEC community', enhanced mutual understanding, and a sound foundation has been laid for future actions. The annual APEC summit, highly valuable to all its members, has become one of the most prominent events in the world and has attracted the attention of the international community.

Nevertheless, APEC has obvious shortfalls and is increasingly facing a credibility problem. To cope with changing circumstances, APEC must further consolidate its position on trade and investment, develop a more effective implementation mechanism, and find better ways to carry out its ecotech agenda. In addition, its leaders should act together to produce focused and results-oriented outcomes, in making responsible decisions about important issues in the region. APEC also needs to work more closely with the business community and broaden its outreach to involve a wider segment of the business sector. These are crucial elements in ensuring healthy and sustainable development from APEC's future endeavours.

NOTES

[1] Merit Janow, Professor in the Practice of International Trade of Columbia University, provides details of the historical background and rationale for the setting up of APEC in her recent paper (see Janow 1997).
[2] The 15 sectors identified by APEC ministers and leaders in Vancouver in 1997 included: environmental goods and services, fish and fish products, forest products, medical equipment and instruments, energy, toys, gems and jewelry, chemicals, telecommunications mutual recognition arrangement, oilseeds and oilseed products, food, natural and synthetic rubber, fertilisers, automotive, civil aircraft. The first sectors are classified as 'fast-track' sectors.
[3] See introductory material *Asia-Pacific Economic Cooperation 1998*, and *Selected APEC Documents 1998*, both published by the APEC secretariat.
[4] See *APEC Introduction* available online at http://www.apecsec.org.sg/97brochure/97brochure.html

[5] In his speech addressed to the Council on Foreign Relations, President Clinton called the economic crisis the 'biggest financial challenge facing the world in a half century'. *The New York Times*, 14 September 1998.

[6] OAA specifies that ecotech should be conducted on the basis of 'mutual respect and equality, mutual benefit and assistance, constructive and genuine partnership and consensus building'. Its purpose is to attain sustainable growth and equitable development in the Asia Pacific region, while reducing economic disparities among APEC economies and improving economic and social well being.

[7] The 15 areas in trade and investment liberalisation and facilitation include: tariffs, non-tariff measures, services, investment, standard and conformance, customs procedures, intellectual property rights, competition policy, government procurement, deregulation, rules of origin, dispute mediation, mobility of business people, implementation of the Uruguay Round outcomes, information gathering and analysis. The 13 areas under ecotech include: human resources development, industrial science and technology, small and medium enterprises, economic infrastructure, energy, transportation, telecommunications and information, tourism, trade and investment data, trade promotion, marine resources conservation, and agricultural technology.

[8] According to China's customs statistics of 1997, China's trade with APEC members reached US$240.2 billion, accounting for 73.9 per cent of its total trade. Foreign direct investment (FDI) from APEC members stood at US$37.7 billion, accounting for 83.7 per cent of the total FDI it attracted during the whole year. The top six investors—Hong Kong, Japan, Chinese Taipei, United States, Singapore, and the Republic of Korea—were all APEC members.

REFERENCES

Janow, Merit, 1997. 'APEC: an assessment,' *Northwestern Journal of International Law and Business*, January.

Pacific Economic Cooperation Council (PECC), 1996. 'Assessment of MAPA', published by PECC for the APEC Secretariat, Singapore.

——, 1995. Survey of Impediments to Trade and Investment in the APEC region, published by PECC for the APEC Secretariat, Singapore.

AUSTRALIA–CHINA COOPERATION IN APEC

4

AUSTRALIA'S APEC AGENDA— IMPLICATIONS FOR AUSTRALIA AND CHINA

CHRISTOPHER FINDLAY & CHEN CHUNLAI[1]

Trade between two countries can be impeded by a variety of constraints. Some are the consequences of government policy; for example, border barriers to trade. Others include internal constraints, such as local business practices in the importing country. These too may be the consequence of deliberate policy choices. They may also reflect features of local markets and the stage of development of the importing country, including the depth of its institutions which reduce transactions costs. This chapter considers both types of impediments. The focus is on the economic relationship between Australia and China, and Australia's APEC agenda is examined to determine how it might affect some of these impediments.

An APEC member's commitments are codified in its Individual Action Plan (IAP). The IAPs were first released at the Manila meetings of APEC in 1996 and further developed—to involve a greater degree of standardisation in the format— during the Vancouver meetings in 1997.

All the IAPs are organised under 15 headings: tariffs, non-tariff measures, services, investment, standards and conformance, customs procedures, intellectual property rights, competition policy, government procurement, deregulation, rules of origin, dispute mediation, mobility of business people, implementation of Uruguay Round outcomes and information gathering and analysis.

Some features of the IAP for Australia are examined in the next section. We identify its implications for the reduction of Australian tariffs. We then review some aspects of Australia's proposals for the early voluntary sector liberalisation process, and its implications for bilateral trade. Later, the role of government in reducing the costs of doing business between Australia and China is considered and the issue of whether the Australian IAP makes a contribution to reducing those costs is discussed.

LIBERALISATION

Our main focus in this section is on the implications of Australia's commitments on tariffs for the bilateral relationship. Towards the end of this section, however, we also offer some brief remarks on other aspects of the IAP relatively important to China.

TARIFFS

The features of Australia's tariff commitments in its IAP are

- commitments on tariffs are only made up to the year 2000, rather that 2010 which is the target date for developed countries in the APEC process
- the exceptions are the sensitive sectors of passenger motor vehicles (PMV) and textiles, clothing and footwear (TCF), where commitments are made to 2005
- the general commitment is for tariffs in the range of 0 to 5 per cent by 1997 and a review by 2000 or earlier
- PMV tariffs are to fall from 22.5 per cent (15 per cent for parts) in 1997 to 10 per cent in 2005 and a review of post-2005 tariffs in 2005
- TCF tariffs are to fall from an average of 34 per cent in 1997 to 17.5 per cent in 2005 with a review of post-2005 tariffs in 2005
- other specific provisions are listed for sugar, vegetables and cheese.

The tariff policies on PMV and TCF were announced in 1997. They represent a retreat from earlier Australian commitments to programs of steady reductions in tariffs. The average tariff applied to PMV is to fall to 15 per cent in 2000, where it will remain until 2005, after which it will drop to 10 per cent. Similarly, while the average tariff on TCF products will fall to 25 per cent in 2000, it will stay at that level until 2005, when it will drop to 17.5 per cent.

These 'pauses' in the schedules of tariff reductions between 2000 and 2005 were contrary to the advice of the Productivity Commission. The Commission argued that a schedule of regular cuts is preferred to a relatively long period of no change. It proposed a series of reductions in tariff rates to 5 per cent by mid-2008.[2]

Furthermore, the pause and the manner in which it was decided is likely to make it more difficult in the process of reviewing tariffs beyond 2005 to commit to further schedules of reductions. By adopting a 'pragmatic' position, the government has increased the expectation of future rewards to political activity by the interest groups who stand to gain from a pause.

There is some evidence, however, that the broad commitments to APEC were important in leading to commitments by Australia to cut tariffs in 2005. The risk was that without commitments, the schedules might have been open-ended, finishing with a simple commitment to later reviews rather than a tariff cut in 2005.

Our particular interest here is the impact of the Australian tariff commitments and of these commitments on trade with China.

We summarise those effects by calculating Australia's average tariff as perceived by each APEC member. This average is calculated by weighting the Australian tariff in each commodity group (at the 6 digit HS tariff classification) by the value share of imports from a country in that group. The results, obtained from the APEC Impediments Measurement System (AIMS), are reported in Table 4.1. The 1997 column refers to current most-favoured nation tariff rates (preferential rates are not taken into account) and that for 2005 assumes that all the listed IAP commitments on tariffs are implemented. Weights used to calculate the average in both columns are the shares in total imports from the source country of each commodity group in 1996.

Australia's IAP commitments will lead to significant reductions in Australia's average tariff, from 4.3 per cent in 1997 to 3.5 per cent in 2005—a reduction of 19 per cent in the average tariff. It also leads to a significant reduction in tariffs applied to imports from non-APEC members.

The average tariff applied by Australia to imports from China in 1997 was 12.2 per cent, over 2.5 times the APEC average. In 2005, the average tariff applied by Australia to imports from China was 7.4 per cent, now about twice the APEC average.

The high average tariff applied to imports from China reflects the high share of textiles, clothing and footwear in Australia's imports from China (Findlay and Song 1996). As China continues to grow over the next decade, the share of these products in China's exports might be expected to decline and therefore the extent of the impediments applying to Australia's imports from China would also decline. Further work on modelling bilateral trade flows as China grows could be used to capture these effects.

The average tariff rate by country in 1997 is plotted against each country's GDP per capita (Figure 4.1). A simple regression line is fitted to these data. When a dummy variable is added to the equation to test China's outlier position, the regression line becomes horizontal and the China dummy is highly significant. Apparently the composition of China's trade with Australia is driving China to an outlier position.

The IAP commitments will have the effect of the reducing the extent of this impact on China of Australia's tariff structure. Completing those commitments will therefore make an important contribution to an even closer economic relationship between the two economies.

OTHER LIBERALISATION COMMITMENTS

Other elements of Australia's IAP may attract particular interest from China in terms of its access to Australian markets. These include

- the phasing out of bounties on ship building which will facilitate market access to Australia by suppliers in Northeast Asia, to which China may be a contributor
- the removal of investment restrictions in the hotels, restaurants, travel agencies, tour operators and tourist guide services, which may be important for Chinese firms aiming to serve the market for Chinese travellers in Australia (and which facilitates Australian exports of those services to China)
- the commitment to review cabotage policy applied to shipping by 2000, the result of which may be more opportunities for Chinese shipping companies

Table 4.1   Australia's import weighted average tariffs[a] by source

Trading partner	1997 weighted average tariff	2005 weighted average tariff
Total	4.3	3.5
APEC members	4.5	3.6
non-APEC members	4.1	3.4
Brunei	22.7	11.7
Canada	2.3	2.2
Chile	1.0	1.0
China	12.2	7.4
Hong Kong	4.3	3.0
Indonesia	3.2	2.3
Japan	5.4	4.4
Korea	7.0	4.8
Mexico	3.9	3.6
Malaysia	3.4	3.2
New Zealand[b]	4.8	3.8
PNG	0.1	0.1
Philippines	6.0	5.5
Singapore	1.0	1.0
Thailand	4.5	3.6
Chinese Taipei	4.1	3.6
United States	3.3	3.0

Notes: [a] Tariffs included in the calculations are most-favoured nation tariff rates. Import values used as weights are those for 1996. The same weights are used for 1997 and 2005. [b] Tariffs on imports from New Zealand are also calculated at most-favoured nation rates. The New Zealand number therefore refers to tariffs that would have been imposed on imports from New Zealand had preferences not applied.

Source: APEC Impediments Measurement System (AIMS), compiled by Malcolm Bosworth and Gerard Durand at the Australia–Japan Research Centre at the Australian National University for the Pacific Economic Cooperation Council (PECC).

- the alignment of Australia's non-preferential rules of origin with harmonised rules when adopted by the World Trade Organization (WTO), which removes some of the uncertainties associated with anti-dumping issues and with labelling of goods, in particular when origin of goods has to be defined.

In other cases, commitments in Australia's IAPs will have greater effects on China's purchases from Australia. For example, the commitment in Australia's IAP to remove export licensing arrangements on exports of natural gas, coal, mineral sands, bauxite and alumina, will add to the security of supply in trades in which China may become a more important buyer.

EARLY VOLUNTARY SECTOR LIBERALISATION

The tariff rate data illustrate the concentration of Australia's most sensitive sectors in its trade with other APEC members. The APEC process, including the implementation of IAPs by other members, creates opportunities to deal with these sectors (although defining the counterfactual and thereby specifying APEC's contribution to that outcome is difficult). Furthermore, these data highlight the importance of APEC continuing to deal with the sensitive sectors, not only in Australia but in all member countries: it is important for the Australia-China

Figure 4.1 The relationship between Australia's average tariff rates and per capita GDP of APEC member economies (with a dummy variable for China), 1997

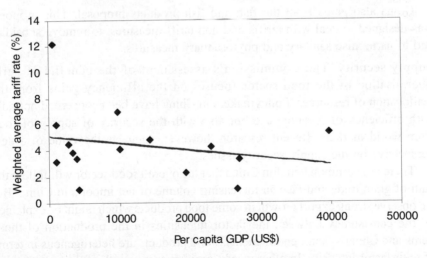

Source: Authors' calculations.

relationship that sensitive sectors not be backloaded in any concerted efforts at liberalisation in APEC.

The priorities for liberalisation are being discussed in APEC in the process of determining sectors for early voluntary sector liberalisation (EVSL).

Australia's nominations taken up in the EVSL process were energy products, chemicals and food. Chemicals was also nominated by China (whose other nomination was toys—textiles and clothing was not included in this process). Chemicals was a first tier EVSL sector and food was located in the second tier. We illustrate some of the issues and opportunities involved by reference to the food sector.[3]

FOOD

The food sector as defined for the purpose of the EVSL discussions included some parts of non-grain crops, beverages and tobacco and some other food products. Milk products, meat and livestock, grain crops and processed rice were not included. Fish and fish products are covered by a separate EVSL discussion in the first tier.

The Productivity Commission reports that the original specification of the food sector for EVSL discussion would lead to a loss of real income in a number of APEC economies.[4] This is due to incomplete coverage of the definition of the sector. The Commission simulates an extension of the coverage of this sector and shows that if the coverage is broad enough then all economies can gain from its liberalisation. According to the Commission's modelling work, however, China gains at all levels of coverage.

China also gains from the fish and fish products proposal. This proposal was designed to deal with tariffs and non-tariff measures, to remove subsidies and to harmonise sanitary and phytosanitary measures.

Supply security. The Commission's assessment of the benefits of early liberalisation of the food sector focuses on the efficiency gains from the reallocation of resources. Policymakers in China have been concerned not only with efficiency of resource use but also with the security of supply of food from world markets. Recent research, however, suggests the value of a new perspective on the supply security issues.

There is a common belief in China that the overall food sector will follow the path of grain trade and face an increasing volume of net imports in China. But we observe strong export growth in some food products which might be explained by the consistency between the factor intensities in the production of those items and China's factor endowments. Food products are heterogenous in terms of their factor intensity. In other words, rapid export growth of those items may be consistent with China's comparative advantage within the agriculture sector.

A shift in the focus of policy towards the efficiency objective might therefore lead to the growth of exports of some foods as well as imports of others.

An important question exists: who will feed China? One response has been that China will feed itself through trade; for example, the export of labour-intensive manufactured products which will finance the imports of grain. From that perspective, China has strong interests in seeing developed economies dealing with sensitive sectors like textiles and clothing. This is significant in the bilateral relationship since Australia at the same time is seeking access to China's grain markets.

There is another way in which China can feed itself and that is through the exchange of 'food for food'. Sources of export income to finance grain imports might emerge, not only from the other export sectors of the economy, but also from within the food sector itself.

This argument applies to food produced at the farm level, for example the export of fruit and vegetables concurrent with the import of grains. The argument also applies at the level of manufactured products, which are also covered by the EVSL process. This point can be illustrated by reference to the trade in manufactured food products between Australia and China.[5]

Australia's net export ratios[6] in bilateral trade with China in the manufactured food product sector in 1996 are shown in Figure 4.2. Australia has high ratios for meat products (not shown here) but also for animal feed, wine, beer, sugar products, dairy products and fish products. China, on the other hand, is a large net exporter to Australia of processed fruit and vegetables, bakery products and spirits. Even within this small group of products, there are substantial differences in the patterns of trade in the bilateral relationship. These data also illustrate the scope for China to gain from the liberalisation of this sector in other economies to which China does or might export these products.

Economic and technical cooperation. As Elek and Soesastro point out in Chapter 10, a feature of the EVSL process was to note that liberalisation is linked to economic and technical cooperation, which can improve the productivity of resources employed in the sectors exposed to increased international competition.

The food products sector in China receives a relatively high level of protection. The simple average tariff rate for this sector is nearly 32 per cent, about twice the average for all manufactured product imports into China. In fact, all the rates for this sector are above the average for the rest of manufacturing except that for animal feed. Yet in trade with Australia, it is clear that some of these sectors have the potential for a high degree of international competitiveness. The distribution of tariff rates between sub-sectors (showing the simple average for each sub-sector and the high and low rates within that sub-sector) highlights the degree of variation in this sector and also the high rates on average (Figure 4.3). Relatively high rates are shown for beverages, dairy products, vegetables, and grain mill products (some rates may be redundant).[7]

Figure 4.2   Australia's net export ratios in the bilateral food product trade with China, 1996

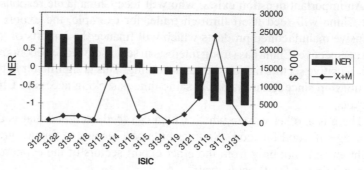

Source: International Economic Databank, The Australian National University, Canberra.

In Australia, the food sector is relatively lightly protected. The average tariff rate is just over 2 per cent (within a range of 0 to 7 per cent). In addition to removing the remaining tariffs, there are other ways in which Australia can contribute to growth in trade in this sector between the two economies, and to China's export performance in third country markets.

There is substantial scope for Australian contributions to economic and technical cooperation programs in each of these sectors as liberalisation occurs. These activities might include the transfer (on a commercial basis) of processing technologies, of experience of food product marketing, of systems of logistics (transport, storage, warehousing) required, and of systems of standards and labelling. These transfers would be facilitated by policy action to develop relevant policy environments, for example, commitments on the protection of intellectual property and the terms and conditions of foreign ownership of Chinese enterprises. The program might also include the mobilisation of funding for the development of appropriate rural infrastructure that removes impediments to the deeper relationships which are valuable between grower and food product processors (for example, the links between potato growers and fast food retailers). All these developments would facilitate a reorientation to international competitiveness in the food sector in China.[8]

TRADE FACILITATION

Other important areas in the IAP are commitments which affect the costs to firms within countries doing business with each other. These include commitments on standards and conformance and on dispute settlement.

Australia has made a number of commitments on standards and conformance which may remove some impediments to Australia-China trade—for example, in automotive parts, food and food products, electrical and electronic equipment, and telecommunications equipment, all of which are likely to become increasingly important export items for China.

Standards and conformance are examples of a set of trade facilitation matters. Trade will be facilitated if there are efficient systems for writing contracts between exporters and importers, for organisation of financial flows alongside the flows of goods and services, and for resolving disputes between exporters and importers. These matters have been important in the China-Australia relationship, reflecting China's stage of development and its transition to a market economy. One example where these issues arise is in the trade of wool between Australia and China.

The wool trade has been a theme in the discussions with China about market access issues and about China's accession to the WTO. Our interest here is in the trade facilitation issues associated with the wool trade. The bilateral experience in this market demonstrates the scope for international cooperation to facilitate trade, the relevance of some Australian IAP commitments in that context and also the value of private sector initiatives in dealing with facilitation issues.

While the wool trade is not an issue of China's market access to Australia— rather the reverse—a high proportion of wool exported from Australia is re-exported from China in processed forms. The management of the raw material component of these series of linkages is therefore critical to China's competitiveness

Figure 4.3 China's food sector import tariffs, 1997

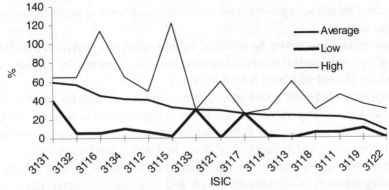

Source: APEC Impediments Measurement System (AIMS), compiled by Malcolm Bosworth and Gerard Durand at the Australia–Japan Research Centre for the Pacific Economic Cooperation Council (PECC).

in other markets, including Australia's own market for textiles and clothing which was the focus of discussion in the liberalisation section of this paper. We argued in an earlier paper that the experience of the wool trade illustrates the importance of

- the transparency and conformance of standards, or their recognition, across countries (this applies not just to the products being traded but also to contractual arrangements such as letters of credit)
- innovative financial systems, which can redistribute risks associated with international transactions
- ways of resolving disputes.

The experiences also highlight the scope for private sector initiatives to deal with these issues. We also reported an important private sector initiative to raise finance to the trade in raw wool. This arrangement provided liquidity for Chinese buyers, and dealt with risks that might otherwise be present in the trade.

Australia's commitments in its IAP to develop bilateral mutual recognition arrangements on conformity assessment, to support the involvement of Australia's technical infrastructure bodies in the development of mutual recognition arrangements, as well as its indication of interest in dealing with dispute resolution systems in APEC, are all relevant to this set of issues.

But should governments be involved? Market processes are also capable of supplying trade facilitating services—such as product description systems, contract drafting, risk shifting instruments and even dispute resolution processes.

The role of government is important where market processes fail to provide sufficient quantities of these services. Examples of efficient forms of government action may be removing impediments to firms setting up to supply these services. This will be relevant if, for example, there are regulations applying to financial services markets or to private sector involvement in some infrastructure services. In that case, an efficient government response is to liberalise policy applying to these sectors.

Governments might also be involved in supporting the provision of services where actors in the market have incentives to free-ride. In that case, an innovation from which all will gain may not be provided.

Cooperation between governments is relevant where one can benefit from the policymaking experience of another, or where joint action is efficient. Australia's IAP commitments to transfer its experience on the development of competition policy and intellectual property legislation is relevant here.

The economic and technical cooperation program in APEC is a vehicle for organising this sort of cooperation. Elek and Soesastro (Chapter 10) discuss that program in more detail and also highlights the importance of making more progress in that area in APEC. The experience of issues in the wool trade recounted here illustrate one principle that might be applied in the development of economic and technical cooperation programs—that is, their complementarity to private sector initiatives that deal with trade facilitation issues.

CONCLUSIONS

We have argued in this paper that the structure of Australian protection is highly biased against China. The average tariff rate faced by Chinese exporters to Australia is much higher than that faced by exporters from other APEC members. The rate will fall by 2005, creating scope for greater gains from trade between the two economies. But that higher degree of integration would have occurred even sooner if Australia had maintained its earlier commitments to a program of steady reductions in tariffs—on TCF products in particular. The tariff pause between 2000 and 2005 has slowed down the rate of integration. Also the commitments to tariff cuts in 2005 still leave China (apart from Brunei), on the basis of its current trade patterns, facing the highest average tariff into Australia. The rate facing China will still be about twice the APEC average. APEC commitments can constrain tariff rate setting processes in Australia and that pressure will be important to realise the potential that still exists in the bilateral relationship.

We examined some of the issues involved in the EVSL process in APEC by reference to the food sector, a second tier sector proposed by Australia. We noted that there is already substantial two-way trade in food products in the bilateral relationship. The data highlight the scope of gain from liberalisation in this sector and the scope for further mutual gain from economic and technical cooperation programs.

We have also stressed here the relevance of various components of the IAPs to trade facilitation. We illustrated the relevance of these issues by referring to experience in the bilateral trade between Australia and China in wool. We argued that efficient delivery systems of this raw material into the textile industry of China was critical for the international competitiveness of that sector. This includes its capacity to penetrate Australian markets.

We noted the value of private sector initiatives in dealing with issues which might otherwise impede trade. The example offered was the innovative arrangements developed by private sector banks to deal with risks in the wool trade. Implicit in this discussion was the value of the development of trading institutions in China. These include not only standards institutions but also those that supply financial instruments that deal with some of the risks in international trade. These developments in China are especially important since the financial market remains relatively closed.

We also discussed the scope for government to play a role in correcting failures in markets for trade facilitation services and the scope to support that activity from within the APEC economic and technical cooperation program. The links to Australia's IAP were noted.

In summary, implementation of the programs included in the Australia's APEC agenda, according to APEC principles, will contribute to a more intense trading relationship between Australia and China. The program also has the potential to extend and accelerate commitments in some of the sensitive sectors in the bilateral relationship. This is partly because of the range of instruments that is available in the APEC process, in particular, the role of economic and technical cooperation programs. It also occurs because of the linkages in policymaking processes of issues in the sensitive sectors, for example food sector policy in China and textiles and clothing sector policy in Australia.

A final question of interest is the effect of these liberalisation and facilitation initiatives on the bilateral relationship. The bias in Australian trade policy against China suggests the gains from liberalisation will be substantial. The gains from the development of markets for trading services may also be large. One methodology for doing this work is to compare Australia's trade relationship with China, and Australia's other bilateral relationships. Through such comparison, the potential for trade between the two economies can be estimated. Comparisons of actual and potential trade will then give some idea, at least, of the quantity impacts of these impediments and the progress towards their reduction. This work could also identify the effects of an acceleration of liberalisation, according to APEC principles, in some sectors where there was a mutual interest and where simultaneous action was expected to facilitate the implementation of the policy change in each economy. This is a topic for further work.[9]

REFERENCES

Drysdale, P., K.P. Kalirajan, Ligang Song and Yiping Huang, 1997. 'Trade among APEC economies: an application of a stochastic varying coefficient gravity model', paper presented to the 26th Conference of Economists, Hobart, September.

Findlay, C.C. and Ligang Song, 1996. 'The China-Australia commodity trade, 1985-1994', in Mackerras, C. (ed.), *Australia and China: Partners in Asia*, Macmillan, South Melbourne.

NOTES

[1] Ian Dickson was a co-author of an earlier version of this paper which contained a longer discussion of issues in the trade in raw wool and which was prepared for the meeting in Beijing, 7 October 1998 at the APEC Policy Research Centre, Chinese Academy of Social Sciences.

2   The Industry Commission considered a number of options. It argued that any advantages associated with a tariff pause outweighed the costs. It stressed the value of maintaining the momentum in a reform program and highlighted the credibility of its preferred option for Australia's trading partners in APEC. See Chapter 11 of Volume 1 of the Industry Commission report on The Textile Clothing and Footwear Industries.

3   We do not discuss the chemical sector in detail except to note the following. The Productivity Commission points out in its modelling work on EVSL ('APEC Early Voluntary Sector Liberalisation' a Staff Research Paper by Philippa Dee, Alexis Hardin and Michael Schuele, July 1998) that the chemicals proposal as defined involves the liberalisation of trade at the upstream end of the processing chain. The consequence is that inputs are cheaper for downstream processors and, depending on the extent of the assistance which they receive, the result can be a less efficient allocation of resources in the economy. For example, liberalising chemicals will encourage a transfer of resources into domestic textiles, clothing and other manufacturing which includes toys and sporting goods. Some of these sectors tend to be highly protected. The Commission's estimates are that the losses for China from this reallocation of resources are significant.

4   See note 3.

5   The scope of this sector defined in terms of ISIC classifications is
   3111-SLGHTRG,PREP,PRESERV MEAT
   3112-MANUF OF DAIRY PRODUCTS
   3113-CANNG,PRES FRUITS VEGS
   3114-CAN,PRES,PRS OF FISH,CRUS
   3115-MANUF VEG,ANL OILS + FATS
   3116-GRAIN MILL PRODUCTS
   3117-MANUF OF BAKERY PRODUCTS
   3118-SUGAR FACTORIES REFINERS
   3119-MANUF COCOA,CHOC+SUG CONF
   3121-MANUF OF FOOD PRODS NEC
   3122-MANUF OF PREPD ANL FEEDS
   3131-DISTG,RECTG,BLENG SPIRITS
   3132-WINE INDUSTRIES
   3133-MALT LIQUORS AND MALT
   3134-SFT DRNKS+CARB WTRS IND
   3140-TOBACCO MANUFACTURES

6   The net export ratio is the ratio of the difference between exports and imports, and their sum.

7   If EVSL sectors were chosen for each economy according to those which are expected to lead to the greatest efficiency gains, then the top ten sectors

for China include (in ISIC categories) 3116, 3132, 3134, 3843 (motor vehicles), 3115, 3112, 3844 (motorcycles), 3131, 3140, and 3901 (jewellery). Thus, all but three of these are in the food sector. The same principles applied to Australia suggest a focus on textiles and clothing, rubber products and motor vehicles. Data are from PECC's work in progress on the principles for selection of sectors for early liberalisation in APEC.

8   This set of activities in the food sector is included in the scope of a proposal being developed by one of the task forces of the APEC Business Advisory Council (ABAC) on the APEC Food System. The food sector is also the subject of a case study in a research project on impediments to trade and investment being undertaken by PECC on behalf of ABAC.

9   There is already some work applying gravity models to this question, see for example, Drysdale et al. 1997 and Drysdale, Huang and Kalirajan in Chapter 15, this volume. As well, Kaleeswaran Kalirajan in his MEc thesis at the University of Adelaide ('Estimating the gravity equation using the stochastic frontier approach') has developed a theoretical basis for using the gravity model and explaining why a stochastic frontier approach is an efficient way of estimating the relationships. These models could be applied to examine the Australia-China bilateral trade.

5

AUSTRALIA AND CHINA— SHARED OBJECTIVES IN APEC AND THE INTERNATIONAL ECONOMIC SYSTEM

ANDREW ELEK

The ability of APEC governments to handle short-term financial or macro-economic crises depends, to a large extent, on awareness of the shared interest in limiting needless underemployment of people and productive capacity. The limited success in terms of responding to the problems which became evident in mid-1997 should not be seen as a failure of APEC leaders in Vancouver, but an indication that more needs to be done to nurture a sense of community in the Asia Pacific. This is not surprising in a remarkably diverse region, whose diversity has been substantially increased by the decision to include Russia in the APEC process.

To strengthen a sense of community, APEC's agenda will need to extend beyond the recent emphasis on liberalising trade and investment. Reducing impediments to international economic transactions remains important. All Asia Pacific economies will benefit considerably from progress towards the 2010/2020 Bogor commitments. But the reforms needed will impose short-term costs of adjustment. The cohesion of APEC will depend on exploiting many other opportunities for mutually beneficial cooperation. Economic cooperation to maximise the sustainable growth potential of Asia Pacific economies needs to extend to a broad-based process of development cooperation, not based on one-way transfers of funds, but on a collaborative approach to dealing with the region's problems. The 1996 'Manila Declaration' of APEC ministers set out a framework of principles and priorities for doing so, but much more needs to be done to intensify development cooperation in the region.

As China continues to upgrade its technology and increase the productivity of its human and other resources, it has the widely acknowledged potential to be by far the world's biggest economy. Achieving this will lead to a considerably greater interdependence with other economies. That, in turn, requires much

59

greater confidence by China about its access to international markets for inputs as well as outputs, combined with confidence about China's external economic policies by the rest of the world. China has the biggest stake in global free and open trade and investment in the twenty first century, which will be achieved only if APEC provides credible and cohesive leadership in international institutions. Both these considerations point to the need to end the delay in including China in the WTO.

Asia Pacific economies cannot expect to realise their potential for development in isolation from the rest of the world. That is why APEC has consistently sought to promote global, not just regional, objectives by pursuing open regionalism. Up to now, open regionalism has been used to distinguish between MFN or preferential liberalisation of border barriers to trade. As APEC governments develop concrete proposals to facilitate trade and investment—for example by harmonising product standards and administrative procedures—the concept of open regionalism will need to be spelt out in more detail.

As APEC gathers momentum, participants will become increasingly aware of the need to ensure that cooperative arrangements among some participants are indeed capable of subsequent region-wide application. They will also need to ensure that new arrangements do not create new sources of discrimination, thereby fragmenting, rather than integrating regional markets. This is likely to lead to the adoption of principles for cooperative arrangements involving APEC economies which generalise the fundamental General Agreement on Tariffs and Trade (GATT)/WTO principles of transparency, non-discrimination and national treatment, and their application to new issues in international economic cooperation.

Such clarification of the concept and principles of open regionalism is also needed for forging closer economic links between APEC and non-APEC economies. In the medium-term, such links can be expected to emerge from the new Asia Europe Meeting (ASEM) process. In the short-term, APEC economies need to think about ways which will allow Russia to maintain and strengthen its economic ties to Europe in ways which preserve the integrity and cohesion of APEC.

ECONOMIC AND TECHNICAL COOPERATION

The need to respond to short-term economic problems confirms that the scope of economic cooperation in the Asia Pacific can go well beyond its current focus on reducing border barriers to trade and investment. The cohesion of APEC will come under strain as the 2010/2020 deadlines for free and open trade and investment loom closer and APEC governments start to think about exposing their more sensitive sectors to international competition. While the greatest share of the benefits of liberalising highly protected sectors would go to the economies which undertake the reforms, this is not the popular perception. It could become difficult to maintain the effectiveness and cohesion of APEC unless the scope of cooperation extends to other matters where the mutual benefits of collective action are more evident.

There are many such opportunities. There is growing awareness that border barriers to trade and investment are not the only important factors which increase the costs and risks of international commerce. Inadequacies of infrastructure— for example, transport and communications facilities—and very different approaches to the regulation of commercial activity are also important issues. The crisis has demonstrated that excessive volatility of exchange rates can be a destabilising influence which weakens the scope for trade and investment among the region's economies.

All of these issues can be addressed, to a significant extent, by a collaborative approach. To be consistent with APEC's fundamental principles of mutual respect and mutual benefit, such cooperation needs to be distinguished clearly from traditional 'foreign aid', which is characterised by one-way flows of money in return for political alliances, preferential access for trade, or enforced changes to economic policies. A new model of development cooperation, suited to the new realities of the region has to rely on a more sound foundation of mutual respect and the mutual beneficial pooling of available information, experience, expertise and technology. As Morrison (1997) has noted

APEC member economies should view development cooperation broadly as a process by which they work together to develop the entire region in mutually agreed-upon ways, and not as a process for resources transfers. In this sense, all members are developing economies, cooperating to achieve common goals such as establishing efficient regional transportation networks, creating world-class telecommunications links, developing the human resources needed for economic growth and protecting the Asia Pacific environment.

Since APEC leaders endorsed the objective of intensifying development cooperation in the region in Bogor, there has been extensive discussion of developing a model of economic and development cooperation designed so that all Asia Pacific economies can contribute to, as well as share in, the benefits of collaborative activities. It has been recognised that economic and technical cooperation is not only essential to support progress towards free and open trade and investment, but is an important ingredient in creating a sense of regional community of interests.

The 'Manila Declaration on an Asia Pacific Economic Cooperation Framework for Strengthening Economic Cooperation and Development' sets out a conceptual framework for a new Asia Pacific model of development cooperation, consistent with the fundamental principles of the APEC process of voluntary cooperation. The guiding principles of that declaration indicate that economic and technical cooperation among APEC governments will be conducted on the basis of mutual respect, including respect for diversity, autonomy, mutual benefit, genuine partnership and consensus-building. Consistently with the voluntary nature of APEC, as well as to move away from the 'donor-recipient' style of cooperation, activities are expected to involve the pooling of resources such as information, experience, expertise and technology, rather than one-way transfers of funds. All APEC economies are expected to make voluntary contributions, commensurate with their capabilities, and the benefits of cooperation are expected to be shared broadly. Cooperative activities are to promote a working partnership with the private sector and the community in general, to ensure that cooperation is consistent with market principles and the efficient allocation of resources.

According to the Manila Declaration, the six priorities of economic and technical cooperation activities are to

- develop human capital
- develop stable, safe and efficient capital markets
- strengthen economic infrastructure
- harness technologies for the future
- safeguard the quality of life through environmentally sound growth
- develop and strengthen the dynamism of small and medium enterprises.

Well over 300 activities have been proposed by APEC committees and working groups, mostly involving the exchange of information and expertise. Some of these are already underway, but the number of potential cooperative arrangements is growing rather more rapidly than the number implemented. It is also proving difficult to set an order of priority among the many ideas that have been put forward. During 1997, it became evident that economic and technical cooperation among APEC economies is lagging somewhat behind the process of trade and investment liberalisation and facilitation.

INTENSIFYING ECONOMIC AND TECHNICAL COOPERATION

APEC provides new means of interaction among Asia Pacific political leaders and officials which can lead to innovative ideas and opportunities for cooperative activities. However, it does not follow that APEC institutions are the only vehicles, or even appropriate vehicles, for financing or managing all such activities. Nor should the APEC process restrict its role to becoming just one more means of funding or implementing economic and technical cooperation in the region. The broader challenge is to act as a catalyst for new ideas, to help achieve a high degree of coherence among the activities of all those involved in economic and technical cooperation in the Asia Pacific, while avoiding duplication or creating needless new bureaucratic structures.

Just as the overall APEC process needs to find constructive ways to complement and cooperate with other institutions such as the WTO, joint efforts to promote economic and technical cooperation among Asia Pacific economies need to find sensible and efficient ways of forging constructive partnerships with the many multilateral, regional and national public and private agencies which are already active in those fields (Table 5.1).

To achieve synergy between all these potential sources of support for economic and technical cooperation among Asia Pacific economies, it will be essential to reach consensus about the comparative advantage of each in terms of financing and/or managing the implementation of the following forms of economic and technical cooperation.

- policy development, such as the exchange of information or expertise and the design of potential cooperative activities
- technical cooperation, such as specific programs to upgrade expertise, institutional capacity or technological capability
- infrastructure-building, especially where additional capacity can benefit several Asia Pacific economies
- financial cooperation to overcome short-term macroeconomic problems.[1]

Different combinations of these four types of economic and technical cooperation are needed in each of the six priority areas identified in the Manila Declaration. For example, human resource development relies mainly on policy development and technical cooperation activities such as training, while infrastructure-building requires a mix of finance and the design of appropriate policy framework relying on the exchange of expertise and experience among APEC officials. All four types can make direct or indirect contributions to trade and investment liberalisation and facilitation (TILF) while joint policy development work and people-to-people exchanges through technical cooperation activities are vital ingredients for nurturing a growing sense of community among APEC participants.

Each of these types of cooperative arrangements has vastly different requirements for funding and for ongoing management. Moreover, various agencies have been pursuing all of these four aspects of economic and technical cooperation since well before the establishment of the APEC process. Their involvement will be essential to implement the new opportunities for economic and technical cooperation which are emerging from the APEC process. For example, at a time of tight budget constraints, the business sector has by far the largest pool of financial resources. Its involvement will be indispensable to finance adequate investment in economic infrastructure during the coming decades, while the direct support of APEC governments will be needed to pursue policy development work as well as many technical cooperation activities.

THE CHALLENGE FOR APEC

Compared to the business sector, or to Asia Pacific governments, the APEC process has very modest funds at its disposal. These can be used to fund, at most, a small proportion of the many economic and technical cooperation opportunities it has already identified. This reality need not imply a passive role for APEC, but a serious effort to concentrate on its comparative advantage and to complement the work of others. It should be possible to design a strategy, based on the relative strengths of APEC and other potential sources of support, to pool the region's diverse resources and to mobilise new contributions to economic cooperation and development from all of these sources.

APEC leaders and officials have potential comparative advantage in designing options for economic and technical cooperation which can draw on information, experience, expertise and technology from throughout the region and make it available to many Asia Pacific economies.

These ideas and initiatives can act as a catalyst for intensifying economic and technical cooperation, provided APEC can evoke a positive response to such new ideas from the private sector and from Asia Pacific governments. Relatively small amounts of resources, allocated to relevant policy development work and to forming partnerships with others, could set examples of innovative technical cooperation activities and mobilise considerably larger contributions from others to help implement many of the options for cooperation identified by APEC.

The following examples illustrate how such a catalyst/response strategy for promoting economic and technical cooperation among APEC economies could be applied to some specific activities.

Table 5.1   Agencies active in the Asia Pacific economies

Private sector	business sector	individual firms or associations of firms
	NGOs	private foundations, research organisations and non-governmental development organisations
Public sector	multilateral agencies	development agencies such as United Nations agencies, World Bank, Asian Development Bank and IMF Asia Pacific governments acting individually or in groups
	APEC institutions	committees or working groups reporting to political leaders

HARNESSING TECHNOLOGIES FOR THE FUTURE

Policy development work by APEC working groups has already identified many options for pooling technological expertise. Such technical cooperation will be essential to implement many of the opportunities for collective action by APEC governments to facilitate trade and investment. This link is recognised in the Vancouver agreements on early voluntary sectoral liberalisation (EVSL). The programs for early reform in sectors such as energy are to be a combination of technical cooperation and facilitation as well as the liberalisation of border barriers to trade or investment.

Another example is the 'Blueprint for APEC Customs Modernisation' which has been endorsed by APEC leaders. It is a comprehensive program to harmonise and simplify customs clearances by 2000. Introducing the new procedures will need the development, installation and testing of compatible software for the electronic interchange and processing of customs information, backed by ongoing training for those responsible for applying the new, streamlined procedures.

These proposals, as well as many others for facilitating trade and investment— often by means of promoting human resource development—have emerged from the new APEC process. But that does not mean that the costs of such technical cooperation and training need to be financed directly from APEC's budget. Existing development agencies of some Asia Pacific governments, or a regional agency like the ADB, might be persuaded to add some of these activities to their priorities. Moreover, since the business sector is aware of the potential benefits of such facilitation, they should be willing to contribute to the cost of the associated need for technical cooperation, possibly through the new 'Partnership for Equitable Growth', described below. In a few cases—for example, region-wide pooling of expertise and training—cooperative arrangements could be pioneered on a small scale using funds from APEC's modest economic and technical cooperation budget. The subsequent continuation and possible expansion of such 'pilot projects' could be financed by a 'consortium' of businesses and existing development agencies.

Table 5.2 illustrates how policy development APEC working groups (marked by C) could catalyse appropriate responses by the private sector or APEC governments (marked by R) to finance and manage the consequent need for technical cooperation. The table also indicates how such a catalyst/response sequence could work in the following examples.

STRENGTHENING ECONOMIC INFRASTRUCTURE

Even if rates of growth were to slow temporarily in East Asia, there remain many commercially viable opportunities for extending or upgrading economic infrastructure in the Asia Pacific. The volume of investment which is expected

Table 5.2   Catalysing economic and technical cooperation within APEC

Type of cooperation	Agency 'Level' within agency	Policy devt.		Technical cooperation		Infrastructure building		Financial cooperation	
		Fund	Manage	Fund	Manage	Fund	Manage	Fund	Manage
Private sector	Business sector			R_1	R_1	R_2	R_2		
NGOs or research institutions				R_1					
Multilateral agencies	IMF							R_3	R_3
	Development agencies					R_2			
Asia Pacific govts	Individual, or groups of govts			$R_{1,2}$	$R_{1,2}$			R_3	
APEC Institutions		$C_{1,2}$ C_3	$C_{1,2}$ C_3						

to be needed is well beyond the resources of existing development agencies to provide concessional funding and it is widely accepted that the overwhelming share of investment in such infrastructure—including power generation, transport, telecommunications, airports, harbours, water and sanitation—will have to come from the business sector, either directly or channelled through multilateral or regional development banks such as the ADB. It follows that APEC's economic and technical cooperation is not expected to finance massive public investment in infrastructure, but to improve the efficiency of existing infrastructure and the prospects for private investment in new facilities.

On the demand side, economic forecasting work by APEC committees and working groups can foreshadow the need for timely investments in economic infrastructure. On the supply side, the development and implementation of policy options such as the harmonisation of customs and safety procedures can add significantly to the capacity of existing infrastructure. Policy development work by APEC officials, combined with technical cooperation, can also improve the framework for attracting commercial investment, including by strengthening financial markets or by creating the policy environment needed in cases where several Asia Pacific economies may need to cooperate in order to facilitate investment in infrastructure—for example, in sub-regional power or irrigation schemes. Such strategic inputs and the potential responses in terms of private investment in infrastructure-building are shown by C_2 and R_2 in Table 5.2.

STABILISING FINANCIAL MARKETS

By monitoring macroeconomic trends and anticipating potential difficulties, the forecasting work of APEC's Economic Committee and regular communications among APEC ministers can help prepare the ground for rapid responses to potential problems, with some individual APEC governments supplementing the resources which can be made available by the IMF (see C_3 and R_3 in Table 5.2).

The links which APEC has established among APEC Finance Ministers and their senior officials, and the mutual understanding of the structures and prospects of the region's economies have already proved worthwhile in facilitating a prompt initial response to the short-term macroeconomic and financial sector problems faced by several APEC economies in 1997.

FORGING NEW PARTNERSHIPS

The prospects for the private sector and existing development agencies taking up and implementing the new ideas for economic and technical cooperation emerging from APEC depend on establishing effective channels of communications and designing effective structures for potential partnerships.

'PARTNERSHIP FOR EQUITABLE GROWTH'

In its 1997 report to APEC leaders, ABAC confirmed the willingness of the business sector to give direct support to APEC's economic cooperation and development agenda. ABAC decided to establish a 'Partnership for Equitable Growth' (PEG) to serve as a new framework to encourage business participation in economic and technical cooperation activities, noting that the private sector can add value by undertaking projects in areas where neither the market nor governments currently meet regional needs.

At their 1997 Vancouver meeting, APEC leaders endorsed the PEG concept and also adopted the 'Vancouver Framework for Enhanced Public-Private Partnerships in Infrastructure Development'. Several export credit agencies and export financing institutions have signed a mutual cooperation protocol to enhance the attractiveness of infrastructure investment by the private sector. Objectives to be promoted by encouraging private-public partnerships in infrastructure-building include

- creating an Asia Pacific information society
- creating an integrated Asia Pacific transport system
- increased energy infrastructure
- infrastructure for sustainable cities
- infrastructure for rural diversification and integration.

During 1998, it should be possible to implement the first phase of some of these programs using the new PEG framework for forging a new form of partnership with the private sector for development cooperation in the Asia Pacific.

PARTNERSHIPS WITH EXISTING DEVELOPMENT COOPERATION AGENCIES

There are reasonable grounds for confidence that the development agencies of APEC governments, multilateral and regional development banks will respond positively to challenges to finance and/or implement new ideas for economic and technical cooperation proposed by APEC leaders.

APEC governments can exercise considerable influence over the priorities of their own international development agencies. Some existing agencies—such as Australia's AusAID—have already provided funds and made arrangements for the management of some technical cooperation priorities identified by APEC working groups. The Chinese government could, together with others, encourage all existing development agencies to shift their emphasis to supporting projects of region-wide significance emerging from APEC committees and working groups, rather than projects with a narrower, bilateral focus.

Once APEC governments have set some priorities for technical cooperation and infrastructure development, they have considerable potential collective influence over the priorities and activities of multilateral development agencies, particularly the ADB. Such development agencies have the institutional capacity to raise the funds required and to select firms best qualified to construct physical facilities and for the day-to-day management of projects.

In these ways, APEC governments can use the policy development capacity of APEC committees and working groups and a modest budget for innovative technical cooperation activities to mobilise substantial commitments from other sources. Moreover, the private sector and existing development agencies can take on the task of implementation. In some cases, private sector interest can be sharpened by contributions from APEC governments with a particularly strong interest in certain forms of economic and technical cooperation.

GLOBAL FREE AND OPEN TRADE AND INVESTMENT

Intensifying economic and technical cooperation using the mechanisms described above will help APEC governments to implement proposals for reducing impediments to trade and investment. Nurturing a sense of community through practical and mutually beneficial collective actions will also pave the way for APEC to tackle the liberalisation of 'sensitive' sectors early in the next century, by means of consensus-building rather than confrontation.

China, Australia and other APEC economies also need to develop a strategy for promoting free and open trade and investment globally, rather than just within the Asia Pacific region. An open, non-discriminatory global economy is needed to accommodate the expected growth of China's economy and trade. It is not realistic to expect that all of the structural changes necessarily will be restricted to within the Asia Pacific. China has the biggest stake in free and open trade and investment and its continued commitment to 'opening to the outside world' is a vital ingredient in sustaining the progress of all APEC economies towards the agreed 2010/2020 targets.

APEC's track record so far is encouraging. APEC governments have implemented the undertakings for 1997 in the 'Manila Action Plan for APEC'[2], while the prospects for sustaining the pace of reform have been improved in several ways. First, by strengthening the Individual Action Plans (IAPs) of APEC economies; second, by the nomination of 15 sectors—ranging from energy and chemicals to food and telecommunications—for early voluntary liberalisation.[3] Proposals for individual and collective actions in nine of these sectors are expected to be endorsed by Trade Ministers in mid-1998.

The sectors agreed for early liberalisation do not include the most sensitive sectors such as agriculture or clothing. However, it is realistic to apply new approaches to sectors where consensus is expected to be relatively easy to reach. Moreover, early agreements will prevent these from becoming the sensitive sectors of the future. The unilateral decision of APEC governments for completely free trade in information technology products in 1996 was followed swiftly by a corresponding WTO-wide agreement. Once APEC governments begin to implement programs for EVSL, they will be justified in expecting a similar response from the rest of the world, improving the prospects for tackling other difficult areas globally.

As the 2010/2020 deadlines approach and attention turns towards the 'sensitive sectors' of each Asia Pacific economy, all governments will need to make politically difficult decisions, in order to help other APEC participants to make correspondingly difficult decisions. It is quite possible that these decisions, involving different sectors in different economies, will need to be orchestrated by negotiations. But that does not imply that the APEC process should be transformed into a negotiating forum. The WTO has been specifically designed for conducting such negotiations and has the advantage that all significant economies take part.

It is very difficult to imagine either East Asia or the United States dismantling all of the protection of their agriculture sectors unless the European Union (EU) is prepared to act similarly. Such globally concerted decision-making could be achieved through WTO negotiations, while APEC economies continue their voluntary cooperation on many other less contentious matters.

Engaging the attention of the rest of the world and providing collective leadership in the WTO, as well as in other multilateral organisations like the IMF, will require APEC governments to act cohesively to promote their interests.

That in turn requires determined attempts to avoid inevitable friction over international trade or investment from leading to unilateral threats of retaliation. It also requires that all APEC economies become members of the WTO.

The post-Uruguay Round dispute settlement procedures are working well and there has been less inclination to try to settle issues by unilateral threats rather than by reference to the WTO. However, the WTO dispute settlement mechanism is not available to China (or to Taiwan and Russia). China's entry to the WTO has been blocked up to now, primarily by the United States, preventing prospects for a real sense of community within the Asia Pacific and APEC governments exercising their full potential for positive collective influence in international forums.[4] Europe is also a problem.

Australia can help to resolve the issue of China's inclusion in the WTO by making an unequivocal statement that, in its view, China's commitment to 'opening to the outside world' and its record of extensive reforms in that direction over the past two decades justify its immediate full membership of the WTO, with an unconditional right to most-favoured nation (MFN) treatment by all other members. There is room for improvement in China's trade policies, but these can be addressed through subsequent negotiations or, in some cases, by referring issues to the WTO's dispute settlement procedures. The time has come for Australia to address China's inclusion in the WTO in a strategic way, rather than looking for tactical negotiating opportunities, while hiding behind the United States on this matter.

THE FUTURE OF OPEN REGIONALISM

The concept of open regionalism has been critically important to APEC since its inception in 1989, reflecting the deep concern of East Asian economies in sustaining and strengthening an open global trading system. There are three main reasons why the Asia Pacific region has adopted a non-discriminatory approach to regional economic cooperation (Garnaut 1996; Drysdale et al. 1997).

First, it is impractical to consider regional trade liberalisation by means of a conventional discriminatory free trade area of the kind sanctioned by the GATT/WTO. The substantial elimination of trade barriers through the negotiation of a free trade area is simply not attainable within the Asia Pacific region, especially following the inclusion of Russia in APEC. Any attempt to negotiate such an arrangement would be highly divisive and delay the process of liberalisation it was supposed to promote (Elek 1995). It would corrode the objective of community-building and lead to the exclusion of major players inside the region who are not yet members of the WTO (such as China, Russia and Vietnam) as well as APEC's neighbours and trading partners. Hence APEC has opted for an alternative, new approach: setting targets for trade and investment liberalisation, rather than negotiating 'free and open trade and investment in the region'.

Second, the trading interests of East Asian and the Pacific economies extend beyond APEC, including to Europe. A conventional free trade area strategy towards trade liberalisation would deter internationally-oriented reform in the region's developing economies and introduce tensions into relations with major partners outside the region. As already noted, emerging giant economies like China (hopefully followed by Indonesia and Russia) can only be accommodated in a global economic system.

Third, trade discrimination involves the unnecessary costs of trade diversion, complicated in the Asia Pacific region by the likelihood of high associated political costs both within and outside the region (Garnaut and Drysdale 1994: Chapter 5).

APEC's agenda has evolved around giving progressively more precise expression and effect to the idea of open regionalism and this process must continue. The GATT/WTO principles of transparency, non-discrimination and national treatment apply strictly only to trade in goods, which dominated international commerce when the GATT was set up in the 1940s. These fundamental principles have yet to be extended systematically to cover other international economic transactions, such as trade in services, and international investment.

Similarly, up to now, the concept of open regionalism has been used to distinguish the reduction of border barriers to trade in a non-discriminatory—or MFN—basis from preferential trading arrangements. As APEC economies enter into new cooperative arrangements to facilitate trade and investment, they need to define how open regionalism can be applied effectively beyond trade in goods; to new areas for cooperation where there are few significant multilateral disciplines against discrimination.

The very different economic structures of the 21 participants of APEC, combined with diverse cultures, political systems and decision-making procedures, can make it difficult to prioritise and act on shared economic interests; one or more APEC participants may resist, or wish to delay, any specific proposal for practical cooperation. It makes sense to expect groups of APEC participants to implement cooperative arrangements to facilitate trade and investment at different speeds. The 'Osaka Action Agenda' contains an explicit provision for some Asia Pacific economies to set examples of cooperative arrangements which can be applied region-wide once their benefits become clear.

Such flexibility can promote the early initiation of cooperative activities to facilitate trade and investment and to exchange expertise and technology. However, such flexibility also carries some risks. Thoughtful management will be needed to ensure that 'variable geometry' does not create needless confusion or divisions by neglecting the interests of other economies. It is possible—and indeed imperative—to find ways to ensure that cooperative arrangements involving some APEC economies take careful account of the interests of others and promote the smooth evolution of region-wide arrangements. In other words, APEC governments will need to design and adopt guidelines which encourage the design of 'open clubs'.

DESIGNING 'OPEN CLUBS'

The main characteristics of 'open clubs' are that they
- do not seek to disadvantage outsiders
- have transparent 'rules', including transparent criteria for admitting new members
- actively promote wider membership.

Few clubs meet all of these conditions, but such criteria can distinguish those clubs which are genuinely seeking to meet high standards of 'openness'. Correspondingly, it is possible to set guidelines or criteria for cooperative arrangements which are designed to reduce impediments to trade or investment consistently with the concept of open regionalism.

Cooperative arrangements to facilitate economic transactions among groups of economies are typically implemented by adopting certain norms for policies which influence such transactions. For example, the 'policy norms' to implement the 1996 decision by Australia, Korea and the Philippines to introduce a streamlined system for business travel, provided for agreed and transparent procedures for the issue of visas and electronic processing of travellers with such visas, making it feasible for others to join once the procedures had been found to be helpful. By the end of 1997, several other Asia Pacific governments volunteered to join the scheme.

Many other options are available for some Asia Pacific economies to set examples for others. An arrangement for the mutual recognition of disclosure requirements and auditing standards for firms would need the economies involved to adopt some agreed norms, or minimum standards, of accounting. If these norms are clearly documented and others are encouraged to adopt them then such mutual recognition arrangements would also be open clubs.

Cooperative arrangements can be described as open clubs if the policy norms of the arrangement are transparent, do not contain provisions which discriminate against products or producers from other economies, and all economies which adopt the relevant policy norms have the right to accede to the arrangement. It is not easy to meet all of these criteria.

It is technically possible to reduce border barriers to trade in ways which do not discriminate against products from any source; this is usually described as liberalisation on a MFN basis. For trade in goods, Article 1 of GATT/WTO requires MFN treatment—at least of products from WTO members—except in some special circumstances, for example in the context of preferential trading arrangements which comply with Article XXIV.

Beyond trade in goods, there are fewer restrictions on discrimination. It is also more difficult to design cooperative arrangements which do not discriminate in some ways against other economies, either by design or by default. For example, free and open trade in services and free and open investment require national treatment of producers as well as of products.

Arrangements to facilitate international economic transactions will tend to divert economic activities even in the absence of any explicit provisions which discriminate against products or producers from other economies. Such arrangements typically involve agreements by a group of governments to adopt a certain set of more convergent, or more compatible, policies. Since these arrangements are designed to reduce the costs or risks of economic transactions among one group of economies, they will create an added incentive for transactions within the group compared to transactions with others.

In some cases, the resulting diversion of trade and investment may be unintended and insignificant. In other cases, diversion may be exacerbated and entrenched by explicit discrimination against products or producers from other economies. Those outside such cooperative arrangements can often reduce any disadvantage to them by voluntarily adopting the relevant policy norms. However, to avoid any diversion they usually need to be admitted to the arrangement.

There are several issues which need to be considered and resolved in designing cooperative arrangements involving APEC economies (Appendix 1). It is not always easy to reduce impediments to international economic transactions without detriment to other economies. It is not surprising that, in practice, markets are fragmented in various ways, not only by explicitly preferential trading arrangements, but also by many other cooperative arrangements among groups of economies. Therefore, if APEC participants want to ensure that cooperative arrangements pioneered by some APEC economies set positive examples and take account of the interests of others, they will need to devise and adopt principles to help ensure that arrangements for practical cooperation take full account of the interests of others and encourage them to join such arrangements.

In designing such guidelines, it is important to follow the basic principle of evolutionary cooperation, acknowledging that complete transparency and non-discrimination are ideals which can only be approached, rather than fully achieved. However, it is possible to agree on ways to ensure that all new arrangements do indeed contribute to an international trading system which is less fragmented and less discriminatory than it is now, and that becomes progressively closer to these ideals.

For example, in relation to trade in goods and services, the WTO has adopted the combination of 'standstill' and 'roll-back' to promote a gradual trend towards non-discriminatory free trade. The liberalisation of border barriers to trade, by individual governments or groups of governments, is expected to reduce some barriers without raising existing ones or creating new obstacles. Such a strategy can be generalised to promote cooperative arrangements to reduce impediments to all international economic transactions.

APEC's already agreed-upon principles of 'standstill' and the commitment to endeavour to apply the principle of non-discrimination can be given effect by guidelines which stipulate that new cooperative arrangements involving APEC economies should not lead to new discrimination. It will also be necessary to generalise the concept of national treatment to deal with the issues involved in reducing impediments to trade in services as well as to international factor movements. Accordingly, new arrangements should not contain any provisions which create additional or new forms of discrimination among products or producers, either on the basis of the location of various stages of production or the 'nationality' of producers.

To be effective, the principles for cooperative arrangements involving APEC economies will need to contain provisions for review of both proposed and existing arrangements. First, prior notice can enhance the prospects of more economies joining these new arrangements at the outset. Second, as illustrated by the examples in Appendix 1. It is not easy to ensure that cooperative arrangements among some economies are genuinely open clubs. While they may be designed in good faith to meet APEC's agreed guiding principles for trade and investment liberalisation and facilitation, their implementation could cause unexpected problems for other economies. Therefore, those involved in these arrangements should be willing—once again in good faith—to respond to constructive suggestions from other economies on how to improve the consistency of these cooperative arrangements with agreed guiding principles.

GENERAL PRINCIPLES OF OPEN REGIONALISM

Based on these considerations, the principles proposed below build on those of the 'Osaka Action Agenda', generalising the concept of open regionalism as well as the fundamental principles of transparency, non-discrimination and national treatment which lie at the heart of the GATT/WTO system.

APEC economies that are ready to initiate and implement cooperative arrangements to reduce impediments to economic transactions or to promote economic and technical cooperation are encouraged to do so, while taking account of the interests of other economies as follows.

TRANSPARENCY
(i) The policies adopted to implement these arrangements should be documented explicitly (typically expressed in legislation or regulations of those economies) and be freely available and accessible, through convenient channels of communication.

(ii) APEC economies should provide reasonable prior notice of the nature and objectives of proposed cooperative arrangements as well as the policies by which these are to be implemented.

NON-DISCRIMINATION

The arrangements should not contain any provisions which result in new or additional discrimination, either against products on the basis of the location of production, or among producers on the basis of their place of registration or ownership.

ACCESSION

(i) Any economy whose government accepts the responsibilities as well as the benefits of following policies compatible with any existing or proposed cooperative arrangements among some APEC economies should be able to, and encouraged to, become parties to these arrangements.

(ii) Existing parties to these cooperative arrangements should be willing to share the information, experience, expertise and technology needed to enable others to adopt the relevant policies.

REVIEW

APEC economies should endeavour to respond positively to constructive suggestions from other economies for improving theconsistency of existing or proposed cooperative arrangements with APEC's agreed guiding principles for liberalising and facilitating trade and investment.

As APEC gathers momentum, participants will become increasingly aware of the need to ensure that cooperative arrangements among some of them are indeed capable of subsequent region-wide application, as well as the need to avoid the proliferation of arrangements which fragment, rather than integrate, regional markets. This is likely to lead to the adoption of principles along these lines to promote the design of cooperative arrangements which are 'open clubs', consistent with these criteria.

Such principles or guidelines are likely to prove very useful in adapting cooperative arrangements which have been implemented in other regions in order to make them consistent with the Asia Pacific model of open regionalism. Most of the options for facilitating or liberalising trade and investment under consideration in the Asia Pacific have already been implemented in other processes of regional economic cooperation. It would be unwise and inefficient for APEC economies to ignore this experience. On the other hand, such arrangements have not always been designed to be 'open clubs'. Most existing cooperative arrangements among groups of economies contain provisions which discriminate explicitly among products and/or producers, thereby creating new market distortions. Moreover, few existing arrangements have well-defined means of accession which can overcome short-term vested interests against wider participation and will need to be modified to fit APEC's style of cooperation.

Once adopted, such principles can also serve as a framework for the design of cooperative arrangements involving both APEC and non-APEC economies. For example, the recently initiated ASEM process is likely to lead to some practical cooperative arrangements to lower the costs and risks of trade and investment between European and East Asian economies. If such arrangements were consistent with the proposed principles, they would be quite consistent with the interests of other APEC participants who are not part of the ASEM process.

The inclusion of Russia in APEC adds to the need for such principles. Russia's economic links with Europe and with other former members of the Soviet Union are considerably stronger than with other APEC economies. This balance will change, but Russia will certainly wish to be free to strengthen economic links with trading partners outside, as well as within APEC. If Russia can be encouraged to abide by the principles proposed for new arrangements involving APEC economies, then such links can contribute to APEC's ultimate objective of reducing impediments to global, rather than just regional, trade and investment.

CONCLUSION

The East Asian financial crisis has been a test of the cohesion of APEC and demonstrates the need for APEC to broaden its horizon beyond trade and investment. China and Australia can work together to help resolve crises of confidence in parts of the region. Australia can also play a more helpful role in ending the delay in China's inclusion in the WTO.

China and Australia can help to intensify development cooperation in the region, building on the conceptual framework of the Manila Declaration. There are many opportunities for forging new partnerships with existing development cooperation agencies, as well as with the private sector, to implement some regional economic and technical cooperation activities identified by APEC working groups. Training programs which share the experience and expertise needed to facilitate early voluntary sectoral liberalisation could be a good starting point.

In addition to ensuring that the commitment to early liberalisation of some sectors proceeds on schedule, the time has come to think ahead and develop a strategy for global action to deal with those 'sensitive sectors' which arc less likely to be opened up through unilateral, voluntary decisions by individual governments. APEC's guiding principles will also need to be refined to ensure that cooperative arrangements involving some APEC economies take full account of the interests of all other economies. This will be important as sub-groups within APEC start to implement arrangements for economic and technical cooperation or to facilitate aspects of trade and investment among themselves. Such principles are also needed to help ensure that practical arrangements for facilitating trade or investment between some APEC economies and non-participants—for example, arrangements emerging from the new ASEM process—remain consistent with the coherence of APEC.

These are complex matters. APEC officials and leaders will take some time to understand and address these issues. Some if not all of them will need further attention in 2001, when China takes up the leadership of APEC. There is an opportunity for Chinese and Australians, with shared interest in the future of APEC and of the international economic system, to work together to propose and promote ways to address emerging issues in Asia Pacific cooperation.

Appendix 1
PROPOSED STRENGTHENED PRINCIPLES FOR APEC

APEC's flexible approach to cooperation allows Asia Pacific governments to determine the sequence of unilateral liberalisation to dismantle border barriers to trade and investment. It also allows groups of APEC governments to implement cooperative arrangements—either to facilitate trade and investment or to intensify economic and technical cooperation—at different speeds. However, they will need a strategy for managing such 'variable geometry'.

As discussed in this chapter, the remarkable diversity of Asia Pacific economies means that it would be counter-productive to insist that all APEC participants be involved in every specific initiative for cooperation. Accordingly, the 'Osaka Action Agenda' encourages those APEC participants who are ready to implement cooperative arrangements to do so ahead of others. This provision can promote rapid progress as long as the initiatives taken by some are positive examples which are designed to maintain the cohesion of APEC and to provide practical means—as well as incentives—to widen the coverage to include all of the region. At the same time, such a '21 - X' provision carries some risks. As already remarked upon, initiatives by some APEC economies to facilitate trade or investment could sow the seeds of division and confusion if these arrangements neglect, or damage, the interests of others. Instead of promoting further market-driven integration of Asia Pacific economies, they could lead to an inefficient and needless fragmentation of markets.

Experience to date with regional economic cooperation indicates that most arrangements to reduce impediments to international economic transactions among one group of economies tend to divert economic activity away from the rest of the world. In some cases, such as preferential trading arrangements—sometimes called 'free trade areas'—the diversion is intended. In other cases, the diversion may be an unintended by-product of practical steps to reduce the costs or risks of trade or investment among some economies.

The following examples illustrate how the policy norms of various cooperative arrangements can be designed to take account of the interests of others and encourage them to join the arrangements in order to share in the benefits, while avoiding any unintended diversion of economic activity.

TRADE IN GOODS

APEC governments have agreed to dismantle all barriers to trade in all goods in a WTO-consistent manner by 2010/2020. Each government will set its own schedule for eliminating—unilaterally—its tariffs and any other border barriers to trade in goods by their respective deadlines.

APEC participants have rejected the option of setting up a formal trading arrangement, so Article 1 of the GATT/WTO will ensure that unilateral liberalisation of border barriers does not discriminate against any member of the WTO. Therefore, as long as all APEC economies join the WTO in the near future, unilateral liberalisation will not lead to any new discrimination.

However, the majority of APEC participants also belong to formal sub-regional preferential trading arrangements, so such unilateral reductions of tariffs and non-tariff barriers to trade in goods will be accompanied by liberalisation within these arrangements. Article XXIV of the GATT/WTO permits liberalisation within these groups to be preferential; that is, to proceed faster than liberalisation with respect to other economies, raising the prospect of some new discrimination by some APEC participants.

Fortunately, most Asia Pacific governments are aware of the advantages of non-discriminatory liberalisation. In practice, liberalisation within sub-regional arrangements is being accompanied by unilateral, non-discriminatory reduction of border barriers to trade. Both Australia and New Zealand have lowered trade barriers against the rest of the world while eliminating barriers to bilateral trade.[5] In the 1996 Manila Action Plan for APEC, ASEAN governments have confirmed that, as well as liberalising trade within AFTA, they would also continue to lower tariffs unilaterally against all trading partners. Some of them—including Indonesia and the Philippines—have indicated that they will extend the liberalisation committed within AFTA to all members of the WTO.

Members of NAFTA are not expected to extend the liberalisation within that preferential trading arrangement to other economies. In that case, there would be some short-term diversion of economic activity away from other APEC economies. The extent of new trade diversion could increase if, as planned, all North and South American economies form a preferential Free Trade Area of the Americas. However, members of NAFTA are committed to eliminate border barriers to trade and investment in the Asia Pacific by 2010.

For these reasons, the 'WTO-consistency' principle of APEC provides an adequate—and also critical—guideline for limiting discriminatory liberalisation of trade in goods on the way to meeting the agreed 2010/2020 targets.

TRADE IN SERVICES

Free and open trade in services requires more than the elimination of border barriers to the delivery of services. It will also be necessary to remove artificial distinctions in the way policies apply among services—for example on the basis of how they are delivered—or to 'domestic' and 'foreign' providers of services, leading towards the national treatment of all firms.

At present, there are few multilateral restraints to prevent governments from discriminating between 'domestic'and 'foreign' firms, or among 'foreign arms' of different 'nationality'. In practice, most cooperative arrangements to liberalise trade in services extend a greater degree of national treatment only to service providers from the economies involved. Other things being equal, such arrangements will divert activity away from economies which are not parties to these arrangements.

The design of practical guidelines for liberalising trade in services among APEC economies must take into account that it would be unrealistic to expect all arrangements to move from highly fragmented markets to automatic MFN treatment of all service providers. The immediate challenge is to ensure that cooperative arrangements to liberalise trade in services among some APEC economies can serve as a stepping stones'to wider arrangements.

For example, it would be counter-productive to expect to move from a system of bilateral agreements on international aviation—most of which are designed to limit competition—to free and open trade in aviation. In practice, reform is likely to proceed by the liberalisation of existing bilateral arrangements towards 'open skies' agreements and the subsequent linking of such agreements to cover more and more of the region. In other service sectors, the liberalisation of trade in services may advance most rapidly within existing sub-regional arrangements. This will rely on the acceptance of guidelines for cooperative arrangements on services which can ensure that liberalisation among some groups of APEC economies will lead smoothly towards the Bogor vision of free and open trade in services.

In line with APEC's 'standstill' principle, such guidelines should rule out any arrangements that create new sources of discrimination either among services or among service providers on the basis of their 'nationality'. While it might be unrealistic to expect all new cooperative arrangements to lack any preferential features, it will be important to anticipate that preferential arrangements tend to set up vested interests to resist the inclusion of additional economies. This suggests criteria to ensure that cooperative arrangements are transparent and provide for the unconditional accession of any economy whose government adopts the policy norms agreed upon by existing parties.

HARMONISING ADMINISTRATIVE PROCEDURES

APEC participants are already implementing a proposal for the electronic interchange of customs information and harmonised clearance procedures. This arrangement is likely to be an 'open club'. The arrangement is not designed to favour any particular sector or economy, but to reduce the costs, uncertainties and delays of customs processing. The resulting improvement in the efficiency of infrastructure will be maximised if more economies join the arrangement.

Accordingly, all APEC economies are expected to take part in the new cooperative arrangement. They also have an incentive to pool the relevant expertise and technology needed to allow all of them to implement the new procedures quickly and smoothly. Moreover, the benefits will be increased if all exporters to, or importers from, APEC economies also adopt the same procedures for customs documentation and clearance, so there are strong incentives for transparency and no incentives for discrimination against non-participants.

This initiative for facilitating trade is just one of the many opportunities for reducing the costs and risks of international economic transactions by promoting more convergent or more compatible procedures for the administration or regulation of commercial activities by groups of governments. There will normally be clear benefits from maximising transparency. The economy-wide benefits of such arrangements to facilitate international economic transactions would be enhanced by widening the group. However, since many of these arrangements are likely to be preferential, they will favour producers within the arrangement relative to outsiders, and there may be sectoral pressures against widening. Therefore it will be helpful to set up guidelines which ensure that new arrangements among groups of APEC economies do not create new sources of discrimination and make clear provisions for accession.

MUTUAL RECOGNITION OF STANDARDS

The evolution of the EU has demonstrated how a cooperative arrangement for the mutual recognition of product and process standards is an essential ingredient of any serious effort to create an integrated market. Experience in Europe and elsewhere has also demonstrated the potential for standards to become new means of protection.

By definition, only those economies which adopt and monitor adherence to comparable standards can be party to mutual recognition arrangements. Since the relevant products can be traded more conveniently among the parties to the arrangements, there will be an incentive to divert some economic activities away from other economies.

If the mutually recognised standards are not transparent, then other economies will certainly be disadvantaged. However, if all the relevant standards are transparent, then producers from any economy can choose to conform to them. If the procedures for demonstrating compliance to these standards are also transparent and applied without discrimination, then products from any source could be marketed in all the economies within the mutual recognition arrangement after being tested in any one of them. Producers from outside the arrangement would still be at some disadvantage compared to those within, since they would still need to have their product tested by agencies of one of the parties to the mutual recognition arrangement. However, such residual disadvantage could also be eliminated if their governments were able to become full parties to the arrangement.

Accession should be feasible if the arrangement makes it clear that any economy which adopts the policies required to implement the arrangement are automatically entitled to join. To join an arrangement for mutual recognition, prospective parties would not only need to adopt comparable standards, but also demonstrate their willingness and ability to monitor their producers' compliance with such standards (with comparable certainty as in existing parties). That may require the strengthening of some institutions which may depend on the willingness of existing parties to share the necessary information and expertise.

TECHNICAL COOPERATION

Many of the proposals for facilitating trade and investment will require the training of people from Asia Pacific economies in the techniques and procedures needed to administer new approaches, such as a harmonised system for recording and processing information needed for customs clearance or for monitoring conformance to mutually recognised standards.

It is sensible to set up joint programmes for training. The smooth administration of such schemes relies on adequate mutual trust in the capacity of counterparts in other Asia Pacific economies to manage the jointly agreed procedures. By far the most efficient way is for these people to be trained similarly in an environment where personal mutual respect can be established. It is therefore quite likely that many such regional training facilities will be established. The private sector, through ABAC's proposed 'Partnership for Equitable Growth', has indicated its willingness to help finance such initiatives.

It is not necessary to wait for all APEC participants to show interest in participating in each training program before they can be embarked upon by some. To be consistent with the spirit of open regionalism, the curriculum and materials should be designed to be relevant to all of the region and be freely available for information and for comment. Moreover, all economies should be encouraged to send people to be trained, provided they take on responsibilities reasonably comparable to those who are already doing so—for example, by bearing the same share of the travel and other costs incurred by trainees, together with a contribution to the costs of the programme in line with other economies with similar attributes.

GUIDING PRINCIPLES

The preceding examples of options to liberalise and facilitate trade and investment and to promote technical cooperation are by no means exhaustive. However, they are sufficient to illustrate that it is not simple to design such cooperative arrangements while avoiding any detriment to, or excluding, other economies. Therefore, it is not surprising that, in practice, markets are fragmented in various ways, not only by explicitly preferential trading arrangements, but also by many other cooperative arrangements among groups of economies.

All such arrangements create an incentive for others to join, in order to avoid any trade or investment being diverted from their economies. At the same time, any arrangements which divert economic activity create vested interests against widening by those who benefit from such diversion. That makes it difficult to keep these 'clubs' open, unless clear rules for accession are built in from the outset. Moreover, many cooperative arrangements to facilitate international economic transactions, such as double-tax agreements or arrangements for mutual recognition of product and process standards, are technically complex to administer. Even if their policy norms are transparent, it will be difficult for others to adopt them in order to join such arrangements, unless those already involved are willing to share the relevant expertise and technology.

These considerations suggest that some guidelines are needed if cooperative arrangements among any groups of economies are to be 'open clubs'. In particular, if APEC participants want to ensure that cooperative arrangements pioneered by some APEC economies set positive examples and take account of the interests of others, they will need to devise and adopt principles for practical cooperation which build on those in the 'Osaka Action Agenda'.

The following criteria may be useful to help ensure that all cooperative arrangements involving APEC economies are consistent with the spirit of open regionalism and which, by taking full account of the interests of all APEC participants, can preserve the cohesion of APEC.

Transparency. Perfect transparency may be an ideal, but it is possible to agree on criteria which cooperative arrangements involving APEC economies should meet. For example, guiding principles for transparency could require that the policies and procedures adopted for these arrangements be set out explicitly, typically in their legislation or regulations. These should be freely accessible to all governments and producers who wish to do so. In practice this can be achieved by preparing (where applicable) an authoritative translation into English, which is the working language of APEC. The policy norms of 'open clubs' should be available to all those interested, free of charge, through one of the more recognised channels. In 1998, that would probably be on a World Wide Web site accessible, among many other ways, through the APEC Secretariat's 'home page'.

A second important aspect of transparency is prior notice of new arrangements (or significant amendments to existing arrangements). This can enhance the prospects of more economies joining these new arrangements at the outset. Prior notice can also allow governments of other economies to comment on the terms of the proposed arrangements. Such comments could improve the effectiveness of these arrangements and help to make them as consistent as possible with APEC's guiding principles for trade and investment liberalisation and facilitation.

Non-discrimination. For trade in goods and services, the WTO has adopted the combination of 'standstill' and 'roll-back' to promote a gradual trend towards non-discriminatory free trade. The liberalisation of border barriers to trade, by individual governments or groups of governments, is expected to reduce some barriers without raising existing ones or creating new obstacles. Such a strategy can be generalised to promote cooperative arrangements to reduce all impediments to all international economic transactions.

APEC's agreed principles of 'standstill' and the commitment to 'endeavour to apply the principle of non-discrimination' can be given effect by guidelines which stipulate that new cooperative arrangements involving APEC economies should not lead to new discrimination. It will also be necessary to generalise the concept of national treatment to deal with the issues involved in reducing impediments to trade in services as well as to international factor movements. Accordingly, new arrangements should not contain any provisions which create additional or new forms of discrimination among products or producers, either on the basis of the location of various stages of production or the 'nationality' of producers.

Accession. As shown by the preceding examples, cooperative arrangements to facilitate trade or investment will tend to divert economic activities to the economies involved. Moreover, those who benefit from the diversion of trade or investment—intended or unintended—will tend to resist accession by additional economies. Therefore, if cooperative arrangements involving APEC economies are to be genuinely open to accession, their design will need to anticipate and minimise such resistance.

To a large extent, this can be achieved if the arrangements are highly transparent and do not create new discrimination among products or producers. In addition, the arrangements should specify at the outset, that the only condition for accession by additional economies will be their demonstrated ability to follow policies consistent with the arrangements. Many arrangements to facilitate trade or investment are technically complex; they will be 'open clubs' only if existing members are willing to share the requisite information, experience, expertise and technology. The 1996 Ministerial 'Declaration on an Asia Pacific Economic Cooperation Framework for Strengthening Economic Cooperation and Development' commits all APEC participants to such pooling of resources.

Review. As shown by the earlier examples of facilitation, it is not easy to ensure that cooperative arrangements among some economies are genuinely 'open clubs'.

While they may be designed, in good faith, to meet APEC's agreed guiding principles for trade and investment liberalisation and facilitation, their implementation could cause unexpected problems for other economies. Therefore, those involved in these arrangements should be willing to respond to constructive suggestions from other economies on how to improve the consistency of these cooperative arrangements with agreed guiding principles.

Proposed principles. A concise set of principles based on these concepts, building on APEC's current guiding principles as well as the fundamental GATT/WTO principles of transparency, non-discrimination and national treatment have been proposed for consideration within this chapter.

REFERENCES

Asia Pacific Economic Cooperation (APEC), 1991. 'Seoul APEC Declaration', Ministerial Declaration, Singapore.

——, 1996. 'Manila Declaration on an Asia Pacific Economic Cooperation Framework for Strengthening Economic Cooperation and Development', Ministerial Declaration, Singapore.

——, 1995. 'Osaka Action Agenda', endorsed by APEC Ministers, November.

Drysdale, P. and Elek, A., 1992. 'China and the international trading system', Pacific Economic Papers, No. 214, Australia–Japan Research Centre, The Australian National University, Canberra.

Drysdale, P., Elek, A. and Soesastro, K., 1997. 'Open regionalism: the nature of Asia Pacific integration, in D. Vines and P. Drysdale (eds), Europe, East Asia and APEC: a shared global agenda, Cambridge University Press, Cambridge.

Elek, K., 1995. 'APEC beyond Bogor: an open economic association in the Asian-Pacific region', Asian–Pacific Economic Literature, 9(1):1–16.

Foundation for Development Cooperation (FDC), 1997. Economic and technical cooperation and the APEC process: issues for consideration, paper prepared for meeting at ISIS Malaysia, Kuala Lumpur.

Garnaut, R., 1996. Open Regionalism and Trade Liberalisation, ISEAS, Singapore.

Garnaut, R. and Drysdale, P. (eds), 1994. Asia Pacific Regionalism: Readings in International Economic Relations, Harper Collins (in association with the Australia–Japan Research Centre), Sydney.

Hai Wen, 1996. China's accession to the WTO and its role in APEC, paper prepared for the Europe, East Asia and APEC Conference, Australia–Japan Research Centre, The Australian National University, Canberra.

Morrison, C., 1997. *Building an Asia-Pacific community: development cooperation within APEC,* in A. Elek (ed) The Foundation for Development Cooperation, Brisbane.

Pacific Economic Cooperation Council (PECC) Trade Policy Forum, 1996. *Perspectives on the Manila Action Plan for APEC*, PECC Secretariat, Singapore.

NOTES

1   For more detailed descriptions of these four types of economic and technical cooperation, see FDC (1997).
2   Independent studies, including by the Pacific Economic Cooperation Council (PECC) indicate that, if sustained, the pace of liberalisation of border barriers to trade is on track for meeting the 2010/2020 deadlines agreed in Bogor in 1994. (PECC Trade Policy Forum (1996).
3   The 15 sectors identified for early voluntary sectoral liberalisation are
    * environment goods and services*
    * fish and fish products*
    * toys*
    * forest products*
    * gems and jewellery*
    * oilseeds and oilseed products
    * chemicals*
    * energy sector*
    * food sector
    * natural and synthetic rubber
    * fertilisers
    * automotive sector
    * medical equipment and instruments*
    * civil aircraft
    * telecommunications mutual recognition arrangements.*
    Detailed proposals for economic and technical cooperation, facilitation and liberalisation are to be prepared by mid-1998 for the nine sectors marked with an asterisk.
4   The urgency of admitting China to the WTO, with unconditional rights for most-favoured-nation treatment, have been set out in many publications, including Drysdale and Elek (1992), Wen Hai (1996) and Elek (1996) and will not be elaborated upon here.
5   Since no APEC participant belongs to any customs union (such as the EU), nothing prevents them from lowering trade barriers to outsiders at any pace they choose.

APEC, STRUCTURAL REFORM AND SECTORAL LIBERALISATION

6

HOW IMPORTANT IS APEC TO CHINA?

YONGZHENG YANG & YIPING HUANG

China has actively participated in the APEC process since its inception in 1989. China seems to accept that APEC is important to its overall economic relations with the rest of the world. This judgment is not without empirical basis. The APEC region accounts for more than 60 per cent of China's trade, and a much higher percentage of its foreign capital inflows. However, China seems to have given a high profile to merchandise trade in the APEC process. This is manifested in President Jiang Zemin's announcement in the Osaka APEC summit in 1995 that China would slash its overall tariff level from 36 per cent to 23 per cent.

In making such a high profile and dramatic announcement, Jiang seemed to have China's WTO membership in his mind. China ultimately wants to enter the WTO, whose membership has strong implications for its trade (Anderson 1997a; Yang 1996). The announcement serves to demonstrate China's willingness to integrate with the world economy and to rally international support for its WTO bid. Whatever is on China's APEC agenda, there are questions. How important is APEC in its own right? How might China's participation in the APEC process help negotiations on its WTO membership?

Perhaps the most important question to ask is how APEC membership might help China in its domestic reform. Chinese negotiators have recently stressed the importance of WTO membership to domestic reform (Long 1998). After all, the long-term benefits of China's WTO membership to itself and the rest of the world are not going to come from China's free trade *per se*, but from its sustained growth. Further reform is essential to maintain the strong growth that China has achieved since it embarked on reform two decades ago.

There are significant differences in the nature of the institutions of the WTO and APEC and, thus, in the implications of their membership for China (Elek 1992; Anderson 1997b). While the WTO has binding rules of economic policies for its members, APEC relies largely on consensus and peer group pressure to achieve desired policy outcomes. Can APEC help facilitate China's reform to the same extent as the WTO?

In this chapter we first examine China's APEC strategy in relation to its WTO membership, economic diplomacy and overall economic reform. Particular emphasis is placed on the importance of the two institutions to the political economy of reform in China. We then evaluate the potential benefits of the proposed APEC trade liberalisation to China using a global general equilibrium model. These benefits are contrasted with those from hypothetical unilateral and global trade liberalisation in order to highlight the significance and limitations of the APEC initiative to China. Some sensitivity analysis is then undertaken to test the robustness of the simulation results and policy implications are drawn.

CHINA'S APEC STRATEGY

While APEC provides large potential for China's trade expansion, APEC's role in China's overall international economic relations goes far beyond this. APEC has become an important international forum for China to demonstrate its willingness to integrate with the world economy. APEC is made all the more important by the fact that China is not a member economy of the WTO, nor of the Organisation for Economic Cooperation and Development (OECD) (Garnaut and Huang 1995). As most of the APEC member countries are also economically the most important trade and investment partners for China, China can address important issues with its major economic partners in a more efficient and consistent way under the auspices of APEC. Bilateral negotiations are not only costly, but are also often seen as being discriminatory.

China wants to be perceived as a responsible member of the Asia Pacific community. By joining and participating in APEC, China reassures its smaller East Asian neighbours that it is committed to regional prosperity and stability. This is directly reflected in the announcement of the tariff reduction at the Osaka APEC Summit and the recent decision to maintain the yuan exchange rate in the wake of the Asian crisis despite strong economic pressure for devaluation.

China sees advantages of being an APEC member in dealing with the United States, especially in forming alliances with other East Asian member countries. China believes it is discriminated against by the United States. This belief is re-enforced by the alleged reluctance of the United States to accelerate negotiations on China's WTO accession and the recent disputes between the two countries over the issue of intellectual property rights. China argues that violation of intellectual property rights is widespread in East Asia, and it resents being singled out on the issue by the United States. Such economic issues are intertwined with political issues, such as the disputes over human rights. Since many other

Asian countries have a similar stand to China on trade and social issues, China feels more confident in dealing with the United States when it has support from its East Asian neighbours.

Perhaps central to China's APEC strategy is its intention to use APEC to build support for its WTO membership. By showing its commitment to the APEC region and its support for some of its East Asian neighbours over such issues as human rights and the proposed formation of the East Asian Economic Caucus, China is consolidating its support in the region. Bilateral talks on China's WTO accession with several key East Asian economies—most notably Japan and Korea—have made significant progress. China seems to have won more support for its WTO bid from its neighbours with a series announcements of the yuan exchange rate policy in the wake of the Asian currency crisis.

Finally, and perhaps most importantly, the APEC trade liberalisation process may help China's domestic reform. The Chinese leadership may not have set this as an explicit objective of its APEC agenda, but the impact will be significant if the APEC process succeeds. Officially, China gives its WTO membership great weight in helping domestic reform—also a bargaining chip (Long 1998). However, as WTO accession keeps eluding China, it may increasingly resort to APEC for external pressure for economic reform. Whether or not the Chinese government deliberately uses external pressure to push forward domestic reform, the APEC process will serve as a stimulus to trade liberalisation in China. In conforming with the commitments made by the Chinese government at the APEC Osaka meeting, China lowered its tariff rate for over 4,900 items on 1 April 1996 and the simple average tariff rate was brought down from 36 per cent to 23 per cent. On 1 October 1997, China further reduced its average tariff rate to 17 per cent, another significant drop of 26 per cent. In 1997, non-tariff measures on 17 items of products were eliminated. China will eliminate all non-tariff barriers that are inconsistent with the WTO agreements by the end of 2010. China also advanced its commitment to the free convertibility of the Chinese currency for transactions in current accounts. The experiment on Chinese currency business by foreign banks is underway and nine foreign banks have been granted approval for it.

In its Individual Action Plan (IAP) submitted to APEC in October 1997, China made commitments for continued economic liberalisation in the near future. These include

- further reducing the average tariff rate to 15 per cent before the turn of the century
- increasing progressively the number of operational subsidiaries of foreign banks
- continuing and expanding the pilot programs of equity and contractual joint ventures in retail, wholesale and foreign trade businesses

- opening 5 more cities—on top of the existing 12—for state-level joint ventures in tourism.

None of these reforms can be solely attributed to APEC. The pace of China's economic reform—and trade liberalisation in particular—is still largely determined by domestic political forces. Like in many other countries, a mercantilist approach to trade policy is pervasive in China. Although extremely high protection is now often regarded as protecting backwardness, 'moderate' protection is still widely considered necessary to protect indigenous industries. With growing open unemployment, it has become increasingly difficult politically for China to reduce its protection further. The willingness to liberalise unilaterally may come to a halt once China's overall tariff levels are comparable to those prevailing in other developing countries. Accession to the WTO should restore the process, but it is difficult to assess how fast China can move towards free trade from then on. If no substantial progress is made in the next round of WTO trade negotiations, then China's trade liberalisation process may begin to slow. If this happens, the APEC process would become even more important to China. The question is, can the APEC process continue to move forward rapidly if the WTO process is stalled?

China's past trade reform can largely be characterised as unilateral and it was one of the driving forces behind the economic success of the past two decades (Garnaut 1992; World Bank 1997). The impact of unilateral liberalisation can be significantly enhanced by similar liberalisation by China's trading partners (Yang 1996). Both APEC free trade and China's WTO accession can increase the prospects for continued export expansion. Despite the potentially substantial welfare gain from unilateral liberalisation, China feels more confident in opening its own market if it sees others are doing the same.

Irrespective of the prospects for APEC trade liberalisation, one should not overstate the stimulus effect or the external pressure that APEC can exert on China. In its approach to trade liberalisation, APEC opted for consensus and peer-group pressure (Drysdale and Garnaut 1992; Soesastro 1993). This seems to suit China's political need for flexibility in undertaking domestic reform in terms of timing and depth. However, this creates loopholes and reduces the disciplinary effect on domestic policy. Thus, APEC does not have the same effect on China's economic policy as the WTO may have, as the latter imposes binding rules on the policies of member countries. Both APEC and the WTO will help increase the transparency of China's trade regime, but the rules of the WTO and its trade policy review mechanism would probably exert greater pressure on China than the APEC harmonisation process.

In terms of geographical coverage, there is also a significant difference between APEC and the WTO. The WTO currently has more than 130 members, while APEC includes only 21 countries from the Asia Pacific region. While it may be cost-effective for China to negotiate on trade and investment issues with a smaller group of major trading partners within APEC, engaging other trading partners in the liberalisation process is also important. After all, non-APEC economies account for nearly 40 per cent of China's trade. In addition, the WTO will provide a major forum for China to settle trade disputes with other countries once it becomes its member, although China may not be able to avoid potential discrimination against it, as some of these measures are likely to be incorporated in China's protocol of accession (Zhong and Yang 1998).

APEC is unable to address some important issues to China, especially in relation to the MFA and trade disputes. Despite its enormous importance to China and many other APEC economies, the MFA has not been a focus of APEC trade liberalisation. This is partly due to the Uruguay Round Agreement on Textiles and Clothing which will lead to the phasing out of MFA quotas by 2005 for WTO members. APEC free trade by 2010 for developed members cannot be of any help to China unless it is still outside the WTO by then. Recent trade disputes between China and several of its trading partners further demonstrate the inadequacy of the APEC process for China. Mexico, for example, recently imposed anti-dumping duties of 54–500 per cent on Chinese textiles and clothing. China had to rely entirely on bilateral efforts to deal with the problem as it is not a WTO member.

Disputes of a similar nature will probably be of increasing importance to China as its exports expand rapidly while its economy continues to be regarded as transitional. While the Uruguay Round has tightened the rules governing trade among WTO members, more discriminatory measures may be directed against China. A recent agreement between the United States and China, for example, stipulates that US quotas for Chinese textiles will continue well after the phasing out of the MFA.

As far as China is concerned, APEC cannot substitute for the WTO. APEC should be seen as both a forum for China to demonstrate its commitment to WTO rules and an opportunity to reform its trade regime. While APEC may provide an external environment conducive to trade liberalisation, it is the WTO that will serve as a more powerful force in ultimately placing China's economy under a rules-based trade regime. It is therefore in China's interests to continue to make efforts to join the WTO while pushing forward with unilateral liberalisation, both as a demonstration of its commitment to economic openness and as part of the APEC process. Such a strategy will not only prepare China for eventual WTO membership, but also bring economic benefits to China, and through cooperation with other APEC countries, overcome the resistance to domestic reform.

THE VALUE OF APEC

In this section we employ a 9 x 12 (nine commodities and 12 regions) version of the GTAP model to evaluate the impact of APEC trade liberalisation on China. The model was implemented and solved using GEMPACK (Harrison and Pearson 1996). To capture the impact of APEC trade liberalisation, the world economy is first projected to the year 2005. We then assume that the full effect of the Uruguay Round reform takes place in 2005. As free trade in the APEC region will not occur until 2020, we further project the world economy to that year, assuming that by then the full impact of APEC liberalisation will be felt. The projected 2020 equilibrium of the world economy provides a benchmark for subsequent comparative static simulations of trade liberalisation.

The projections follow the methodology used in Hertel et al. (1996) and Yang et al. (1998). Essentially, forecasts of real GDP growth and primary factor accumulation are imposed on the world economy, and the implied (neutral) technological change—the difference between the growth of primary factors and real GDP—is deduced. Forecasts of major macroeconomic variables for various regions over the period 1992–2005 are obtained (Table 6.1). We base our projections of GDP growth and primary factor uses on Hertel et al. (1996) and the World Bank (1995). In light of the recent Asian crisis, the growth rates for the ASEAN, the newly industrialising economies (NIEs) and Japan are adjusted downward. Because only economy-wide GDP forecasts are available, only technological change at the economy-wide level can be deduced. It should be noted, however, that sectoral GDP does not grow at the same rate in the projection even though only the economy-wide GDP growth rate is projected. Because of variations in factor intensity among sectors, different rates of factor accumulation mean that sectoral growth will differ among sectors—the Rybczynski effect. In addition, consumer preferences are non-homothetic, so that the growth of demand for various products differs as income rises.

In the projection, all prices and sectoral quantities endogenously adjust to exogenous changes in macroeconomic variables. Labour and capital are perfectly mobile across sectors while land is partially mobile. Regional savings are a fixed proportion of income and are pooled together in a 'global bank'. Global savings are allocated to investment in such a way that each region retains its share in global investment. This effectively constrains large changes in the trade balance. No policy change is implemented in the projection from 1992 to 2005. Based on the evidence provided by Gehlhar (1997), the trade elasticities in the GTAP model are doubled in the projection and subsequent comparative static simulations. Gehlhar found that structural changes in the Asia Pacific economies over time would be best replicated if the trade elasticities are doubled. Full details of the GTAP elasticities and other data can be found in McDougall (1997).

Table 6.1   Projected annual average growth of macroeconomic variables, 1992–2005 (per cent)

	Population	Labour	Capital	Real GDP
Australasia	0.7	0.6	2.1	2.5
North America	0.7	0.9	2.8	2.7
EU-12	0.2	0.2	1.3	2.2
Japan	0.3	-0.2	2.5	2.0
NIEs	0.9	0.9	5.0	5.0
ASEAN	1.6	2.2	6.0	6.0
China	1.3	2.4	9.3	8.9
South Asia	1.8	2.4	7.1	5.2
Latin America	1.7	2.2	1.2	3.6
Central and Eastern Europe	0.9	0.9	6.0	6.0
Former Soviet Union	0.0	0.0	4.4	4.4
Rest of the world	1.3	2.4	2.5	2.5

Source: Based on Hertel et al. (1996), World Bank (1995) and Yang and Zhong (1998).

The post-Uruguay Round equilibrium of the world economy in 2005 is created by simulating the Uruguay Round reforms at the projected baseline in 2005. Following Yang et al. (1998), our estimates of tariff cuts and agricultural liberalisation are based on GATT (1993, 1994) and UNCTAD (1995). Essentially, domestic support for agriculture is reduced by 20 per cent, and export subsidies and tariffs (including their equivalents of quantitative restrictions) by 36 per cent. Tariffs on textiles and clothing are reduced by 18 per cent in North America, 16 per cent in the European Union (EU) (15 per cent for imports from developing economics), and 33 per cent in Japan. For developing countries, domestic support for agriculture is cut by 15 per cent, export subsidies by 24 per cent, and tariffs by 26 per cent. Tariff reductions in developing countries are two-thirds of that in industrial countries.

Once the Uruguay Round trade liberalisation is carried out, the world economy is projected to 2020, following the same procedures as those used for the projection to 2005. The projection was made from the 2005 post-Uruguay Round database by accumulating factors of production and increasing real GDP across the regions consistent with the forecasts. In most cases, trend forecasts for the period 1992–2005 are extrapolated to the year 2020. In the case of China, we have projected a slowing down of GDP growth for the period 2005–2020 (to 7.3 per cent per year). Unlike in the period 1992–2005—when the labour force grows much more rapidly than population—we have assumed that over the period 2006–2020, labour force growth is the sum of population growth, which is based on the SSB (1996) projection, and any unemployment left over from the period 1992–2005 (Yang and Zhong 1998). Again, no policy changes are incorporated in the projection.

The same model closure is used in the Uruguay Round reform experiment for the year 2005 and all other comparative static simulations for 2020. This closure is similar to the one used in the projections. In the comparative static experiments, however, land, labour, capital stock and technology are all fixed. Unlike dynamic models, such as the G-Cubed model (McKibbin and Wilcoxen 1995) and the Monash model (Dixon and Rimmer 1997), GTAP is a one-period model. Investment therefore does not augment capital stock in the next period, although it affects final demand in the current period.

Two scenarios are postulated for APEC trade liberalisation. In the first scenario, all border barriers to trade in the APEC economies, including those to agricultural trade, are eliminated on a MFN basis. On the import side, these barriers include tariffs, quotas, variable import levies and any other import restrictions, such as anti-dumping duties. On the export side, export subsidies, taxes and MFA quotas (which are modelled as export taxes) are abolished altogether. Output subsidies are also removed. In the second scenario, we assume that distortions in agriculture are retained while all those in other sectors are eliminated as in the first scenario. This scenario is intended to highlight the importance of agricultural liberalisation in the APEC process. To put in perspective the potential benefits to China of concerted MFN trade liberalisation in the APEC region, a third experiment on unilateral MFN trade liberalisation by China was also undertaken. In this scenario, China eliminates all its trade distortions without any other countries reciprocating. The results for these three scenarios are reported in Table 6.2.

Under the scenario of comprehensive APEC trade liberalisation, China's real GDP increases by nearly 3 per cent (column 1 of Table 6.2). This large expansion of domestic production reflects the extent of trade distortions in China. Measured in equivalent variation, however, the welfare gain to China is not as significant as the increase in domestic production suggests. The US$23.9 billion welfare gain is equivalent to only 0.6 per cent of GDP in 2020. The discrepancy between production expansion and welfare gain results from a substantial decline (4.1 per cent) in China's terms of trade following APEC trade liberalisation. Decomposition of the welfare effect shows that the deterioration of the terms of trade translates to a US$74.4 billion welfare loss. The massive efficiency gain from trade liberalisation, however, more than compensates for this loss. Further decomposition of the allocative efficiency gain indicates that the massive expansion of imports is largely responsible for the higher efficiency, although export expansion also contributes significantly. This suggests that it is China's own liberalisation that is most important for its welfare position in the APEC process. Both exports and imports expand substantially, but the latter expand

Table 6.2 The impact on China of APEC and unilateral trade liberalisation, 2020

	Comprehensive APEC	APEC excluding agriculture	Unilateral trade liberalisation
Equivalent variation (US$b)	23.9	16.3	17.2
Allocative efficiency	98.3	92.4	98.9
Terms of trade effect	-74.4	-76.1	-81.7
Real GDP (per cent)	2.9	2.7	2.9
Terms of trade (per cent)	-4.1	-4.2	-4.5
Real exports (per cent)	41.8	41.3	41.1
Real imports (per cent)	70.3	69.4	68.1
Trade balance (US$b)	-20.1	-20.7	-21.2

Source: Simulations of the GTAP model, database version 3.

more than the former, leading to a US$20 billion reduction in China's trade surplus in 2020.

If agriculture is excluded from APEC trade liberalisation, the increase in China's GDP is only slightly lower, but the overall welfare gain to China—as measured by equivalent variation—is reduced by nearly one-third (column 2 of Table 6.2). Not only is the efficiency gain smaller, but the adverse terms of trade effect also becomes larger. The terms of trade further deteriorate despite the fact that both exports and imports expand less if agriculture is excluded from APEC trade liberalisation. China has moderate levels of agricultural protection compared to many other economies in the APEC region. When agriculture is liberalised, the terms of trade for China's agricultural sector improve as export demand rises.

Judging by the welfare effects, APEC trade liberalisation without agriculture would be a less desirable option for China than unilateral trade liberalisation. As shown in the last column of Table 6.2, the large efficiency gain from unilateral trade liberalisation more than compensates for the increased terms of trade loss. Real GDP growth is also higher under unilateral trade liberalisation than under APEC without agriculture. Comparison of the results between full APEC and unilateral trade liberalisation shows that the main benefits to China from the APEC process come from the terms of trade effect. Simultaneous liberalisation by other countries increases China's welfare by over US$7 billion.

The most noticeable effect of full APEC liberalisation on different sectors is observed in the food processing industry, which has been highly protected by tariffs. The removal of tariffs leads to substantial contraction of this industry, in turn weakening demand for crops and livestock products. As a result, production in the two industries also falls. Combined with strong export demand from other APEC economies—especially Japan, the NIEs and North America—lower domestic prices lead to a surge in agricultural exports, albeit from a small base (projected agricultural exports in 2020 are quite small) (Table 6.4). Crop imports, on the other hand, decline because of the removal of import subsidies, while imports of livestock products increase moderately with the elimination of tariffs (Table 6.5).

Output in the clothing industry also expands, despite the removal of the high tariff for the industry. This results largely from the removal of MFA quotas and

Table 6.3 The impact on China's production of APEC and unilateral trade liberalisation, 2020 (per cent)

	Comprehensive APEC	APEC excluding agriculture	Unilateral trade liberalisation
Crops	-5.2	-6.7	-6.7
Livestock products	-0.7	3.1	1.7
Natural resources	-6.5	-7.5	-9.1
Processed food	-50.2	-41.4	-41.2
Textiles	-27.4	-21.0	-27.0
Clothing	44.2	45.3	43.9
Automobiles and equipment	6.4	5.0	7.5
Basic manufactures	-1.3	-1.8	-3.7
Services	0.5	0.5	0.6

Source: Simulations of the GTAP model, database version 3.

Table 6.4 The impact on China's exports of APEC and unilateral trade liberalisation, 2020 (per cent)

	Comprehensive APEC	APEC excluding agriculture	Unilateral trade liberalisation
Crops	135.8	26.5	41.0
Livestock products	148.9	15.3	27.7
Natural resources	23.7	18.4	8.0
Processed food	-13.2	67.4	35.7
Textiles	79.1	94.4	71.9
Clothing	79.4	81.3	81.4
Automobiles and equipment	33.5	31.8	35.3
Basic manufactures	38.9	38.7	25.0
Services	9.7	8.6	11.1

Source: Simulations of the GTAP model, database version 3.

Table 6.5 The impact on China's imports of APEC and unilateral trade liberalisation, 2020 (per cent)

	Comprehensive APEC	APEC excluding agriculture	Unilateral trade liberalisation
Crops	-37.9	-20.2	-23.8
Livestock products	4.4	-2.6	-2.4
Natural resources	13.2	14.6	16.2
Processed food	509.6	410.1	400.0
Textiles	143.8	140.0	136.2
Clothing	1349.5	1358.5	1332.2
Automobiles and equipment	148.5	149.5	149.4
Basic manufactures	53.8	54.0	53.5
Services	-3.6	-3.2	-4.5

Source: Simulations of the GTAP model, database version 3.

relatively high tariffs (compared with other manufactures) imposed by North America and Japan. In addition, the removal of tariffs on textiles significantly reduces the input costs for clothing production. Nevertheless, the strong demand from the clothing industry fails to prevent a decline in the output of the textile industry. The elimination of high tariffs on textiles does improve the competitiveness of Chinese textiles in overseas markets. Together with the removal of MFA quotas and tariffs in other APEC economies, this leads to considerable expansion of textile exports.

Imports of clothing increase dramatically following the elimination of high tariffs. It should be noted, however, that this occurs from a very small base as China has a strong comparative advantage in clothing production and most of the high tariffs on clothing products are probably redundant. The simulation result on clothing imports is therefore likely to be biased upward.

The automobile and equipment industry expands following APEC liberalisation, but basic manufactures suffer a small contraction. The service sector expands slightly as its internal terms of trade improves. Despite the widespread negative impact on production after APEC trade liberalisation, trade (imports plus exports) expands for virtually all commodities, although exports of processed food and imports of crops and services decline marginally. This shows that under the assumption of differentiated products, exports and imports can expand simultaneously with APEC trade liberalisation, leading to a more open Chinese economy in the process. It is this openness that improves the overall efficiency of resource allocation in the Chinese economy.

Excluding agriculture from the APEC trade liberalisation scenarios has little impact on sectoral output, but the outcome for agricultural exports is drastically different in the scenario of APEC without agriculture. Instead of massive expansion, agricultural exports increase only moderately, more slowly than the exports of most other commodities. With import subsidies retained, imports of crops fall less. Without tariff reductions, imports of livestock products decline, while they increase in the case of full APEC liberalisation.

Sectoral results under unilateral trade liberalisation are very similar to those under APEC trade liberalisation without agriculture. Agricultural exports do expand more with unilateral trade liberalisation, as other exports expand less when there are no increases in demand from other APEC economies. Imports of crops, on the other hand, fall even more strongly.

Caution is warranted in interpreting the sectoral results presented in the tables. The GTAP database includes perhaps the most comprehensive trade distortion data that one can find in any global model. China's protection data, however, leaves much to be desired, as it does in virtually all models. Extensive non-tariff barriers in the Chinese trade regime are hardly covered in the GTAP database. Thus, trade liberalisation implemented for China in the above simulations represents at best, tariff reductions. Without the removal of non-tariff barriers—especially quantitative restrictions—estimates of sectoral results can be biased, as can welfare results. In addition, there are great variations in the tariff levels among commodities. This tends to lead to greater welfare losses than under uniform tariffs of the same average level. Offsetting these biases are the extensive tariff exemptions and rebates mentioned earlier. It is difficult to evaluate the net effect of these factors. One such an attempt has been made by Bach et al. (1996).

Aggregation may also lead to biases in sectoral results, and this can result in difficulties in the interpretation of results. For example, the basic manufactures industry includes a lager number of sub-industries with a wide range of factor intensity and protection levels. The automobile industry would probably have contracted had it been separated out from the more aggregate automobile and equipment industry. To obtain more accurate sectoral results, a more disaggregated database is desired, but this needs to be balanced against the increased complexity of results and computing requirements.

How important is APEC and unilateral trade liberalisation compared to the global trade liberalisation that the WTO aims to achieve? By global trade liberalisation, we mean that all countries undertake to eliminate all their trade distortions, including tariffs, non-tariff barriers, export subsidies and taxes, and domestic support for agriculture. The results of global trade liberalisation are reported in the first column of Table 6.6. In the next three columns, the results for the previous three scenarios are reported as percentages of the outcomes of global trade liberalisation. As expected, welfare benefits to China from global

Table 6.6 APEC and unilateral trade liberalisation versus global trade liberalisation, 2020

		As per cent of global trade liberalisation		
	Global trade liberalisation	Comprehensive APEC	APEC excl. agriculture	Unilateral trade liberalisation
Equivalent variation (US$b)	43.7	54.6	37.3	39.3
Allocative efficiency	99.8	98.5	92.6	99.1
Terms of trade effect	-56.1	132.6	135.7	145.6
Real GDP (per cent)	2.9	100.0	93.1	100.0
Terms of trade (per cent)	-3.1	134.1	136.7	146.9
Real exports (per cent)	43.6	95.9	94.7	94.3
Real imports (per cent)	74.0	95.0	93.8	92.0
Trade balance (US$b)	-8.1	248.7	256.4	262.1

Source: Simulations of the GTAP model, database version 3.

trade liberalisation are larger than from both APEC and China's unilateral trade liberalisation. A comprehensive APEC program would generate 55 per cent of what China would gain from global trade liberalisation, and APEC liberalisation without agriculture would give China 37 per cent of its potential benefits from global trade liberalisation. Unilateral trade liberalisation scores slightly better than APEC without agriculture as far as welfare impact on China is concerned. As in the case of the comparison between full APEC and unilateral trade liberalisation, the larger gain from global trade liberalisation is primarily a result of the improved terms of trade for China, although in comparison with APEC liberalisation excluding agriculture, efficiency gains are important as well. The improvement in China's terms of trade is more or less proportional to the regional coverage of trade liberalisation. The non-APEC region accounts for about 38 per cent of China's total trade. Trade liberalisation in these countries reduces the adverse terms of trade effect of APEC on China by about one-third.

Under global trade liberalisation, China's GDP increases to a similar extent to that in the three previous scenarios. The greatest difference between global liberalisation on the one hand, and APEC and unilateral liberalisation on the other, occurs in the trade balance. In the simulations, we allowed the trade balance to adjust. Despite similar trade expansion, APEC and unilateral trade liberalisation lead to a reduction in the trade surplus one-and-a-half times larger than global trade liberalisation. The much more favourable export prices under global trade liberalisation explain a large part of the difference. China has a large current account surplus in the base year. Reductions in the trade surplus do not pose a balance of payments problem.

SENSITIVITY ANALYSIS

Simulation results in the previous section show that China suffers large terms of trade losses from trade liberalisation despite overall welfare gains. It is well known that in the Armington-type demand systems, such terms of trade losses are related to the elasticity of substitution among sources of supply as well as country size. In this section, we test the sensitivity of the simulation results to two sets of elasticities: the elasticities of substitution between domestic goods and imports, and those between various sources of imports. We first halve these elasticities across all commodities and then double them. Other possible variations in the elasticities are not cosidered here because of the excessive computing resources they would require.

The welfare results of trade liberalisation are sensitive to the magnitude of the elasticities of substitution (Table 6.7). With lower elasticities, China loses in every scenario except global trade liberalisation. In contrast, higher elasticities lead to large welfare gains in every scenario, and these gains are several times those in the central scenarios of the previous section. When the elasticities are lower, not only are the negative terms of trade effects larger, but the allocative efficiency gains are smaller. In fact, it is the decline in allocative efficiency gains that is mainly to blame for China's welfare losses. The results for the higher elasticity scenario confirm this. Thus, while the terms of trade effects vary considerably between the lower and higher elasticity scenarios, differences in allocative efficiency largely determine the overall welfare results.

Table 6.7   The impact of trade liberalisation on China: sensitivity analysis, 2020

	Unilateral trade liberalisation		Compre- hensive APEC		APEC excluding agriculture		Global trade liberalisation	
Elasticity of substitution =>	Low	High	Low	High	Low	High	Low	High
Equivalent variation (US$b)	-25.5	115.3	-20.5	112.7	-19.8	98.3	0.7	125.1
Allocative efficiency	45.2	212.1	47.5	183.9	42.6	191.0	47.9	182.2
Terms of trade effect	-70.7	-96.8	-68.0	-71.2	-62.4	-92.7	-47.2	-57.1
Real GDP (per cent)	1.3	6.2	1.3	5.5	1.2	5.6	1.3	5.4
Terms of trade (per cent)	-4.2	-4.6	-4.1	-3.4	-3.7	-4.4	-2.8	-2.7
Real exports (per cent)	18.8	84.0	19.0	87.0	19.0	82.7	19.8	87.8
Real imports (per cent)	29.3	143	29.3	153.6	30.5	142.1	31.2	155.4
Trade balance (US$b)	-25.4	-6.9	-21.4	-12.0	-22.8	-11.0	-7.9	-2.4

Source: Simulations of the GTAP model, database version 3.

These sensitivity results must be interpreted with caution. If the elasticities of substitution were indeed as low as in our lower elasticity scenario, it is possible that China has nothing to gain from APEC trade liberalisation as far as its static effects are concerned. As discussed earlier, however, the value of APEC to China is not merely a one-off increase in allocative efficiency. Although this static gain is important, the largest benefits of APEC are probably from its facilitation of domestic reform and China's WTO accession. The simulation results show that China is more likely to benefit from multilateral trade liberalisation under the auspice of the WTO (even with lower elasticities). This is not surprising, as by 2020 China is so large that its own trade liberalisation can exert considerable negative terms of trade effects on itself. Multilateral liberalisation is most effective in mitigating the terms of trade effect.

It should also be borne in mind that our simulation results tend to underestimate the welfare gains of trade liberalisation. Simulations using models incorporating economies of scale and imperfect competition generally show larger welfare benefits of trade liberalisation (Francois et al. 1997; Harrison et al. 1996). Despite its large domestic market, China has not been able to exploit economies of scale for its industries, nor has it been able to improve competition substantially in many key industries, such as telecommunications and banking (Cao 1993; He and Yang 1998). One would expect that welfare gains from the exploitation of these economies of scale and increased competition in China are large.

CONCLUSION

APEC seems to be an imperative for China's economic diplomacy. Having been denied earlier accession to the WTO, China sees APEC as an important forum to show its commitment to economic openness and to demonstrate the importance that China attaches to its neighbours. Concerted liberalisation in the APEC region reduces the adverse terms of trade effect of China's own trade liberalisation. All these help to maintain the momentum of reform by reducing domestic resistance. APEC is not a stepping stone to WTO membership, but it gives China an opportunity to rally international support for its early entry into the WTO.

To build a more open, rules-based economy, China must continue to seek early entry to the WTO. This is not only because the WTO framework provides greater security for market access for Chinese exports and potentially larger gains to the Chinese economy, but also because it imposes legal bindings on China's trade policy once it becomes a member.

In facilitating China's trade liberalisation, APEC and the WTO seem to be mutually re-inforcing. APEC prepares China for the WTO and the WTO accession pushes China to go along with the APEC process. Both APEC and WTO accession propel domestic reform. At a critical time of state enterprise reform, it is important to lock China's domestic reform into a process of economic integration with the rest of the world. While such a process cannot replace hard work in fostering domestic support for further reform, it helps reform both by providing tangible economic benefits and by encouraging rules-based institutions.

APPENDIX A
REGION AND COMMODITY DESCRIPTIONS

Table A6.1   Region descriptions

Region	GTAP region descriptions
Australasia	Australia and New Zealand
North America	United States and Canada
EU-12	12 member states
Japan	Japan
NIEs	Hong Kong, Republic of Korea, Singapore and Taiwan
ASEAN	Indonesia, Malaysia, the Philippines and Thailand
China	China
South Asia	Bangladesh, Pakistan, India, Sri Lanka, and rest of South Asia
Latin America	Mexico, Central America and the Caribbean, Argentina, Brazil,
Chile, rest of South America	
Central and Eastern European Associates	Poland, Hungary, Czech Republic, Slovakia, Romania, Bulgaria
Former Soviet Union	Former Soviet Union
Rest of the world	Regions not included above

Table A6.2   Commodity descriptions

Commodity	GTAP commodity descriptions
Crops	Paddy rice, wheat, other grains, non-grain crops and processed rice
Livestock products	Wool, other livestock, meat products, and milk products
Natural resources	Forestry, fishery, coal, oil, gas, and other minerals
Processed food	Other food products, and beverages & tobacco
Textiles	Textiles and leather products
Clothing	Clothing
Machinery and equipment	Transport equipment, machinery and equipment, other manufactures
Basic manufactures	Lumber, pulp & paper etc., petroleum & coal, chemicals rubber & plastics, non-metallic minerals, primary ferrous metals, non-ferrous metals, and fabricated metal products
Services	Electricity water & gas, construction, trade & transport, other services (private), other services (government), and ownership of dwellings

APPENDIX B
TRADE ELASTICITIES

Table B6.1   Central scenario trade elasticities used in this study

	Elasticities of substitution between imports and domestic products	Elasticities of substitution among imports by place of production
Crops	4.4	8.8
Livestock products	4.9	9.3
Natural resources	5.6	11.2
Processed food	5.0	9.9
Textiles	5.3	11.6
Clothing	8.8	17.6
Machinery & equipment	7.1	13.7
Basic manufactures	4.5	9.0
Services	3.9	7.6

REFERENCES

Anderson, K., 1997a. 'On the complexities of China's WTO accession', *The World Economy*, 20:749–72.

—— (ed.), 1997b. *Strengthening the Global Trading System: from GATT to WTO*, Centre for International Economic Studies, University of Adelaide, Adelaide.

Bach, C.F., Martin, W. and Stevens, J., 1996. 'China and the WTO: tariff offers, exemptions, and welfare implications', *Weltwirtschaftliches Archiv*, 132:409–31.

Bergsten, C.F., 1994. 'APEC and the world economy: a force for worldwide liberalisation', *Foreign Affairs*, 73:20–6.

Cao, Y., 1993. The Chinese iron and steel industry in transition: towards market mechanisms and economic efficiency, PhD dissertation, The Australian National University, Canberra.

Dixon, P.B. and Rimmer, M.T., 1997. Monash: a disaggregated, dynamic model of the Australian economy, Centre of Policy Studies and Impact Project, Monash Univesity, Melbourne. (mimeo)

Drysdale, P. and Garnaut, R., 1992. 'The Pacific: an application of a general theory of economic integration', in C.F. Bergsten and M. Noland (eds),

Pacific Dynamism and the International Economic System, Institute for International Economics, Washington, DC.

Elek, A., 1992. 'Trade policy options for the Asia Pacific region in the 1990s: the potential of open regionalism', *American Economic Review*, 82:74–8.

Francois, J.F., McDonald, B. and Nordstrom, H., 1997. 'The Uruguay Round: a global general equilibrium assessment', in D. Robertson (ed.), *East Asian Trade after the Uruguay Round*, Cambridge University Press, Cambridge.

Garnaut, R., 1992. 'China's reforms in international context', in R. Garnaut and G. Liu (eds), *Economic Reform and Internationalisation*, Allen & Unwin, Sydney, in association with the Pacific Trade and Development Conference Secretariat, The Australian National University.

—— and Huang, Y., 1995. 'Trade liberalisation and transition in China: opportunities and challenges for OECD countries', report prepared for the Trade Directorate, OECD, Paris.

General Agreement on Tariffs and Trade (GATT), 1993. *An Analysis of the Proposed Uruguay Round Agreement, with Particular Emphasis on Aspects of Interest to Developing Economies*, Geneva, 29 November.

——, 1994. *News of the Uruguay Round of Multilateral Trade Negotiations*, April, Geneva.

Gehlhar, M., 1997. 'Historical analysis of growth and trade patterns in the Pacific Rim: an evaluation of the GTAP framework', in T. Hertel (ed.), *Global Trade Analysis Using the GTAP Model*, Cambridge University Press, Cambridge.

Harrison, G.W., Rutherford, T.F. and Tarr, D., 1996. 'Quantifying the Uruguay Round', in W. Martin and A.L. Winters (eds), *The Uruguay Round and the Developing Countries*, Cambridge University Press, Cambridge.

Harrison, W.J. and Pearson, K.R., 1996. 'Computing solutions for large general equilibrium models using GEMPACK', *Computational Economics*, 9:83–127.

He, J.M. and Yang, Y., 1998. 'The political economy of trade liberalisation in China', National Centre for Development Studies, The Australian National University, mimeo.

Hertel, T. (ed.), 1997. *Global Trade Analysis: modeling and applications*, Cambridge University Press, Cambridge.

——, Martin, W., Yanagishma, K. and Dimaranan, B., 1996. 'Liberalising manufactures trade in a changing world economy', in W. Martin and A.L. Winters (eds), *The Uruguay Round and the Developing Countries*, Cambridge University Press, Cambridge.

Huff, K.M. and Hertel, T.W., 1996. *Decomposing Welfare Change in the GTAP Model*, GTAP Technical Paper No. 5, Center for Global Trade Analysis, Purdue University, Western Lafayette.

Long, Y., 1998. 'China's integration into the world economy: challenges from the new global prosperity', presentation made at the international conference 'China's Integration into the Global Economy', 17 January 1998, Harvard University, Cambridge.

McDougall, R.A. (ed.), 1997. *Global Trade, Assistance, and Protection: the GTAP 3 Data Base*, Centre for Global Trade Analysis, Purdue University, West Lafayette.

McKibbin, W.J. and Wilcoxen, P.J., 1995. *The theoretical and empirical structure of the G-Cubed model*, Brookings Discussion Papers in International Economics, No. 118, Brookings Institute, Washington, DC.

Soesastro, H., 1993. 'Pacific economic cooperation: the history of an idea', in B.K. Bundy, K. Weichel and S.D. Burns (eds), *The Future of Regional Cooperation in the Pacific Rim*, Center for the Pacific Rim, University of San Francisco.

State Statistical Bureau (SSB), 1994. *Kua shiji de zhongguo renkou (China's population into the next century)*, China Statistical Publishing House, Beijing.

UNCTAD, 1995. *An Analysis of Trading Opportunities Resulting from the Uruguay Round in Selected Sectors: agriculture, textiles and clothing, and other industrial products*, UNCTAD, Geneva.

World Bank, 1995. *Global Economic Prospects and the Developing Countries*, World Bank, Washington, DC.

——, 1997. 'China engaged: integration with the global economy', *China 2020 Series*, World Bank, Washington, DC.

Yang, Y., 1996. 'China's WTO membership: what's at stake?', *The World Economy*, 19:661–82.

—— and Zhong, C., 1998. 'China's textile and clothing exports in a changing world economy', *The Developing Economies*, XXXVI:3–23.

Yang, Y., Duncan, R.C. and Lawson, T., 1998. 'Trade liberalisation in the European Union and APEC: what if the approaches were exchanged?', in P. Drysdale and D. Vines (eds), *Europe, East Asia and APEC: a shared global agenda?*, Cambridge University Press, Cambridge.

Zhong, C. and Yang, Y., 1998. 'China's textile and clothing exports in the post-Uruguay Round', in P. Drysdale and L.G. Song (eds), *China's Entry into the WTO: issues and quantitative assessments*, Routledge.

NOTES

This is a modified version of an article that appeared in *The Australian Economic Papers*, September 1999. (reproduced with permission here)

The authors are grateful for comments and suggestions made by the anonymous referee and the participants at the International Conference *APEC and its Impact on the Chinese Economy*, held at The Australian National University, Canberra, 16 February 1998.

7

APEC INVESTMENT, TRADE LIBERALISATION AND CHINA'S ECONOMIC ADJUSTMENT

SUN XUEGONG

The 15th National Congress of the Chinese Communist Party (CPC), concluded in September 1996, reaffirmed that China would continue its reform and open-door policy. Investment and trade liberalisation are important parts of the strategy to bring a prosperous and stable China into the new millennium. At the APEC Osaka summit, China pledged to take an active part in the APEC liberalisation process. Since then, China has unilaterally taken major steps to cut tariff rates and dismantle non-tariff barriers, bringing China's average tariff rate from 36 per cent—almost the highest in the world—to 15 per cent—the target set for 2000—and abolishing import control measures such as quotas, licensing and other direct administrative controls on more than 170 frequently traded commodities. Further liberalisation is also on the agenda. China's commitment to liberalisation is strong and it has made substantial progress in implementation.

ECONOMIC STRUCTURAL ADJUSTMENT: REAPING THE BENEFITS OF LIBERALISATION

There is unanimous agreement (World Bank 1997; Zhang et al. 1997) that trade liberalisation will bring enormous welfare benefits to China's economy. In particular, it will dramatically expand the labour-intensive sectors of the economy without causing output in other sectors to decline, if China's offers of tariff reductions and the phasing out of non-tariff barriers are implemented. This will help China maintain its momentum of economic growth in the long run and promote its industrialisation drive. However, to realise the expected potential benefits and to cope with the challenges that will accompany liberalisation, adjustment of China's economic structure is essential. The experience of other countries shows that without a sound economic structure, liberalisation does not necessarily bring benefits. China's present inefficient economic structure will likely decrease its chances of realising the benefits, and magnify the risks, of liberalisation. As a transitional country with a long experience of a closed market and a planned economic system, and as the largest developing economy in the world undergoing rapid industrialisation, China's need for economic structural adjustment is much more fundamental and comprehensive than that of other countries undergoing a similar transition process.

While there are many facets of China's economic structural adjustment in response to proposed trade liberalisation, this chapter seeks only to identify and deal with a few key fields that are crucial to preparing China adequately for liberalisation. Considering that China is still in the throes of transition from a planned to a market economy, the first key field is reform of the economic system, an aspect of fundamental importance in the context of liberalisation. The notion that a country will necessarily benefit from free trade is predicated on the assumption that the market mechanism in that country functions well. If not, the story is totally different. After 20 years of concerted efforts, China has basically established a market system but there is still much work to do. Last year, the party congress called for strategic readjustment of the state-owned economy. This was a signal that China's policy of incremental reform—which had proved very effective in the past two decades, and was characterised by allowing the non-state sector to develop freely while avoiding dramatic reform in the troublesome state sector—had come to an end. Further reform will focus on state-owned enterprises (SOEs), and bolder reform measures will be introduced. Although not intended to deal with the issues raised by free trade, SOE reform is relevant to the process of trade liberalisation. SOEs are the parts of the Chinese economy most vulnerable to external shocks. However, SOEs have strong bargaining power to influence government policymaking. If the SOE reform program cannot be implemented smoothly, the adjustment costs of liberalisation will be very high and this, in turn, will damage the process of trade liberalisation.

The market structure of China's industries is another matter of concern for trade liberalisation. It is an undeniable fact that all countries want to profit from participation in international competition. But nowadays, the possession of comparative advantage does not necessarily guarantee that a country will be competitive in a world market dominated by huge multinational corporations. China's unique experience of decentralised incremental reform has left its industrial organisational structure ill-prepared for fierce international competition. The overall size of China's economy is approaching that of a developed country, but individual Chinese enterprises are far smaller than their counterparts in developed countries. The relatively small size of its enterprises has weakened China's competitiveness in many ways, particularly in terms of capability in worldwide marketing and R&D. China is now encouraging its enterprises to establish conglomerates through mergers or other means of capital reorganisation. Adjustment of its market structure will help China gain the confidence to integrate more aggressively with the global economy and set the country firmly on the path of trade liberalisation.

As the most populous country in the world with a long history of struggles against starvation, the importance of the grain sector in China cannot be overemphasised. Adjustment in the grain sector is one of the most sensitive and controversial issues both in China and abroad. In response to changing comparative advantage, adjustment in this sector is already underway. However, given China's large territory and the wide disparities among regions, we argue that this adjustment will be initiated by reallocating domestic resources and reforming the institutional framework to tap the remaining potential of China's grain production. Inevitably, China will integrate with the world grain market. But it will take time, and the speed of this process will not only be affected by economic factors but also by political ones, given the strategic nature of food production.

China's process of trade liberalisation is undoubtedly conditioned by adjustments in these key fields. Coordination of the trade liberalisation process with domestic structural adjustment is essential if China is to achieve its goal at least possible cost and minimal instability.

ECONOMIC STRUCTURAL ADJUSTMENT IN KEY FIELDS AND ITS IMPLICATIONS FOR TRADE LIBERALISATION

STATE-OWNED ENTERPRISE REFORM

One of the main benefits of trade liberalisation is that it intensifies domestic competition, providing incentives for domestic enterprises to improve performance and efficiency, the real engines of economic development. However, this only occurs when domestic enterprises are sensitive to market changes.

Within the Chinese economy, there is a distinct dichotomy between the state-owned sector and the non-state-owned sector. The market-oriented non-state sector—a byproduct of incremental reform—is heavily concentrated in labour-intensive industries in which China's comparative advantage is believed to reside. Trade liberalisation will boost the development of the non-state sector through increased flexibility and accessibility to bigger markets and previously unavailable resources. The state sector, however, presents a different picture. While the state sector has undergone dramatic change, the transformation falls far short of government objectives. State-owned enterprises—to which the majority of China's economic resources are allocated—cannot be considered as enterprises in the true sense of the word until the establishment of a modern enterprise

111

system is complete. State-owned enterprises continue to lack the incentives and vitality necessary to participate in market competition. This defect in the market mechanism will diminish the real benefits of trade liberalisation.

Inefficiency and relative concentration in capital-intensive industries, combined with weak international competitiveness, make the state sector the part of China's economy most vulnerable under trade liberalisation. In recent years, there has been increasing evidence of the linkages between the poor performance of SOEs and external competition, especially in the capital goods industries, such as machine building and electrical equipment. At the introduction of the open-door policy, domestically-produced capital goods accounted for over 90 per cent of total supply, but by the mid-1990s, their market share fallen to less than 40 per cent. Basic mechanical equipment such as machine tools lost more than 70 per cent of their market share (Hu 1996). This has raised major concerns about the role of trade liberalisation and provoked heated debate on policy options. Some people argue that China's long-term dynamic advantage lies in capital-intensive sectors. They are pessimistic about the further expansion of China's labour-intensive sector in the light of deteriorating terms of trade and trade barriers in destination countries. Accordingly, they advocate slowing the process of trade liberalisation to protect these emerging industries. This opposition to liberalisation—especially from the industry sector—is so strong that it cannot easily be ignored by policymakers.

Another concern centres on employment. Ongoing SOE reform and downsizing campaigns in the state-owned sector have already caused more than 10 million workers to be laid off, bringing the real unemployment rate to a record high since reform. Despite government assurances that every laid-off worker will be re-employed, more than half remain unemployed, and the situation is even worse in some interior provinces where SOEs are concentrated. This is regarded as a potential threat to social stability, an issue of real concern to policymakers in China. A rush to liberalise will inevitably exacerbate the unemployment situation. Zhang et al. (1997) estimate employment losses due to trade liberalisation in certain sectors dominated by SOEs. Their findings illustrate that more than 20 per cent of workers will lose their jobs in an average industry, and the industry most strongly affected—the automobile industry—will lose 67 per cent of its jobs (Table 7.1).

Furthermore, the production factors—both capital and labour—in the state sector are stickier than those in the non-state sector. The inertia in the state sector makes it difficult to channel redundant resources into more productive industry. This will create very high adjustment costs as the trade liberalisation process outpaces SOE reform.

It is clear that SOE reform has lagged behind trade liberalisation and has increasingly become an impediment to further liberalisation. Synchronising SOE

Table 7.1   The effect of trade liberalisation on employment in selected industries

Industry	Employment before liberalisation (10,000)	Change in employment (10,000)	Rate of change (%)
Colour TVs	17.58	-1.68	-9.54
VCRs	3.27	-0.95	-29.06
Motorcycles	14.41	-5.13	-35.57
Air conditioners	5.62	-3.36	-59.35
Steel	66.66	-17.40	-26.11
Bronze	16.17	-1.07	-6.63
Aluminium	20.71	-8.29	-40.01
Gasoline	26.55	-5.98	-22.53
Diesel oil	59.78	-13.14	-21.98
Synthetic fibres	19.56	-2.93	-14.98
Synthetic rubbers	14.12	-3.85	-27.30
Plastics	78.70	-32.16	-60.86
Automobiles	10.94	-7.42	-67.85
Personal computers	8.13	-1.03	-12.66
Color kinescopes	12.40	-2.48	-20.01
Switchboards	13.33	-3.84	-28.84

Source: Zhang, S., Zhang, Y. and Wan, Z., 1997. 'Measuring the cost of China's trade protection', *Economic Research*, 2:12–22.

reform and trade liberalisation will lead to smoother and less costly adjustment. Speeding up SOE reform rather than slowing the scheduled pace of liberalisation appears to be an efficient and logical solution. The government has pledged that in the coming three years, large and medium-size state-owned enterprises will resolve their current difficulties. China's target for trade liberalisation over the same period is to lower the tariff rate to the average level of developing countries, a new milestone in the drive towards trade liberalisation.

MARKET STRUCTURE

Unlike traditional trade theory—which is based on assumptions of perfect market competition and constant returns to scale—the assumptions of new trade theory are more realistic. Under this theoretical framework, market structure is an important factor in determining whether a country can benefit from free trade. When the domestic market structure corresponds to the international market structure, free trade is the optimal option, just as traditional trade theory predicts. But when the domestic market is in a state of perfect competition, and the international market is characterised by imperfect competition—such as the presence of monopoly or oligopoly—a country will suffer under free trade because of the existence of monopoly rents as well as the unfair advantage multinationals have over domestic producers.

Unfortunately, China is faced with this unfavourable case. Sheng (1996) compares the market structure of China's manufacturing sector with its international counterparts. He finds that the majority of China's manufacturing industries fall into the category of perfect competition, while their foreign counterparts are in a state of imperfect competition (Table 7.2). There is no single industry in China in which the production concentration exceeds 50 per cent, even those industries where scale economies are notable—such as transport equipment and steel.

Another obvious fact is that there is no Chinese enterprise listed among the Fortune 500 biggest companies, although China ranks first in the output of many industrial products around the world. This is partly due to China's unique experience of decentralised reform. This reform has empowered local governments and SOEs to make their own decisions about investment, although they are not true market players. Many of their investment decisions have proven to be short-sighted and irresponsible, resulting in long-standing problems of duplication and uncoordinated regional industrial structures, usually the result of hasty decision-making. China's industrial organisational structure can be described as large, scattered in distribution and disorderly in conduct.

This fact raises the concern that liberalisation will damage domestic enterprises, even if they have comparative advantage or the potential to be productive, due to a biased market structure. Taking the steel industry as an example, China's steel output is ranked the first in the world, but individual firm size is small in relation to foreign competition. The sales volume of Baoshan Steel Corporation— the largest steel company in China—is less than one-tenth that of steel plants in Japan and Korea. Other industries—such as domestic electronics and building materials—are in a similar position. Under these circumstances, multinationals will easily drive domestic enterprises to the wall with the aid of their monopoly power. This will frustrate China's ambition to compete in the world market and may even cause China to pull back from its commitments on trade liberalisation. This partly explains China's reluctance to open some sectors in which it appears to have a comparative advantage.

China is attempting to change its current industrial organisation structure so that it can adapt to international competition. Many people believe that there is still great potential for China to exploit increasing returns to scale in the domestic market, as distinct from the path taken by China's export-led Southeast Asian neighbours. Some policy incentives have been set up to encourage the establishment of conglomerates, although there is some scepticism as to the effectiveness of such artificial incentives. The recent financial crisis in Korea—

Table 7.2   Market structure of manufactures and expected trade policy Industry

ISIC	Industry	C4[a] (%)	Scale of economy	Domestic structure	Foreign structure	Expected trade policy
311–312	Food	9.5	0.97	Perfect	Imperfect	Rent transfer/tariff
313	Beverages	7.6	1.29	Perfect	Imperfect	Rent transfer/tariff
314	Tobacco	31	2.33	Imperfect	Imperfect	Free trade
321	Textiles	..	0.77	Perfect	Imperfect	Rent transfer/tariff
322–324	Apparel, footwear	..	1.07	Perfect	Imperfect	Rent transfer/tariff
323	Leather	..	1.04	Perfect	Perfect	Free trade
331–332	Wood & furniture	..	0.29	Perfect	Perfect	Free trade
341–342	Paper & printing	..	0.77	Perfect	Imperfect	Rent transfer/tariff
353–354	Oil refining & coking	30	0.91	Imperfect	Market split	Rent transfer/tariff
351	Chemical	8.5	1.02	Perfect	Imperfect	Rent transfer/tariff
3522	Pharmacy	11.0	1.23	Imperfect	Imperfect	Free trade
352	Chemical fibres	32.4	1.44	Imperfect	Imperfect	Free trade
355	Rubber	10.9	0.52	Perfect	Market split	Rent transfer/tariff
356	Plastic	..	0.89	Imperfect	Imperfect	Rent transfer/tariff
36	Building materials	2.2	0.91	Perfect	Imperfect	Rent transfer/tariff
371	Steel	23.6	0.55	Imperfect	Market split	Rent transfer/tariff
372	Non-ferrous metals	12.9	1.35	Imperfect	Imperfect	Rent transfer/tariff
381	Metal products	3.2	1.09	Perfect	Imperfect	Rent transfer/tariff
382	Machinery	3.8	0.40	Perfect	Imperfect	Rent transfer/tariff
384	Transport equipment	28.3	1.16	Imperfect	Imperfect	Free trade
383	Electrical	9.8	1.06	Imperfect	Imperfect	Free trade
	Electronic & telecomms	11.3	0.95	Imperfect	Imperfect	Free trade
385	Instruments & meters	17.4	1.48	Imperfect	Imperfect	Free trade

Note: [a]   C4 denotes the percentage of the largest four companies in the total output of their industry; the scale of economy is measured by the sum of a and b, coefficients of the Cobb–Douglas production function.

Source: Sheng, L., 1996. 'Market structure of China's manufactures and its implications for trade policy', *Economic Research*, 8:62–70.

where the economic structure is dominated by large conglomerates backed by government—has added weight to these concerns and may lead to policy adjustments. However, there have already been several cases of mergers of big companies. In Nanjing, four chemical companies originally belonging to different central and local government departments merged into a giant corporation, forming the largest enterprise in China's chemical industry. In Shanghai, China's largest business, Baoshan Steel Corporation, also purchased a smaller firm, Shanghai Steel Corporation. Many people believe that adjustment in industrial organisational structure is necessary to reconcile the large gap between the size of Chinese firms and their foreign competitors, although how this is to be achieved requires further discussion. Most importantly, the emergence of conglomerates will build up China's confidence to participate aggressively in international competition, and hasten China's integration into the global economy.

To complement these changes in structural policy, China needs to improve its legal system and strengthen the enforcement of competition policy. Even more important is the need to enhance legal awareness within Chinese enterprises. Until recently, no anti-trust or anti-dumping investigations had been launched by Chinese enterprises. At the end of 1996, MOFTEC received its first complaint. Seven Chinese paper-making companies are to sue Canadian competitors for dumping their product on the Chinese market. Using these laws, China's domestic enterprises may find alternative ways to protect their interests rather than closing the door to the outside world in the face of unfair competition from powerful multinationals.

GRAIN SECTOR ADJUSTMENT

Of the major developing countries, China is the most poorly endowed with land. The area of arable land per capita in China is only about one-fifth of the world average. Sooner or later, China will lose its comparative advantage in this field, and adjustment is inevitable. In fact, some adjustment in response to changing comparative advantage has already taken place. Since reform, grain production has gradually shifted from the southern coastal region to the northern interior provinces, despite the former region's more favourable natural conditions for grain production. This is a result of the rapid industrialisation of the coastal region in past decades. As industrialisation spreads through the country, China will eventually liberalise its grain sector and integrate into the world grain market. The percentage of imported grain in total grain consumption will increase steadily. Nevertheless, it is still too early to predict by how much the proportion of imported grain will rise, due to the wide variation in projections made by various sources—from almost 50 per cent to only 3 per cent. Adjustment in the grain sector from an inward to an outward looking approach will take time. There are several reasons for the uncertainty and slow progress.

First, there is still room for China to undertake internal adjustment in the grain sector, both physically and institutionally. Exploitation of unused land, introduction of high-yield varieties, increasing and balanced use of fertilisers, and improvements to the agricultural infrastructure—especially in water conservation and irrigation systems—are often cited as steps that China should take to tap its potential in grain production. Adjustments like these will allow China's grain production to grow rather than contract. In contrast to the predictions of Lester R. Brown, the dramatic decline in grain production that occurred in the newly industrialising countries will not occur in China. Improvements in the domestic trade infrastructure and grain distribution system will make the country more integrated as a common market and help China take advantage of its large territory and the disparities among regions so that they can develop their own specialisations. This will create more regional trade and even replace some of the international trade that occurs now. Maize exports from the northeast of China may be replaced by imports by Guangdong, for example, something not yet possible due to the poor internal transportation system. Reform of the existing grain trade regime can be seen as another stimulus to grain production. In 1997, a bold measure was taken to reform the state grain trade regime with the aim of streamlining and increasing efficiency. Many people claim that the current regime is merely seeking rent from its control over the grain trade and that this has lowered grain production without protecting the interests of farmers or consumers. Reform of the international grain trade regime is also underway. In the past decade, efforts to regulate shortages or surpluses of grain supply have not proved effective. A net import year often coincides with a good harvest year while a net export year usually occurs in a bad harvest year. This unreasonable trade behaviour has exacerbated fluctuations in grain prices on the domestic market, especially in 1993 when grain price hikes triggered a new round of severe inflation and slowed China's growth rate. More reasonable and stable trade behaviour can be expected under the new regime.

Second, the speed of liberalisation of China's grain sector will be heavily dependent on the openness of China's trade partners to China's labour-intensive production. China's withdrawal from the agricultural sector is only possible if labour-intensive industries accommodate the thousand million farmers moving out of the agricultural sector. China's labour-intensive industries face a serious problem of redundant production capacity. Data from the third national industrial census show that over one-third of industries utilise only half of their production capacity or less. Those industries need the international market to make full use of their production capacity and draw farmers out of the traditional sector. But unfortunately, some trading partners limit the access of Chinese products to their markets through quota controls or under the pretext of anti-dumping. Under these circumstances, no one can expect China to open its grain market quickly.

Finally, political concerns also play a role. China's demand for food security and its desire to reduce risk to a manageable level are justifiable. China needs to deal with external concerns that it will exhaust the world's tradable grain supplies or at least increase grain prices on the international market. Some developing countries—whose grain supplies depend heavily on the international market, and are likely to suffer greatly under this scenario—have openly expressed such concerns. All this should prompt China to be prudent in liberalising its grain sector. It is to be expected that the extent of China's involvement in the international grain market will vary with its perceptions of the international environment.

REFERENCES

Hu, C., 1996. 'The impact of openness on China's industrial development', Beijing (mimeo).

Sheng, L., 1996. 'The market structure of China's manufacturing sector and implications for trade policy', *Economic Research*, 8:62–70.

World Bank, 1997. *China 2020,* World Bank, Washington, DC.

Zhang, S., Zhang, Y. and Wan, Z., 1997. 'Measuring the cost of China's trade protection', *Economic Research*, 2:12–22.

8

TRADE PROTECTION IN CHINA'S AUTOMOBILE AND TEXTILE INDUSTRIES AND ITS IMPACT ON TRADE LIBERALISATION

LI KAI

China has become a significant player in the international market and foreign trade has assumed an important role in China's economic development. In 1997, China's total foreign trade volume was recorded as US$325 billion, an increase of 15 per cent on the previous year, ranking the country as the tenth largest trader in the world. In the same year, China's trade surplus was approximately 4.4 per cent of GDP.

With such a large external orientation, it is essential for China to investigate the impact of global trade liberalisation before further integrating itself into an increasingly open international trading system. The impact on the major domestic industrial sectors, including both labour-intensive and capital or technology-intensive sectors is of particular importance.

Generally speaking, China has a comparative advantage in the labour-intensive sectors, so production in those sectors will expand following the adoption of a more open trade regime. Although China has less advantage in capital and technology-intensive sectors, it still needs to foster some of these important industries in the light of its large population and domestic market, the limited world market in labour-intensive goods, and the tendency towards deterioration in the terms of trade for developing economies.

In order to calculate the impact of trade liberalisation on both sectors, the Chinese textile and automobile industries are chosen as examples of each of these sectors and the level of trade protection is measured in each sector. The costs of trade protection—or in other words the welfare of trade liberalisation—is also investigated. A caveat is necessary: due to data limitations, the investigation should be considered preliminary, and further work remains to be done in the area.

119

MEASURING TRADE PROTECTION IN THE AUTOMOBILE AND TEXTILE SECTORS

FORMS OF PROTECTION OF CHINA'S AUTOMOBILE TRADE

Non-tariff trade protection measures and their characteristics. Since the 1980s, the major measures adopted by China in this regard have included

- regulation of approval for automobile imports. For example, in 1985 China stipulated that all imports of luxury cars, luxury jeeps, luxury tourist automobiles and common sedans were forbidden except those approved by the State Council
- regulation of types of imports
- inclusion of automobile imports in national plans
- limits to the issue of licences
- implementation of quotas on automobile imports
- implementation of an import licensing system
- collection of fees and taxes in a manner different from those levied on domestic automobiles
- imposition of import inspection by customs
- nomination of special automobile import units
- selection of special automobile import harbours.

China's restrictions on automobile imports have been greatly relaxed. Now the main non-tariff measures in place are import quotas and licence administration.

Tariff protection measures. In the past few years, tariffs on imported automobiles have been characterised by

- declining tariff rates. Tariffs on cars have been further lowered by an average of 80 per cent since 1 October 1997. Tariffs on other vehicles and parts have followed the same trend
- narrowing the categories of automobiles that enjoy exempt or reduced tariffs, and reduced tariff rates
- the frequent application of preferential tariff rates
- a system whereby special purpose motor vehicles enjoy the lowest tariff rate, with the rate for trucks higher than that for motor vehicles, large buses higher than trucks, medium-sized buses higher than large buses and mini-buses and sedans highest in the hierarchy of imported automobiles.

MEASURING CHINA'S AUTOMOBILE TRADE PROTECTION

The price comparison method is usually employed internationally when describing the degree of trade protection. It involves

- comparison of retail prices of the same imports in the domestic market and world market (excluding factors that cannot be compared, such as freight, insurance and distribution charges among enterprises in different countries)

- comparison between the CIF price of imports and the factory-gate prices of domestically-made commodities of similar quality
- comparison between the CIF value and price, including the CIF and price of trade protection measures on imports.

Due to the lack of price data in the international market and the difficulties in selecting domestically-made commodities that are of the same quality as imports, a third means is tentatively applied to estimate the degree of trade protection in the Chinese automobile industry, as follows. Suppose

ATP = the level of automobile trade protection

ACIF = CIF value of imported automobiles

APV = price variation due to trade protection measures,

then ATP = (ACIF+APV)/ACIF.

Generally speaking, trade protection measures that result in variations in automobile price can be divided into two types: taxation including tariffs, and non-taxation protection measures including import quotas and licensing systems. Thus,

ATP= ATP1+ATP2

ATP1 = level of taxation protection

ATP2 = level of non-taxation protection.

MEASURING THE DEGREE OF PROTECTION IN THE FORM OF TAXES AND FEE COLLECTION

Retail price constituents of imported automobiles in the domestic market are analysed as follows: retail price = the CIF price of imported automobiles + other pre-sale charges

1. tariffs
   tariff volume = CIF price of imported automobiles × tariff rate = ACIF × tariff rate
2. consumption tax
   consumption tax volume = (ACIF + tariff volume) × consumption tax rate / (1 − consumption tax rate)
3. value-added tax
   Value-added tax on imported automobiles can be divided into two components: the value-added tax levied through customs, labeled value-added tax 1.
   Value-added tax 1 = (ACIF + tariff volume + consumption tax volume) × value-added tax rate;
   and the value-added tax levied by taxation bodies when the imported automobiles are sold. This is labeled value-added tax 2 [cf. expense (4)]

4   other importation expenses, including commodity inspection charges, bank charges, foreign trade agency charges and sundry charges for port entry

The four expenses mentioned above plus the CIF of the imported automobiles equal the total cost of automobile imports.

5   other expenses incurred between the time automobiles are declared at customs and the time they are sold, including

a) the operational and management expenses of enterprises engaged in the distribution of imported automobiles, including management expenses, interest, storage expenses and the profits taken by the distribution enterprises. It is generally stipulated that such expenses should be less than or equal to the import cost of the automobile × 6.5%. Expenses (1) + import cost of the automobile = automobile sales cost

b) value-added tax 2 = (automobile sales cost − automobile import cost) × value-added tax rate

c) urban maintenance construction tax and instruction surcharges = value-added tax 2 × 8%

d) automobile purchase surcharges = (automobile sales cost + expense b + expense c) × 10%

The sum of expenses (1) to (4) including the CIF of imported automobiles makes up the theoretical sale price of the imported automobile, including taxes in the domestic market (that is, without taxation exemption).

As the CIF of imported automobiles is theoretically the same as the factory-gate prices of those made domestically without trade protection, automobile trade protection by means of taxation is actually reflected in the price discrepancy between the sale price of imported automobiles (including taxes) in the domestic market where the tariff rate and the commodity inspection charge equal zero, and the sale price where the tariff rate and the commodity inspection charge do not equal zero. Suppose,

a = tariff rate on imported automobiles

b = consumption tax rate on imported automobiles

c = value-added tax rate on imported automobiles

d = commodity inspection charge (generally $D = ACIF \times 0.003$)

e = other expenses excluding commodity charges in expenses (3) (generally $E = 4.5\% \times ACIF$)

tariff volume = $TT = ACIF \times a$

consumption tax volume = $CT = (ACIF + TT) \times b/(1-b)$

value-added tax 1 = $AT = (ACIF + TT + CT) \times c$

operational and management expenses = $(ACIF + TT + CT + D + E) \times 6.5\%$

The discrepancy between the sale price of imported automobiles in the domestic market (including taxation) where the tariff rate and commodity inspection charge equal zero, and that where the tariff rate and commodity inspection charges do not equal zero can be calculated as

$$APV1 = ACIF [a (1 +bc +c) /(1-b) + 0.3\%] \times 1.1847$$

Thus, the degree of automobile taxation trade protection can be expressed as

$$ATP1 = APV1/ACIF = [a (1 +bc + c)/(1-b) + 0.3\%] \times 1.1847$$

In the light of such a formula and the 1996 edition of the catalogue of customs tariffs and customs taxation, the level of China's automobile taxation trade protection can be estimated (Table 8.1).

MEASURING THE DEGREE OF PROTECTION IN FORMS OTHER THAN TAXES AND FEES

When non-taxation protection measures such as import quotas and licensing systems are implemented, the domestic automobile industry is protected, since

Table 8.1   Protection in the form of taxes and fees for automobiles (per cent)

Auto types	Tariff rate (a)	Consumption tax (b)	Value-added tax (c)	Tax protection rate (ATP1)
Heavy-duty trucks 1	30	0	17	42
Heavy-duty trucks 2	50	0	17	70
Medium trucks	50	0	17	70
Light trucks	50	0	17	70
Dumping trucks	15	0	17	21
Buses	60	0	17	84
Medium buses 1	90	3	17	130
Medium buses 2	90	5	17	133
Mini-buses 1	100	3	17	144
Mini-buses 2	100	5	17	147
Mini-buses 3	120	5	17	177
Sedans 1	100	3	17	144
Sedans 2	100	5	17	147
Sedans 3	100	8	17	153
Sedans 4	120	8	17	183
Jeeps 1	100	3	17	144
Jeeps 2	100	5	17	147
Jeeps 3	120	5	17	177
Derrick cars 1	10	0	17	14
Derrick cars 2	20	0	17	28
Ambulances	20	0	17	28
Concrete mixers	25	0	17	35
Arithmetic mean	71	3	17	104

Source: *Customs Statistics Yearbook*, 1996.

these measures do not directly add to the cost of imported automobiles, they limit the quantity. Nevertheless, due to limitations, it is still difficult to measure the degree of protection in any standardised way. To get a rough idea of the current level of non-taxation protection in the automobile trade, the key domestic distributors of automobiles have been investigated and the CIF and sale price (including taxation) on some imported automobiles have been compared with the real domestic retail price. On the basis of the analysis of the cost of imported automobiles, the assumption can be made that the difference between the real sale price and the sale price with taxation included is the result of non-taxation protection measures. Thus, the level of non-taxation protection on some imported automobiles can be roughly calculated (Table 8.2).

FORMS OF PROTECTION IN CHINA'S TEXTILE TRADE

Tariff trade protection measures
- Nominal tax, which has been high, has dropped sharply in recent years. In 1997, the overall tariff level was 17 per cent, whereas the average textile tariff level dropped to 17.1 per cent (Table 8.3).
- The structure of textile tariffs shows that the tariff rate has risen steadily and progressively with growth in the processing trade. An example of

Table 8.2   Level of non-tax protection of selected imported automobiles

Name	CIF (US$)	Tax-included price (10,000 yuan)	Domestic retail price (10,000 yuan)	Non-tax protection degree (%)
Honda 1.6	14000	28.74	29.50	6.55
Ford Tempo 2.2	9000	18.47	21.50	40.50
Chrysler Neon	12000	24.63	29.60	49.87
Daewoo Espero 2.0	8000	16.42	21.50	76.47
Corsica 2.2	12000	24.63	25.80	11.72
Honda Accord 2.0	15000	30.79	34.50	29.79
Honda Accord 2.2	18000	36.95	40.05	20.75
Daewoo Cielo	7500	15.40	19.40	64.33
Toyota Camry 2.2	18000	36.95	38.00	7.03
Crown 3.0	23000	48.25	49.30	5.48
Hyundai 2.0	12000	24.63	31.50	68.94
Hyundai 3.0	15000	31.47	34.00	20.32
Mitsubishi Jeep	15000	30.79	36.00	41.84
Kamaza DumpingTruck	17000	17.09	31.00	98.56
Kamaza Truck	26000	36.61	41.00	20.33

Source: Author's calculations.

the operation of the tariff system in 1996 shows that the tariff rate for fibre materials was 10.3 per cent, 17.6 per cent for yarn, 29.1 per cent for textile fabrics and 41.8 per cent for garments.

- At present, the highest levels of tariff protection are found in the chemical fibre and garment industries which are in their infancy.
- The best feature of the Chinese system is that the actually applied tariff rate is low. The applied tariff rate for imported textiles is, on average, only 2.2 per cent. This is mainly because 90 per cent of imported textile products are for the processing trade, which is duty free (Table 8.4).

Table 8.3   China's textile import tariff rates structure

Material	Degree of processing	Tariff number (%)	Basic rate rate (%)	Favourable
Silk type	Material (including preliminary processing)	5001–5003	54.30	8.10
	Yarn	5004–5006	72.50	15.00
	Fabrics	5007	100	30.00
Wool and other	Material (including preliminary processing)	5101–5105	29.40	12.80
	Yarn	5106–5110	52.20	20.00
	Fabrics	5111–5113	100	35.00
Cotton type	Material (including preliminary processing)	5201–5203	13.20	7.20
	Yarn	5204–5207	30.60	13.30
	Fabrics	5208–5212	59.40	22.00
Textile fibres from other plants	Material (including preliminary processing)	5301–5305	18.90	6.50
	Yarn	5306–5308	37.10	12.30
	Fabrics	5309–5311	55.00	23.00
Chemical fibre filament yarn	Yarn	5401–5406	46.50	21.40
	Fabrics	5407–5408	100	44.20
	Material (including preliminary processing)	5501–5507	40.30	17.10
Chemical fibre abort yarn	Yarn	5508–5511	65.70	23.40
	Fabrics	5512–5516	100	41.30
Various material	Garments &	61,62	90.30	41.80
Various material	Other textile	58,60,63	80.40	35.80
Various material	Other textile	56,57,59	61.60	32.00

Note: Basic rate refers to the concession base on which China re-entered GATT negotiations, and that used by China and other signatories participating in the WTO.

Source: *Customs Statistics Yearbook*, 1994.

Table 8.4   Import trade structure of textile products and their applied tariff rate, 1994 (per cent)

		Structure			
	Total	General trade	Material-supplied processing	Material-imported processing	Barter
Share in total textile imports	99.1	8.8	62.6	26.7	1.0
Average real implemented tariff rate	2.23	23.1	-	-	20.0

Notes: 1. Import structure is taken from the report conducted under the auspices of the Department of Trade, China Textile Association by Wang Lie.
2. The average real implemented tariff rate is calculated from the Customs Tariff Rule, 1996.
Source: *Customs Statistics Yearbook*, 1994.

Non-tariff protection measures include
- import quotas
- import licences
- authorised agencies
- a textile import registration system.

MEASURING CHINA'S TEXTILE TRADE PROTECTION

Tariff protection in the textile sector. Tariff rates for textile products have sustained several cutbacks in recent years, but this figure is still behind what was required of China by American and European states during the Uruguay Talks. The full requirements place great pressure on the future development of China's textile industry. An examination of China's import structure for textile products and its pattern of trade shows that China's actual tariff rate is zero because over 90 per cent of imported textile products are brought into the country for the processing trade (mainly raw materials for textiles, yarn and a small proportion of textile fabrics). Therefore the current high nominal taxation only affects garments and other textile products imported by way of general trade transactions and barter trade.

Because of the low volume that general trade and barter trade occupy in textile imports, it can be concluded that the actual tariff rate for China's textile imports is significantly lower than average nominal tariff rates.

Non-tariff protection in the textile sector. Degree of non-tariff protection = ex-factory price of products of the same kind (quality) / (CIF price of imported products (1+ tariff rate)) × 100%.

In the above formula, the ex-factory price of domestic products already includes value-added taxes, so to facilitate a comparison between the two prices,

Table 8.5   Textile price comparison of imported and domestic products (yuan)

Type	Import (c.i.f)	Tariff rate	Real implem-ented tariff rate	Domestic producer price	Comparable producer price	Degree of non-tariff protection n^1 (%)	Degree of non-tariff protection n^2(%)
Calico	5.8	45	-	8.6	7.4	-12.0	27.6
Medium-length textile cloth	11.1	80	-	15.0	12.8	-36.0	16.4
Cotton yarn	18.0	25	-	22.1	18.9	-16.0	5.0
Woollen yarn	43.2	50	-	72.5	62.0	-4.3	43.5

Notes: ^{1}CIF (yuan) is calculated as CIF (dollars)*exchange rate (8.4). ^{2}Tariff rate and applied tariff rate are expressed as two types such as the rate for general trade and that for the processing trade.

Source: *Customs Statistics Yearbook* (1994); *China Industrial Products Yearbook* (1994); author's calculations.

value-added taxes need to be distinguished from the ex-factory price of domestic products.

Due to lack of adequate data, we are unable to provide an overall measurement of the full range of non-tariff protection for traded textile products. However, an approximate calculation can be made of the range of non-tariff protection by selecting a typical commodity for comparison.

It is clear that the range of non-tariff protection is of negative value (Table 8.5). In the case of a general transaction for an imported assignment of products, due to the presence of high tariff protection, the domestic prices of home commodities retain price competitiveness even in the absence of non-tariff protection, whereas if the import pattern shifts to the processing trade the import tariff rate becomes zero. In this case, the imported commodities assume price competitiveness, and domestic commodities need to be protected by non-tariff measures. According to the data in Table 8.5, in 1994, the average non-tariff protection for selected Chinese textile products was about 23.1 per cent.

THE IMPACT OF TRADE LIBERALISATION IN BOTH SECTORS ON THE CHINESE ECONOMY

THE COSTS OF AUTOMOBILE TRADE PROTECTION AND THE IMPACTS OF LOWERED TARIFFS ON THE NATIONAL ECONOMY

Theoretically, implementation of automobile industry trade protection would have several direct effects, including

- raising the price of imported automobiles, thus sparking a price rise on the domestic automobile market
- stimulating domestic automobile production and restricting domestic market demand for automobiles because of the rise in prices, resulting in a reduction in the import volume of automobiles
- increasing China's fiscal revenue through the tariffs levied on imported automobiles and their components.

According to this analysis, three formulae must be used to calculate the impacts of automobile trade protection

- imported automobile sales price = f1 (level of automobile trade protection)
- automobile import volume = f2 (imported automobile sales price, domestic demand)
- domestic automobile output = f3 (imported automobile sales price, domestic demand).

Unlike taxation protection—the main component of which is tariff protection (rises in tariffs themselves and in other taxes resulting from the tariff)—the major components of non-taxation protection are regulations and measures restricting imports. These changes are comparatively frequent and irregular and, as a result, it is difficult to quantify their real protection effect. At the same time, tariff protection has the same effect as non-tariff protection from the perspective of quantity. When we consider the impact trade protection has on other components—that is, tariff and non-tariff measures—the quantity of imported automobiles is restricted by influencing the price of imported automobiles. In this sense, an estimation of the impact on import volume and the national economy exerted by import price variations due to tariff changes may likewise be applied to an analysis of the impact of non-tariff measures that cause the same import price change. Therefore, with respect to the formulae above, we will replace all trade protection measures with tariff protection. But as trade systems and channels differ and there still exist some tariff-exemption and tariff-reduction measures in the field of automobile imports, the actual applied tariff rate (automobile tariff volume/cost of automobile imports) is lower than the nominal tariff rate in the automobile trade. The important factor in the automobile import trade is the actual applied tariff rate, so it is more reasonable to adopt the actual applied tariff rate in our study. However, as data on tariffs for automobile imports in recent years are unobtainable, we tentatively adopt the applied tariff rates of the total import trade instead of the applied tariff rate in the automobile trade in the following analysis. This is because the applied tariff rate for automobile imports is a linear function of the applied tariff rate for the total import trade provided that tariff and import structures remain comparatively stable. That is,

applied tariff rate of automobiles = a × average applied tariff rate of total import trade (a being a constant).

Therefore, the applied tariff rate for the total import trade can take the place of the applied tariff rate for automobiles when we study the relative influence that variations on the applied automobile tariff rate exert on other aspects (elasticity analysis).

A further consideration is that domestic demand for automobiles in the above formulae is jointly influenced by domestic investment in fixed assets and domestic commodity prices. On the basis of the above analysis, let us suppose that

FAD = nominal domestic investment in fixed assets

OPR = domestic commodity price indices

RTF = applied tariff rate of the total import trade

CARQ = automobile import volume

CARDP = domestic automobile production output

CARG = ACRQ + CARDP = domestic automobile supply volume

By using 1983–94 data and regression technology, we obtain the following formulae

$$\text{Log (cardp)} = 0.99219 \times \text{Log (FAD/OPR)} + 0.34687 \times \text{Log (1 + RTF)} + 8.847$$
$$(R^2 = 0.96 \quad DW = 1.97)$$

$$\text{Log (carg)} = 0.00107 \times W \text{ (FAD/OPR)} - 0.66212 \times \text{Log (1 + RTF)} + 14.7205$$
$$(R^2 = 0.71 \quad DW = 2.38)$$

Here W (FAD/OPR) is the variation rate of FAD/OPR.

In what follows, the above formulae are employed to study the influence on other aspects, of variations in the tariff rate. Estimations using the data of the past few years yield

average nominal tariff rate from 35.9 per cent →0, then RTF from 2.7 per cent → 0

and automobile import volume, automobile production output and domestic automobile supply volume are as in Table 8.6.

The above suppositions lead to the conclusion that the actual executive tariff rates for automobile trade and total trade fluctuate in the same manner. This being so, we can work out the effect on producer surplus, consumer surplus, efficiency gain and the actual executive tariff revenue in the light of trade liberalisation.

Producer Surplus Variation $(\Delta PS1) = 0.5 \times (P1 - P0) \times (Q1 + Q2)$

Consumer Surplus Variation $(\Delta CS1) = -0.5 \times (P1 - P0) \times (D1 + D0)$

(Efficiency gain) EG $= -0.5 \times (P1-P0) \times (IM0 - IM1)$

The results of these estimations are detailed in Table 8.7. From these results, the nominal tariff rate for China's total trade was 35.9 per cent in 1995. Given that the actual tariff rate is 2.7 per cent, domestic automobile enterprises raked in earnings of 2.458 billion yuan from the price rises in automobiles and the expansion of domestic automobile production that resulted from automobile trade protection. Concurrently, the price rise resulted in a loss to consumers of 2.761 billion yuan, meaning that automobile trade protection leads to a net welfare loss of 303 million yuan. In the same way, the net losses of automobile trade protection in the light of other schemes can also be calculated.

Table 8.6   Effect of tariff changes on automobile imports and domestic supply under different schemes

Scheme	Nominal tariff (%)	Real applied tariff (%)	Auto import (units)	Rate of change (%)	Domestic made autos (units)	Rate of change (%)	Domestic supply (units)	Rate of change (%)
Standard value	35.9	2.7	157378	..	1452697	..	1610075	..
Scheme 1	23.0	1.725	172315	9.5	1447903	-0.33	1620218	0.63
Scheme 2	15.0	1.125	181339	15.2	1444998	-0.53	1626337	1.01
Scheme 3	5.0	0.375	192860	22.5	1441366	-0.78	1634226	1.50
Scheme 4	-	-	198613	26.2	1439477	-0.91	1638090	1.74

Note: The change in auto sale prices is calculated on the basis of after-tariff sale prices of autos compared with CIF prices.
Source: Author's calculations.

Table 8.7   Cost of automobile trade protection under different schemes

Scheme	Nominal tariff (%)	Real applied tariff (%)	Auto import (units)	Domestic output (units)	Change in auto sale price (%)	Change in producer surplus (RMB 100m)	Efficiency gain (RMB 100m)	Change in consumer surplus (RMB 100m)
Standard value	-	-	198613	1439477	..	..	..	..
Scheme 1	35.9	2.7	157378	1452697	17.5	24.58	-0.35	-27.61
Scheme 2	23.0	1.725	172315	1447903	11.4	15.99	-0.15	-18.04
Scheme 3	15.0	1.125	181339	1444998	8.1	11.35	-0.07	-12.84
Scheme 4	5.0	0.375	192860	1441366	2.4	3.36	-0.00	-3.81

Note: The change in auto sale prices is calculated on the basis of after-tariff sale prices of autos compared with CIF prices.
Source: Author's calculations.

ESTIMATION OF THE IMPACT OF TEXTILE TRADE PROTECTION ON THE CHINESE ECONOMY

MEASURING PRICE ELASTICITY OF DEMAND AND SUPPLY FOR TEXTILE PRODUCTS

The estimation focuses on the main products of the textile industry, divided into three groups

- textile fibres, including various kinds of yarn such as silk, wool and some chemical fibres
- textile fabrics, including chemical fibre cloth, wool fabrics and silk fabrics
- garments, including various kinds of garments, handkerchiefs, silk scarves and gloves.

By using time-series data from 1981 to 1993, we can generate econometric equations concerning domestic output and the total quantity of demand for the abovementioned three textile products.

- Home production equation for textile fibre

  LOG (GP01) = 0.34863LOG (GDPI) + 0.48088LOG ((1 + RTF) × PIMM)
  − 0.09819D84 + 4.3140)
  RSQ = 0.9655   DW = 1.3838

- Equation of total demand for textile fibre

  LOG (DP01 + IMP1/(PIMM × 3.14)) = 0.74151LOG (GDPI) −
  0.62299LOG (1 + RTF)   + 4.59209
  RSQ = 0.9774   DW = 1.9183

- Home production equation for textile fabric

  LOG (DP02) = 0.24483LOG (GDPI) + 0.4923LOG ((1+ RTF) × PIMM) + 6.28265
  RSQ = 0.9266   DW = 2.6183

- Total demand equation for textile fabric

  LOG (DP02 + IMPZ/(PIMM × 2.861)) =0.36245LOG (GDPI) −
  1.54526LOG (1 + RTF) + 8.06926
  RSQ = 0.9804   DW = 2.4216

- Home production equation for garment

  LOG (DP03) = 1.32197LOG + 1.04359LOG ((1 + RTF) × PIMM)
  − 2.45408D84 − 4.16089
  RSQ = 0.9832   DW = 1.652

- Total demand equation for garment

  LOG (DP03 + IMP3/(PIMM × 4.04)) = 0.9169LOG(SQTC) − 4.92151LOG
  (1 + RTF) − 2.20964D84 − 4.03162
  RSQ = 0.9884   DW = 1.9924

In the above equations,

GDPI = actual increase index of the fixed base for GDP

RTFI = applied and average tariff rates for the total amount of imported products

PIMM = CIF price index for the total amount of imported products

DPOI = domestic output for textiles under category i (i= 1,2,3)

IMPi = imported amount for textiles under category i (i= 1,2,3)

SQTC = total sales amount of garments on the domestic market.

From the previous part of the analysis, (1 + RTF) shows the effect of the tariff applied on the sale price of imported products. Likewise, a change in the prices of imported products cause the price of the same kind of domestic products to change, and therefore the price of the product on the home market is the linear function for (1 + RTF).

According to these equations, we know that domestic output for the three categories of textile products is affected by the interaction between (1 + RTF) and the elasticity of domestic production, or 0.48088, 0.49231 and 1.04359, respectively. That is, for every percentage point increase in (1 + RTF), the domestic output of the three categories of textiles will increase by 0.48088, 0.49231 and 1.04359 percentage points, respectively. The elasticity

Table 8.8   Impact of tariff rate change on selected textile products' imports, domestic production and total demand

	Actual value (1994, 100m yuan)	Scenario I (%)	Scenario II (%)
Fibre			
Domestic production	5441	-0.401259	-0.687873
Imports	755.7324	1.951597	3.345594
Total demand	6226.88	1.550337	2.657721
Fabric			
Domestic production	23754.12	-0.891894	-1.528962
Imports	2373.076	12.45764	21.35596
Total demand	48804.75	11.56574	19.82699
Garments			
Domestic production	6367.82	-1.02	-1.75
Imports	126.24	5.92	10.15
Total demand	6494.06	4.9	8.4

Source: Author's calculations.

Table 8.9   Effect of textile import protection

	RTF = 1.125%	RTF = 2.7%
Fibre		
Producer surplus	190.42	451.57
Consumer surplus	-568.01	-1346.94
Efficiency gain	23.54	62.86
Fabric		
Producer surplus	736.34	1781.50
Consumer surplus	-1528.64	-3661.10
Efficiency gain	74.09	178.78
Garments		
Producer surplus	280.12	674.90
Consumer surplus	-286.03	-688.82
Efficiency gain	5.91	13.92

Note: RTF is the average applied tariff rate of the total import trade.

Source: Author's calculations.

of demand in respect of changes in (1 + RTF) for the three categories of textiles is –0.62299, –1.54526 and –4.92151. In other words, for every percentage point increase in (1 + RTF), total demand for the three categories of textiles will drop by 0.62299, 1.54526 and 4.92151 percentage points, respectively.

ESTIMATE OF THE IMPACT OF TRADE PROTECTION ON TEXTILE PRODUCTS

Based on this analysis, the effect of changing the level of trade protection in the textile industry can be calculated. In view of the fact that the average nominal tariff rate governing total import trade is 35.9 per cent and the applied tariff rate is 2.7 per cent (RTF), if the average nominal tariff rate is cut from 35 per cent to 0, RTF will go from 2.7 per cent =>0.

We calculate the effects of changing the tax rate on the import volume, domestic output and total demand of the three categories of textiles. The results of the calculations are shown in Table 8.8. Consequently, we can calculate the effects of trade protection on textiles imports, producer surplus, consumer surplus and the change in efficiency benefit.

Change in producer surplus (Δ PSi) = $0.5 \times (Pi - Poi) \times (Qi + Qoi)$

Change in consumer surplus (ΔCSi) = $- 0.5 \times (Pi - Poi) \times (Di + Doi)$

Efficiency gain (EG) = $-0.5 \times (Pi\ 0150 - Poi) \times (Moi - Mi)$

In 1993, the nominal tariff rate for China's total import trade was 35.9 per cent, and the applied tariff rate—supposing the applied tariff rate for textile imports is similar to this—was 2.7 per cent (Table 8.9). In that case, the benefit gained by the three categories of textile enterprises that take advantage of the rise in price and the consequent expansion of production as a result of trade protection, is US$451.57, US$1781.50 and US$674.90 million, respectively. However, the welfare losses to Chinese consumers, from the rise in prices, are US$1346.94, US$3661.10, and US$688.82 million, respectively. Subsequently, the net loss resulting from trade protection for the three categories of textiles are US$895.37, US$1879.4,and US$13.92 million, respectively, representing a total loss of $2788.69 million.

CONCLUSION

The nominal reduction of tariffs will not have a significant influence on the Chinese economy in its early stages because of the large gap between nominal and applied tariff rates. This situation gives the Chinese government scope to push the process of tariff reduction and to ease non-tariff protection measures.

High tariff rates continue to be far more important than non-tariff measures in current automobile trade protection policies. In fact, the high rate of protection, allows the domestic automobile industry makes additional profits from other sectors of the domestic economy through pricing and distribution rents. Given that protection reduces competition, the original purpose of protecting the automobile industry has actually hindered the inflow of advanced technology and slowed the development of the domestic automobile industry. Furthermore, since the main automobile makers in China operate as joint ventures, the protection policy does not encourage foreign investors to use and improve technology.

Due to the low applied tariff rate and the dominance of the processing trade in the textile sector, there is little real protection in the domestic textile industry in China. It would be logical for China to select the textile sector as one of the early sectors for liberalisation.

In view of the larger price elasticity of demand in the textile industry, it is necessary to ensure, in the course of reducing the nominal tariff level, that the scope of applicable taxation be gradually expanded in case the applied trade protection decreases too rapidly and extensively. In other words, in the process of transforming the traditional industry to a modern industry, open competition is the key to improving efficiency, but it is necessary to maintain some protection in China for a period. The gradual reduction of trade protection is an inevitable trend, and domestic enterprises should make use of current opportunities to improve the competitiveness of their products to enable them to gain a favourable position in the future.

9

THE COMPETITIVENESS OF CHINA'S CHEMICAL SECTOR: ASSESSMENT AND IMPLICATIONS FOR EVSL POLICY

SUN XUEGONG

The negotiation of the APEC early voluntary sectoral liberalisation (EVSL) policy has gone through a critical stage. Among the nine pilot sectors nominated by the APEC summit in Vancouver, the chemical sector is of most concern to policymakers in China and its major trading partners. This is not only because the chemical sector is the largest sector in terms of trade volume and output, but also because the chemical sector has a significant impact on other industrial sectors, and on people's lives. Subsequently, the question of the inclusion of China's chemical sector in early sectoral liberalisation is an important one for China, and will have long-term and strategic effects on the Chinese economy. This chapter examines the potential impact of the participation of China's chemical sector in APEC EVSL, and its policy implications. Because the international competitiveness of a sector is important in determining whether that sector will benefit from EVSL, a careful assessment of the international competitiveness of China's chemical sector is undertaken.

THE INTERNATIONAL COMPETITIVENESS ASSESSMENT SCHEME

There is no universally accepted definition for the international competitiveness of an industrial sector. In what follows, the international competitiveness of China's chemical sector is assessed in light of five aspects

- market performance
- product identification—price and quality
- productivity
- development capability—equipment and research and development (R&D)
- industry environment—degree of concentration, upstream and downstream relations, market volume.

The assessment scheme measures the competitiveness of China's chemical sector from different perspectives and at different levels. Some aspects reflect current competitiveness—for example, market performance—while others demonstrate long-term and potential competitive capablity. Some aspects can be observed directly in the market—such as price and market share—while others are more fundamental factors—for example, productivity.

COMPETITIVENESS ASSESSMENT OF CHINA'S CHEMICAL SECTOR

THE MARKET PERFORMANCE OF CHINA'S CHEMICAL SECTOR

The competitiveness of an industry is embodied in its ability to satisfy both the quantitative and qualitative needs of the market. In light of this, the trade competitiveness index (TC), revealed comparative advantage (RCA), and market share can be used to measure the current international competitiveness of an industry or product.

Based on the TC criteria, the chemical sector, in general, is still weak in terms of competitiveness. The TC for China's chemical sector has been negative since 1992. The trade deficit for the chemical sector also remains high, at US$6.5 billion. The sector clearly still lacks the ability to meet demand in the domestic market.

In 3-digit SITC, there are 33 categories of chemical products. Among them, there are only 14 categories in which TCs are positive. The categories of products in which China has a comparative advantage are products that are little traded across the border, accounting for only 32.2 per cent of total trade volume. In the harmonised tariff system (HS), the same picture is revealed. Among 13 chapters in 2 sections, the TCs are positive for only 5 chapters, with a meagre 30 per cent of trade volume.

RCA is another type of index widely used to measure the competitiveness of an industry. It is generally accepted that when the RCA of an industry or product is equal to or larger than 2.5, the industry or product is considered to be a strong comparative advantage industry; when the RCA is between 1.25 and 2.5, the industry or product is fairly competitive; when the RCA lies between 0.8 and 1.25, the industry or product is moderately competitive; and, when the RCA is lower than 0.8, the industry or product has a comparative disadvantage. The RCA index gives a grim picture of China's chemical sector. Among 33 products items in the SITC, only 5 have RCA indexes above 2.5, accounting for 15 per cent of the total. Nine items' RCA indicate fairly strong or moderate competitiveness. The lion's share of product items—58 per cent of the total—still fall in the comparative disadvantage group. Most of the products in China's chemical sector are under-represented in total exports, compared with China's competitors.

Table 9.1   Trade competitiveness index of the chemical sector (HS)

	1997 (US$10,000)			1992 (US$10,000)			1992–97 change
	export	import	IC	export	import	IC	
Total chemical Section VI	1519013	2175891	-0.1778	595187	1248445	-0.3543	0.1766
Chemical or allied	939162	1030228	-0.0462	412289	717572	-0.2702	0.2240
28 inorganic	238660	77452	0.5100	104953	37759	0.4708	0.0391
29 organic	339636	306037	0.0520	140345	187557	-0.14398	0.1960
30 pharmaceutical	63962	24352	0.4485	46011	31872	0.1815	0.2670
31 fertiliser	21192	299491	-0.8678	2966	300370	-0.9804	0.1126
32 tan, dye, pigments, etc.	92215	104705	-0.0634	35447	49978	-0.1701	0.1067
33 essential oil, etc.	26644	7258	0.5718	18074	3299	0.6914	-0.1195
34 soap, agents, etc.	22087	25769	-0.0769	10229	16529	-0.2354	0.1585
35 albuminoidal, etc.	7244	33499	-0.6444	2325	13411	-0.7045	0.0601
36 explosive, pyrotech	23799	146	0.9878	15518	374	0.9529	0.0349
37 photographic	13282	17145	-0.1269	3763	9116	-0.4156	0.2887
38 miscellaneous Section VII	90442	134375	-0.1954	32656	67307	-0.3466	0.1512
Plastic and rubber	579851	1145663	-0.3279	182898	530873	-0.4875	0.1596
39 plastics & article	484389	1019882	-0.3560	151642	475405	-0.5163	0.1603
40 rubber & article	95461	125781	-0.1370	31257	55469	-0.2792	0.1421

Source: Customs Statistics, 1997, 1992; author's calculations.

International market share—gauged here by the percentage of one country's exports in total world exports—is another important indicator of industrial competitiveness. In 1996, the products of China's chemical sector constituted 2.1 per cent of the world market, much lower than the share of China's exports to the world total (3 per cent). Among 33 items, only 1 item's share exceeded 10 per cent; 5 items lay in the range of 5 to 10 per cent; 15 items were between 1 and 5 per cent; and 13 items were lower than 1 per cent.

PRODUCT IDENTIFICATION

The market performance of a product is jointly determined by its cost, price, quality and—more fundamentally—the productivity of its producer. Market competition, in most cases, takes the form of price competition among homogenous products. However, another form of competition—based on differential in function, quality and grade of product—is of increasing importance. These factors are examined in turn.

Table 9.2   Domestic to international price ratio for selected products

Product	Price ratio	Product	Price ratio
methylbenzene	1.15	ethylene polymer	1.24
vinylbenzene	1.42	polystyrene	1.01
dimethylbenzene	1.04	PVC	1.53
methyl alcohol	2.01	propylene	1.08
glycol	1.53	ABS	1.22

Notes: 1. The price of international market is CIF in Far East Market. 2. The exchange rate for the renminbi (RMB) is US$1=RMB8.29.

Source: Calculation based on data from *Price Weekly* of Jihua Corporate.

Price. Price is a crucial factor in determining the competitiveness, and hence the market performance, of a product. However, the prices of chemical products in China are generally higher than those in the international market (Table 9.2). In some cases, the price of products is as much as twice the international market price. High prices have seriously weakened the competitiveness of China's chemical products.

Quality, variety and grade. Product differentials in terms of quality, variety and grade characterises high-level competition, such as that prevalent in the international market. Unfortunately, the quality, variety and grade differential between China and other countries is even greater than that in respect of price. Usually, the export to import price ratio is used to measure the quality differential between export and import goods. There is no question that the quality of most of China's exports is inferior to its imports (Table 9.3).

Table 9.3   Export to import price ratio for selected products, 1995

Product	Price ratio	Product	Price ratio
organic chemical	3.62	soap, agent, etc.	0.69
pharmaceutical	0.40	albuminoidal	1.00
fertiliser	0.50	explosive, pyrotechnic	0.16
tan, dye, pigment, etc.	0.86	photographic	0.80
essential oil, etc.	0.59	miscellaneous	0.44

Source: Jin Pei *et al.*, 1997. *The International Competitiveness of China's Industry*, Economic Management Press, Beijing.

Limited variety and low grade of products are other important issues troubling China's chemical sector. Plastic is one example. In the United States, there are roughly 300–500 varieties of specifications in ethylene polymer and propylene polymer; in Japan, there are 793 varieties of high density ethylene polymer, 2450 in low density ethylene polymer, and 9169 in propylene polymer. But in China, China Petrochemical Corporation (Sinopec)—the main Chinese producer of plastic—only has 187 varieties and some firms produce only one or two varieties. There are more than 100,000 varieties of specialty chemicals, abroad; but China has only 18,000. In the field of electronic chemicals, foreign producers produce more than 17,000 products; the same trade in China only produces 360 varieties. For consumption chemicals, Chinese enterprises have lost large market share because of the small number of varieties and low grade of products. The percentage of specialty chemical to total chemical products also demonstrates the general level of product grade. This figure is only 35 per cent in China—far below 60 per cent, the average level for developed countries.

PRODUCTIVITY

Labour productivity. Labour productivity is an important indicator of the efficiency of production factor utilisation. Strong competitiveness is necessarily linked with high factor efficiency. Labour productivity for the chemical sector as a whole in 1992 was 478,300 dollars per person per year in Japan, 274,000 dollars per person per year in the United States and 263,000 dollars per person per year in France. In China, the figure was only 619,000 yuan per person per year in 1995, less than one-thirtieth of that in developed countries.

Sinopec is among those enterprises with the highest labour productivity in China. However, when compared with its foreign competitors, Sinopec lags far behind. In 1996, Sinopec processed 118 million tonnes of crude oil, produced 2.45 million tonnes of ethylene; in the same year, Sinopec's workforce reached 665,000. Labour productivity was 177.4 tonnes of crude oil per person per year, or 3.7 tonnes of ethylene per person per year. In 1995, the labour productivity of Exxon was 2250 tonnes of crude oil per person per year, or 41.3 tonnes of ethylene per person per year, 12.7 times and 11.2 times that of Sinopec, respectively. If labour productivity is measured by turnover per person, we find that while the workforce at Sinopec was the same size as that of the world's 7 largest companies, its turnover was less than one-third that of the world's tenth-largest company.

Installation productivity. Modern chemical industry depends heavily on large and complicated installations, so capacity and utilisation have become important factors determining enterprise efficiency. China's chemical sector, however, suffers from low capacity of installation and high consumption of raw materials due to low investment intensity and overlapping construction. In 1996, the average capacity of ethylene splitting installations in China was 226 kilotonnes per year, while the world average was 354 kilotonnes per year—1.6 times that of China—and the US average was 637 kilotonnes per year—2.8 times that of China. Since the beginning of the 1990s, 7 ethylene installations with capacity of less than 150 kilotonnes per year—with notable diseconomies of scale—have been built. This inherent inefficiency brought some of these projects to bankruptcy as soon as they began their operations.

The installation utilisation rate also plays a role in the determination of costs; this is especially true for huge production installations with heavy investment. The losses due to even short-term overhaul are considerable. Compared with foreign installations, China's installations need more frequent overhauls due to a low level of maintenance. The frequent overhauls not only lower the productivity of installations, but also increase the cost of examination and repairs.

Overall cost. The high cost of China's chemical sector products can be attributed to low installation, low labour productivity and poor management skills. High consumption of energy and materials is also a serious problem. For instance, although China's chemical sector has made substantial progress in energy savings—evidenced by the fact that the energy consumption for 10,000 yuan worth of output in 1995 was only half of that in 1990 (a reduction of 13.75 tonnes to 5.26 tonnes of standard coal), there is still a big gap between Chinese and foreign companies. China's energy consumption per unit of output is still as much as three times that of the United States, and nine times that of Japan. In 1996, Sinopec's energy consumption for producing one tonne of ethylene was 8.49 million kilocalories, much higher than the average level for a foreign company, 6–7 kilocalories. In high density ethylene polymer production, Sinopec has been left even further behind; its energy consumption per unit of output is almost twice that of foreign companies.

Cheap labour is the greatest advantage of China's industry. Labour cost in chemical production in China is lower than that of its foreign competitors. However, this only holds true for individuals, and not for the workforce as a whole. There are several reasons for this. First, the social burden of Chinese enterprises is very heavy. Enterprises are responsible for providing residency, medical insurance, pensions and even kindergarten education to their employees' families. Second, labour productivity is much lower than in a developed country, so the labour cost per unit of output is not as low as the low wages seem to indicate. Third, employees who are not engaged in production—such as auxiliary staff, logistics and administrative personnel—account for a much larger share of the workforce than their foreign competitors. All these factors conspire to create no advantage in labour cost in China's chemical industry. It is estimated that the ratio of labour cost to total cost in China's chemical industry just matches the foreign ratio.

Table 9.4   Equipment status of large and medium-size chemical enterprises, 1995

Equipment	Total	International advances		Domestic advances		Domestic average	
		Quantity	Proportion	Quantity	Proportion	Quantity	Proportion
Ethylene	20	6	30.00	6	30.00	4	20.00
glycol	10	2	20.00	8	80.00	0	0.00
polyethylene	20	2	10.00	10	50.00	4	20.00
polypropylene	76	4	5.26	4	5.26	22	28.95
polyester	12	0	0.00	6	50.00	4	33.33
vinylcyanide	14	2	14.29	2	14.29	4	28.57
caprolactam	4	2	50.00	0	0.00	2	50.00
carbamide	156	30	19.23	31	19.87	90	57.69
phosphate fertiliser	244	16	6.56	34	13.93	190	77.87
sulphuric acid	235	2	0.85	56	23.83	109	46.38
pure alkali	51	1	1.96	8	15.69	27	52.94
PVC	77	9	11.69	25	32.47	37	48.05
dye	495	4	0.81	47	9.49	437	88.28

Source: *China, Third National Industrial Census*, Beijing.

DEVELOPMENT CAPABILITY

Equipment levels, R&D input and the labour force of scientists and technicians are keys to fostering and sustaining the competitiveness of an enterprise. These factors indicate the potential of an enterprise to grow, and reflect its capability to attract investment and financing.

Equipment levels. Equipment is the physical base from which an enterprise can compete. In general, the quality, grade and cost of products are closely related to the equipment employed by an enterprise. The uncompetitiveness of China's chemical sector can partly be explained by the poor equipment in Chinese enterprises. Data from the *Third National Industrial Census* show that for large and medium enterprises in most chemical industries, internationally advanced equipment accounts for less than 20 per cent of the total (Table 9.4). The situation is worse in large enterprises. Furthermore, the most important and large equipment used in China's chemical sector is imported. This situation, coupled with weak innovation capacity and slow assimilation of imported technology, make it impossible for China to keep pace with world progress in equipment improvement.

R&D input. R&D is believed to be an essential element for an enterprise to establish and maintain its competitiveness in the market. The level of R&D is

Table 9.5 R&D activities by large and medium enterprises, 1995

Industry	R&D expend. (RMB 10,000)	Scientists & technicians	Turnover of new product (RMB 10,000)	Turnover (RMB (10 million)	R&D input to turnover (%)	Turnover of new product to total turnover (%)
raw materials & product	82848.6	78586	1846271	2200	0.3792	8.45052
pharmaceutical	48050.3	25059	615318	573	0.8385	10.7385
rubber	23566.4	12248	355891	381.4	0.6178	9.33116
plastic	8513.3	8372	328109	300.5	0.2833	10.9187

Source: Calculations based on data from *China, Third National Indusrial Census*, Beijing.

indicative of both an enterprise's present and future potential. Again, there is a big gap between Chinese companies and world chemical giants. On average, large chemical enterprises in China spent less than 1 per cent of their turnover on R&D activities, much less than 5 per cent, the rule of thumb for world chemical giants (Table 9.5). China's competitiveness can improve very little if this situation does not change.

Quantity and proportion of scientists and technicians. Scientists and technicians are the source of innovations. The quantity of scientists and technicians and their proportion of total staff are important indicators of innovative ability. Data shows that neither the quantity nor proportion of scientists and technicians in China's firms are less than in developed enterprises; some firms are even world leaders in this area. This is an important potential resource for China's chemical sector to tap.

ENTERPRISE ENVIRONMENT

INDUSTRIAL CONCENTRATION

Industrial concentration reflects the market structure, distribution of an industry, economies of scale and intensity of competition. Industrial concentration is thought to be a very important contributor to competitiveness in those industries where economies of scale or scope are notable. The chemical industry—especially the petrochemical industry—is one such industry. We use C4 and C8 (shares of the top 4 or 8 firms) to measure the concentration level of China's chemical sector (Table 9.6). The trends in the change in concentration ratios for different sub-sectors have differed. However, it is obvious that the concentration ratio of

Table 9.6   Change in industrial concentration in China's chemical sector

Industry	1990		1994	
	C4	C8	C4	C8
Raw materials & product	12.1	15.6	8.5	11.9
Daily use chemical	n.a.	n.a.	10.6	15.8
Pharmaceutical	6.5	9.7	7.7	13.2
Plastic	4.5	6.1	1.9	3.2

Source: Calculations based on data from China industry 100, *China Statistic Yearbook 1995.*

the chemical sector has not increased. This conclusion is also supported by the decreasing number and declining position of chemical firms in the 500 biggest companies listed. In 1991, there were 40 chemical companies in the top 500; by 1994, the number had decreased to 35, and no chemical company appeared in the top 10. The ranking of chemical companies fell. In 1991, half the chemical companies in the top 500 ranked in the 300–500 range. In 1994, 63 per cent lay in this range.

These trends are the result of market reform. The removal of entry barriers has led to an influx of small and medium-sized enterprises into a highly concentrated industry. Industrial diffusion, on the one hand, intensifies domestic competition and in turn encourages firms to improve their competitiveness. However, it tends to reduce the efficiency of resource utilisation and is a difficult process in an open economy because the industry faces fierce competition from foreign chemical giants.

The petrochemical industry is characterised more notably by economies of scale than other chemical sub-sectors. We take examples such as ethylene, ethylene polymer, propylene, and styrene polymer to examine the concentration of China's petrochemical industry and cite the Japanese case as a reference (Table 9.7).

Table 9.7   Degree of concentration of selected products in China and Japan

Product	China		Japan	
	C4	C8	C4	C8
ethylene	44.1	68.9	55.2	82.9
polypropylene	42.3	65.3	50.9	78.1
polystyrene	52.4	72.5	29.9	45.2
ABS	100	100	64.1	93.5

Source: Information Institute of Jilin Petrochemical Co.

Table 9.8   Current and planned capacity of ethylene (kilotonnes)

1987	1990	1992	1995	1996	1997	Planned capacity
172.2	195.0	219.5	297.	359.0	412.0	823.5

Source: China petrochemical economic information 1998.1.

Compared with other developed countries, the extent of concentration in Japan is small. China's concentration level is even lower. This situation has already undermined the competitiveness of China's petrochemical industry.

Relation to upstream and downstream industry. The most important upstream inputs of the chemical sector in China—such as oil, coal, electricity and grain—are natural monopolies. As is well known, when one industry is closely linked with another upstream or downstream industry, the market risk and transaction costs are higher than for an industry where this does not hold. The reason is that the monopoly buyer or seller may make use of its strong bargaining power to extract supernormal profit. To counteract this disadvantage, big chemical companies in developed countries are often vertically integrated so as to expand the boundary of the firm, reducing the market risk and transaction costs, and improving their competitiveness in the market.

In China, the chemical industrial chain is segmented. There are five big corporations. China Oil and Gas Corporation is responsible for extracting oil and gas, and China Xinxing Oil and Gas Corporation for prospecting resources. China Marine Oil Corporation is responsible for exploiting offshore oil fields. Sinopec was created to process the oil and gas and produce important chemical products, such as ethylene, propylene, synthetic resin, synthetic rubber, synthetic fibre and synthetic fertiliser. China National Chemical Import and Export Corporation almost has a monopoly on the international trade of chemicals. This configuration increases the risks and transaction costs of all these corporations, and weakens the competitiveness of China's chemical sector as a whole. If China is to open its market further, this situation must be changed.

Domestic demand. The scale and trend of demand also play a role in fostering the competitiveness of a firm. Situated in a big and rapidly growing market, a firm has more opportunities to mature as a big and strong producer. In this regard, China's chemical sector enjoys an exceptional advantage. The Chinese chemical market, fueled by China's rapid economic growth, will be expanding for a long period of time and is regarded as the world's largest potential markets. The Asia Pacific region has a strong concentration of both producers and consumers of chemical products. A booming market is emerging within reach of China's chemical sector. A good example is ethylene, one of the most important chemical products. It is estimated that the world's ethylene production capacity will be in surplus in 2000 while in Asia it will be in shortage. In China, even if all ethylene projects now under plan or construction can finish as scheduled, there is still a 20 per cent gap between supply and demand (Table 9.8). China's chemical sector stands to gain from this.

THE COMPETITIVENESS OF CHINA'S CHEMICAL SECTOR

The immediate competitiveness of China's chemical sector—its market performance—is very poor, as indicated by various international trade competition indexes. This situation is to be expected given the inferior quality, high cost and price of China's chemical products. More fundamentally, weak competitiveness results from low productivity and low efficiency of resource utilisation, common phenomena among China's chemical sector. Although there are some favourable factors—such as a big and fast-growing market and a large number of scientists and technicians—substantial improvement in the competitiveness of China's chemical sector cannot be expected in the near future due to some unfavourable factors such as obsolete equipment, meagre R&D input, weak industrial organisation and lack of vertical integration between upstream and downstream industries. The low base from which the chemical sector began has, to date, prevented this sector from doing better. Subsequently, the competitiveness of China's chemical sector remains weaker than its foreign competitors. It has not yet matured sufficiently to participate in APEC's early sectoral liberalisation.

THE IMPACT OF APEC EVSL ON CHINA'S CHEMICAL INDUSTRY

The chemical sector in China is one of the most important sectors, evidenced by the fact that it is the second largest manufacturing sector. It accounts for over 10 per cent of total industry in terms of number of firms, output value, pre-tax profit, original value of fixed assets, and employees.

The competitiveness of China's chemical industry is still weak in comparison with its foreign competitors. China's participation in early chemical sectoral liberalisation will inevitably cause shocks to the domestic industry. The possible negative consequence include over-capacity of industry, deteriorating operation of enterprises, and increasing the number of unemployed. However, trade and investment liberalisation would increase the effective supply in the domestic market, help to introduce advanced equipment and technology, and upgrade the quality and grade of products as well as intensify domestic competition. All these will benefit the long-term development not only of the chemical sector, but the national economy as a whole.

IMPORT SHOCKS

The immediate consequence of trade liberalisation would be to expose domestic enterprises to competition from foreign competitors in the domestic market. Given domestic enterprises' weak competitiveness, their market share will tend to decline. Since the beginning of the 1990s, China has reduced its tariff level by a significant margin. This has reduced the domestic market share of China's chemical sector by 4.6 percentage points, from 86.5 per cent in 1992 to 81.9 per cent in 1995.

Within the chemical sector, the impact on different sub-sectors varies. Here we use residual analysis to rank the impacts. The first assumption is that the production capacity utilisation level is determined by the interaction of supply and demand. The second assumption is that any deviation from average capacity utilisation is a result of import pressure on the domestic industry. The extent of the deviation reflects impact because all industries face similar non-import factors. We regress sales to production ratio (Y) on production to demand ratio (X). For each production to demand ratio, we calculate an expected sale to production ratio, then the residual between the actual and expected value. The smaller the residual for an industry, the more it suffers from import pressure (Table 9.9).

We find that the most affected industries are daily-use chemicals, plastics, special material chemicals, synthetic material and fertiliser. All these industries are mature industries both at home and abroad, for which the products are

Table 9.9   Estimation of the effect of imports on China's chemical sector

Industry	Production to sale	Production to demand	Residual
daily use chemical	89.77	98.00	-3.3259
plastic	92.08	99.58	-0.9958
specialty chemical	92.42	96.83	-0.6905
synthetic material	93.72	53.86	0.0080
fertiliser	93.35	81.98	0.0303
rubber	93.36	98.44	0.2730
pharmaceutical	93.56	97.18	0.4501
organic chemical	94.00	98.42	0.9133
pesticide	94.23	98.19	1.1366
basic material	95.29	98.57	2.2009

Source: Calculations based on data from *The Development Guide of China's Chemical Sector in 1997.*

highly substitutable. In this case, the advantage of foreign companies is maximised and domestic enterprises are driven into a corner. Other industries—such as the rubber industry, the pharmaceutical industry, organic chemicals, the pesticide industry and basic chemical material industry—are characterised by differentiated products, different target markets and stratified demand. In this case, increased imports do not necessarily increase direct competition from foreign countries. Hence, it can be seen that uncompetitive industries are not necessarily subject to import shocks.

We should not only take the present state of the market into account, but its dynamics as well. Ethylene is one example. By 2000, the shortage of ethylene in China will reach 1500–2000 kilotonnes—equivalent to the output of five production installations. Consequently, an open market will not impact on domestic producers at all in the short term. However, ethylene production capacity in Asia is rapidly growing. If the market is opened now without good preparation, there will be fierce competition in the market in the near future.

INVESTMENT LIBERALISATION SHOCKS

Investment liberalisation means that two-way capital flows—both inflow and outflow—are free. However, in China, overseas investments made by domestic enterprises are very few. Here, we will only discuss the effect of foreign capital inflow.

In terms of the extent of foreign capital participation, the chemical sector is among the average of industries. The biggest sub-sector—the chemical raw material and chemical product industry—receives less foreign capital than other sub-sectors—such as the pharmaceutical, rubber and plastic industries (Table 9.10).

Free investment inflow is, in general, even harder to manage for the recipient country than free trade is, and this is especially true where the host is a developing

Table 9.10   Involvement of FDI in China's chemical sector

Industry	Invested assets (RMB bil,)	Proportion of FDI (%)
Raw material and product	130.641	12.28
Pharmaceutical	33.346	14.55
Rubber	18.346	25.96
Plastic	45.946	30.08
Total industry	2155.288	14.37

Source: Calculations based on data from *China, Third National Industrial Census.*

country. The first reason is that there is often a big gap in the scale, financing ability, technology, management level, market networking, product quality and grade, and brand name between China and foreign companies. Second, the multinational can mobilise resources globally to achieve its own global strategy. When its strategy conflicts with the interests of the host country, the host may suffer rather than benefit from capital inflow. Third, there are some institutional arrangements for developing countries in the World Trade Organisation (WTO) and other trade agreements to cushion the shock brought on by trade liberalisation, such as infant industries, exceptional articles and anti-dumping. However, how to manage investment inflows is still a hotly debated issue.

One important manifestation of foreign capital shocks is represented in the domestic market share of foreign funded enterprises (FFE). FFEs in the chemical sector already occupy considerable domestic market share (Table 9.11). Except in the chemical raw material and chemical product industries, the FFE market share for other sub-sectors is higher than the average for all industries. The market share of FFEs in the plastic industry is as much as 10 percentage points higher than the average. Among 40 industries, the plastic industry ranks 6th, the rubber industry 13th, and the pharmaceutical industry 16th, by FFE market share. In more detailed classifications, FFE market shares are even higher. For instance, the FFE market shares in synthetic rubber, daily use chemicals, bubble plastic and cosmetic products fall in the range of 30–40 per cent, soap and synthetic detergent above 40 per cent, and information chemicals above 50 per cent.

Foreign capital inflow also affects competition in the Chinese market. It intensifies domestic competition. However, it can also be destabilising. First, the introduction of foreign capital may bring about a monopoly. China does not have an established anti-trust legal system and is inexperienced in its implementation. Consequently, present institutional arrangements do not effectively prevent monopoly activities. Second, some FFEs infringe on publicly-

Table 9.11 Domestic market share of FFEs in China's chemical sector

Industry	Market share (%)	Rank within industry
Raw materials and product	11.86	22
Pharmaceutical	18.63	16
Rubber	21.19	13
Plastic	26.56	6
Total industry	16.93	n.a.

Source: Wang Zhengzhong, 'On Issues of Present FFE in China', *Reform*, 1998.2.

accepted commercial morals and act uncompetitively towards their Chinese competitors, through big discounts, and worker abuse, for example.

THE SHOCK TO THE NATIONAL ECONOMY

The impacts of early chemical sectoral liberalisation are not confined solely to the chemical sector. Some negative effects on non-chemical sectors may be observed if the domestic chemical market is opened up too quickly. First, if foreign companies dominate the domestic chemical market, upstream industries such as crude oil will be placed in a very weak position. Because the price of domestic crude oil has been kept higher than the international price since 1997, domestic crude oil producers depend heavily on the domestic petrochemical industry. The monopoly of foreign chemical multinationals will further undermine the bargaining position of crude oil producers. Second, chemical products are important intermediate inputs for agriculture, light industry, textiles, building materials, machine building, electronics, automobiles, the military and hi-tech industries. The dominance of foreign chemical companies potentially damages the interests of these downstream industries. Third, the chemical sector accommodates more than 10 million workers in China. Employment concerns are a very important factor in deciding the timing and pace of early chemical sector liberalisation.

POSITIVE EFFECTS OF TRADE AND INVESTMENT LIBERALISATION

Opening the chemical market to a moderate extent will likely promote the development of related industries and cause minimal harm to the domestic industry. There are several reasons for this.

The domestic chemical sector cannot satisfy domestic demand for chemical products. The importance of the chemical sector means that its development influences the development of downstream industries and the national economy as a whole. According to the 1990 China input-output table, the responsive index of the chemical sector is highest in all sectors, reaching 2.7989. This indicates that the development of non-chemical sectors depends heavily on chemical products. If the supply of chemical products does not meet domestic demand, the development of non-chemical sectors is compromised. The data from Table 9.9 indicates that production of chemical products in high demand is still insufficient. Not surprisingly, the largest trade deficit occurred in those product categories. Therefore, in this case, further opening of the market through lowering tariffs will not introduce direct competition to the domestic industry; it will help reduce the import costs of downstream industries of the chemical sector and in turn strengthen the competitiveness of these industries. There is still much room for domestic enterprises to grow in China's huge market, even with an increasingly open environment. It is estimated that domestic demand growth in industries where there are shortages will be sustained for a considerable length of time and that domestic supply will not keep pace with demand due to deficient investment. Opening the market and foreign capital inflow will fill this gap and ease the constraints imposed by these industries on China's economic development.

Even in those industries where production basically satisfies demand, opening the market will not necessarily damage domestic industries. One reason is increasing market stratification, meaning that consumers can no longer be seen as homogeneous. This makes it possible for both domestic and foreign producers to find a niche and target clients in the market. Trade in differentiated products is becoming increasingly prevalent, thus leaving room for domestic enterprises to develop.

The endurance of domestic industries has been strengthened following big tariff reductions. Since 1994, China's tariffs have fallen dramatically. The arithmetic average tariff for chemical products is only 11 per cent—much lower than the overall arithmetic average tariff of 17 per cent. Contrary to expectations, domestic enterprises did not experience strong competition from imports. One possible explanation is that applied tariffs were already very low, so that nominal tariff cuts had little influence on tariffs actually applied. Indeed, in 1997, tariffs on many chemical products were levied at only one-half or one-third of the base tariff. Preferential tariffs for some products are even one-tenth of base tariffs. In addition, smuggling is a serious problem in China. Illegally trafficked goods account for considerable market share and are totally tax free. Consequently, applied tariffs in China are much lower than nominal tariffs. This has two implications. One is that China's chemical sector is not a heavily protected sector as nominal tariffs seem to indicate. The other is that it is still a great challenge to lower the nominal tariff level without sacrificing protection.

It is a good time to attract foreign direct investment (FDI) in the chemical sector. The industries of chemical raw materials and chemical products—the main body of China's chemical sector—receive little FDI, compared with the national industrial average. There is much potential to expand FDI. The international chemical sector is preparing for a new round of restructuring. The chemical multinationals in developed countries are beginning to shift their business to specialty chemicals and the life science industry while transferring their bulky chemicals— mostly raw or primary chemical products characterised by large-scale and huge installation—to developing countries. For instance, the petrochemical industry is growing strongly in the Asia Pacific region. It is estimated that ethylene production in Asia will double within 15 years. This represents a good opportunity for China to develop its chemical sector. The moderate degree participation of APEC's early sector liberalisation will help China attract more FDI. Given that China's neighbouring countries and regions are competing strongly in this field, China must make every effort to grasp this historic opportunity.

POLICY AND MEASURES FOR CHINA'S PARTICIPATION IN APEC EVSL

Given that the benefits and losses arising from EVSL are unevenly distributed among APEC members, the current arrangements of EVSL—in terms of both timing and product coverage—seem unacceptable for those members with weak international competitiveness. Some mechanism should be put in place to balance the gains and losses from EVSL among APEC member economies. However, such a mechanism is not forseeable in the short term. A practical way to deal with the issue is to leave timing and product coverage determination to member economies, so they can balance the benefits and losses internally.

A phased, selective liberalisation process is the best way for China to reap the benefits (and minimise the costs) of liberalisation. China should keep its options open to participate fully in early sectoral liberalisation when the timing is appropriate. The pace of domestic restructuring should be quickened to promote the competitiveness of the chemical sector, China's key to participating in early sectoral liberalisation.

THE MEASURES FOR TRADE LIBERALISATION

Although at present it cannot endure the shock from full participation in APEC EVSL, China should continue the trade liberalisation process according to its Individual Action Plan. Trade policy measures—both tariff and non-tariff—should achieve a dual purpose: satisfying domestic demand and improving the competitiveness of China's chemical sector.

Tariff concessions. To fulfil China's commitment to APEC trade liberalisation and WTO accession, China should further lower its chemical products tariff, especially the nominal tariff, which is still among the highest in the world. Further tariff concessions also pave the way for China to join APEC EVSL in the future. Tariff cuts should be based on the following principles

- lowering the general chemical products tariff. The effect of earlier tariff cuts indicates that China's chemical sector can bear further tariff cuts. As the value-added tax for imported goods is still high, it can counteract the negative effects of tariff cuts. To illustrate China's determination to catch up with APEC early sector liberalisation, it should declare another round of tariff reductions on chemical products when APEC formally launches its EVSL process. Making large cuts to the base tariff—which is much higher than the applied tariff—would be advisable.

- timing the adjustment of the tariff level to match changes in products' competitiveness. This will create a favourable environment for products well-placed to enter the international market.
- adopting a differentiated tariff regime based on the relative importance of products. It is not necessary for China to provide protection for all internationally uncompetitive chemical products. For those products with strategic significance in China's national economy, the exceptional articles in the WTO agreement for imposing protective tariffs can be cited. Protection should be neither too long nor too excessive. For those products less important to the national economy, demand can be met through international labour division. The tariff on these products can be used as bargaining counters in tariff negotiations.

Adjustment in tariff structure. China applies *ad valorem* tariffs to almost all imported goods. To adapt to an open economy, a more flexible tariff structure should be established. Such a structure should

- apply specific tariffs or compound tariffs to selected products
- apply a sliding-scale duty to those products whose price fluctuations are very large in the international market, so as to achieve a relatively stable price in the domestic market
- apply quotas tariff to selected products, within quotas, a low tariff is applied
- establish emergency tariff regulations, including temporary protective tariffs.

Non-tariff measures. China has committed to reduce its non-tariff trade barriers. Dismantling non-tariff barriers was an important part of its earlier tariff cuts package. China will continue its efforts. Gradually, China will abolish quota controls, import licensing and other trade control measures. In line with international practice, China should establish its own competition policy to promote fair competition in the domestic market and import standards to protect consumer rights. It should also

- refine China's anti-dumping laws to promote fair competition in the domestic market
- tighten environmental and sanitary standards on imported goods. Chemical products are environmentally and health sensitive. The production, transportation, storage and consumption of chemical products can have disastrous environmental and health consequences. As a precautionary measure, China should impose stricter standards in this regard.

INVESTMENT LIBERALISATION

China should be more prudent about investment liberalisation. It should proceed in a planned and phased manner. China needs to promote investment liberalisation in the following ways

- continue to promote investment facilitation. Open and transparent laws and regulations regarding foreign investment are the first step to promoting investment facilitation. China has advanced a lot in this regard. A notable event is the promulgation and revision of the 'Provisions on Guiding Foreign Investment Direction Catalogue For The Guidance Of Foreign Investment Industries by the State Development Planning Commission'.
- implement investment liberalisation in a phased and product-specific manner. China has committed itself to achieving investment liberalisation by 2020. If the chemical sector eventually participates in the APEC EVSL process, the deadline for chemical products will be brought forward. Hence, it is important to set out some kind of timeline for liberalisation. Similarly, the products to undergo liberalisation must be specified.
- coordinate investment and trade liberalisation. Priority products in trade liberalisation should also be priority products in investment liberalisation.
- adjust foreign investment policy in a timely manner. The policy stance on FDI is still that it needs to be stepped up. But it must be kept in mind that a level playing field for competition is the ultimate policy target. Special attention to foreign direct investment (FDI) should only be limited to products that are crucial to promoting economic development and improving the competitiveness of China's enterprises.

DOMESTIC RESTRUCTURING POLICY

The key to improving the competitiveness of China's chemical sector is restructuring the sector domestically. Adjustments need to be made in ownership, industrial organisation and product structure. There is also a role for government to create a favourable environment for the development of chemical enterprises. The following measures should be adopted

- speed up state-owned enterprise (SOE) reform. SOEs are the main body of China's chemical sector. Without vigorous and active SOEs, China cannot establish a competitive advantage in the international market. The targets of SOE reform are to establish a modern enterprise system characterised by clearly defined property rights, the demarcation of enterprises and administration, and own responsibility for profits, losses and scientific management. Property rights reform should be prioritised so as to improve the SOE incentive mechanism.
- diversify ownership within the chemical sector. Since reforms began, the entry of the non-state sector has injected vigour into the chemical sector. The non-state sector is expected to play an increasingly active role in international competition.
- reorganise the industrial organisation of the chemical sector according to its technical characteristics. Efforts should be made to promote vertical

integration of the petrochemical industry, through such measures as mergers, acquisitions and the introduction of a shareholding system. Long-standing troubles—such as overlapping construction and undersized enterprises—should be tackled as soon as possible.

- adjust industrial and product structure. Poor industrial and product structure are significant contributors to the weak competitiveness of China's chemical sector. The proportion of petrochemical and specialty chemicals—both high value-added products—is too low. The chemicals of these two industries should be prioritised in chemical industry development.

- speed up technological progress and innovation in the chemical industry. The chemical sector is a technology-intensive industry, so competition in science and technology is the focus of chemical industry competition. The first step is to increase R&D input, and promote cooperation among industry, research and academic circles. Another important aspect is to introduce advanced technology and equipment from foreign countries. A supportive policy should be established to encourage this.

- encourage chemical enterprises to actively participate in international competition. The government should raise tax rebates, increase export credit and reduce the interest rate. Overseas investment by chemical enterprises should also be encouraged.

It is important for the government to create favourable environment for chemical sector development. Besides providing supportive policies and an effective legal system, the government should attempt to prevent rampant smuggling, from which many of China's enterprises suffer greatly.

ECOTECH COOPERATION

10

ECOTECH AT THE HEART OF APEC: CAPACITY-BUILDING IN THE ASIA PACIFIC

ANDREW ELEK & HADI SOESASTRO[1]

The financial crises of 1997 and 1998 reminded everyone in the Asia Pacific region that sustained economic development requires careful attention to its foundations. The institutions of several East Asian economies proved inadequate, especially in terms of financial sector management. These weaknesses, combined with great instability in international capital markets, led to a severe and widespread economic downturn in activity in the region, shaking confidence in the prospects for further rapid improvements in living standards as well as in the prospects for effective economic cooperation in the Asia Pacific.

Until 1997, rapid growth was taken for granted and the success of APEC was measured largely in terms of reducing barriers to trade and investment. When the economic environment changed, the process was not prepared for its new and very different challenge. It has become evident that economic cooperation needs to be far more broadly based than the interaction of regional governments to dismantle obstacles to trade and investment. Undoubtedly, all economies can benefit from further progress towards the Bogor 2010/2020 targets for free and open trade and investment. At the same time, there are many other opportunities for economic cooperation to strengthen the human, institutional and technological capacity for sustainable and rapid economic development.

By mid-1999, the worst of the financial crisis appeared to be over for most of the region. However, much remains to be done to shore up the foundations for resumed rapid growth and to limit the risks of similar crises of confidence. Cooperation among Asia Pacific economies can help to accelerate and facilitate the costly, short-term effort needed to restructure and recapitalise severely damaged financial sectors as well as the multi-year human resource development and institutional capacity-building effort needed to create better-managed and more robust financial sectors for the future. It has been recognised that these are essentially tasks of economic and technical cooperation among Asia Pacific governments, in either a regional or global context. This perception will help to convince the region's leaders that economic and technical cooperation is at the heart of the APEC process, rather than a distraction from the drive towards free and open trade and investment. However, greater recognition of the importance of such cooperation will not guarantee satisfactory outcomes.

First, it will not be easy to develop a model of economic and technical cooperation capable of anticipating the massive changes expected in the political economy of the region. Some of the economies which currently have the greatest need for capacity-building will be among the most influential in the region by the middle of the 21st century. The experience of 1988 showed how hard it is to escape from an expectation that the currently richest and most powerful can insist on, and even consider themselves to be responsible for, imposing their opinions and conditions on those who need urgent short-term support. Second, there will always be excess demand for cooperative arrangements to enhance the potential of Asia Pacific economies for sustainable growth, so it will be important to have realistic expectations. Third, APEC will need to define its role in the 'market' for economic and technical cooperation. APEC leaders will need to build consensus on where the process may have comparative advantage: either in terms of identifying gaps to be filled, or in terms of direct or indirect involvement in filling such gaps.

In addition to these difficulties, APEC will need to solve a self-imposed problem, generated during its first ten years. APEC set out with the broad aim of sustaining the momentum of successful economic growth in East Asia and the Pacific. However, the process has come to be dominated by the issue of trade and investment liberalisation and facilitation (TILF). Within this broad effort to reduce obstacles to trade and investment, pre-eminent attention has been given to traditional issues of trade liberalisation. There is a widespread perception that APEC is essentially a trading arrangement, albeit not a preferential one, with some other ancillary activities designated as economic and technical cooperation (ecotech).[2]

An early focus on trade policy issues was appropriate, since the defence of an open and non-discriminatory multilateral trading system is the most important shared economic interest of Asia Pacific economies. But that need not mean the neglect of other ways to enhance the capacity of Asia Pacific economies for sustainable economic growth; it is a matter of setting and balancing different priorities for cooperation.

ECOTECH'S ENTRY INTO APEC

INITIAL RESISTANCE

Finding an appropriate balance among APEC's priorities has been hampered by the early resistance of some participants to including it in the agenda. As chair of APEC in 1994, Indonesia insisted that the APEC agenda should not be focused on trade and investment liberalisation alone. While Indonesia promotes and, in fact, has given birth to the Bogor goals of free and open trade and investment in the region, it has also made it clear that liberalisation must be accompanied by facilitation measures and 'development cooperation'. It saw these three aspects of economic cooperation as essential for the APEC enterprise. It was well understood by the developing members of APEC that the APEC process can help them keep, and even accelerate, the already established momentum of trade and investment. It was not difficult for all APEC members to see that facilitation measures complement liberalisation. Yet, some members did not immediately appreciate the need for development cooperation.

Indonesia has articulated the importance of development cooperation being accepted as the 'third pillar' of APEC, in order to enhance the capacity of developing economies to take an active part in the process, including in the liberalisation agenda. Its inclusion would demonstrate a kind of solidarity on the part of the developed members towards the developing members. Such solidarity would help assure the both governments and the public in the developing member economies that they could participate confidently in APEC's liberalisation initiative.

The rather negative reactions to this proposition were perhaps motivated by a concern that the inclusion of development cooperation in APEC's agenda would weaken the liberalisation program that had just taken off. Comments were heard from such countries as the United States that APEC was all about trade and investment liberalisation. Other comments pointed to the problems of nurturing mutual respect if APEC members regrouped themselves as donors and clients as well as to the undesirability of turning APEC into yet another aid organisation.

Whatever the arguments were for rejecting the inclusion of development cooperation, it essentially boiled down to a concern by some members that it would divert APEC's attention from trade and investment liberalisation. This was certainly a short-sighted and narrow view of what APEC is all about. It failed to understand the need to accommodate the interests of all members. In that sense, a balanced agenda is essential to the ultimate objective of community-building in the region through APEC.

It needs to be recalled that economic cooperation was the main reason for Ministers to come to the inaugural meeting in Canberra in 1989. In that meeting the ministers identified broad areas of cooperation—including economic studies, trade liberalisation, investment, technology transfer and human resources development, and sectoral cooperation—as the basis for the development of APEC's work program. The work program, which has been translated into a set of work projects, is meant to

- produce tangible benefits
- progress beyond agreement on general principles
- develop a habit of cooperation among such diverse members
- demonstrate that an Asia Pacific community can be nurtured.

Initially seven work projects were designated, and work began following the second Ministerial Meeting in Singapore in 1990. Three more work projects were added a year later at the third meeting in Seoul. The number of sub-projects under those work projects soon proliferated. By the time development cooperation was accepted as APEC's third pillar in the 1994 Bogor Declaration, there were about 200 projects.

In Osaka in 1995, the term 'development cooperation' was officially changed to 'economic and technical cooperation'. The Osaka Action Agenda noted that facilitation and liberalisation were indivisible components of work towards the Bogor vision of free and open trade and investment. On the other hand, it contained an ecotech agenda which was quite clearly identified as a parallel to, but separate from, the TILF agenda.

Three additional broad ecotech work projects were introduced, so that the ecotech agenda now covers 13 areas (broad work projects) of economic and technical cooperation. They are trade and investment data, trade promotion, industrial science and technology, human resources development, regional energy cooperation, marine resources conservation, fisheries, telecommunications, transportation, tourism, small and medium enterprises (SME), economic infrastructure, and agricultural technology.

The Osaka Action Agenda also proposed three essential elements in the implementation of ecotech, namely the development of common policy concepts, collective action, and policy dialogue in individual areas. It also defined the modality of cooperation, which emphasised a departure from the conventional donor-recipient relationship, consistency with market mechanisms, and encouragement of private sector participation.

By the time of the Manila meeting in 1996, the work projects had further proliferated to a total of 320. The largest number of work projects was in human resources development (86), followed by energy (43), industrial science and technology (41), and agricultural technology (35). These numbers, however, did not give any indication of what was going on in each of the 13 areas and of the priorities for APEC: the many projects were inherited from a largely incoherent process. Yamazawa (1997) observed that a typical ecotech activity was a 'pet project' proposed and coordinated by one particular APEC member, financed mainly by the proponent, and partly supported by APEC's Central Fund. A closer examination of the work projects showed that they were mostly seminars, studies or information gathering. Such activities have their value, but they can be undertaken (perhaps more efficiently) by public or private agencies outside APEC. Yamazawa explained this poor performance as resulting from a lack of practical guidelines which permitted the dominance of pet projects of individual members, and from a failure to involve conventional donor and multilateral aid agencies.

Yamazawa argued that Japan's Partners for Progress (PFP) proposal was meant to boost ecotech beyond studies and seminars by formulating an overall program, providing some seed money (10 billion yen), and establishing an agency within APEC to administer it (Pomfret 1998). This proposal failed to gain acceptance and eventually it was watered down to an initiative that involved technical cooperation in improving administrative capability and transferring technology in just three specific areas of TILF—standards and conformance, intellectual property rights, and competition policy.

THE 1996 MANILA DECLARATION

1996 saw the start of a more serious effort to provide a conceptual and operational framework for economic and technical cooperation and to achieve a new consensus on the balance of APEC's activities. Under Philippines leadership, APEC leaders adopted the 'Manila Declaration on an Asia Pacific Economic Cooperation Framework for Strengthening Economic Cooperation and Development'. That declaration set out the objectives, guiding principles and priorities for promoting economic and technical cooperation, defining a model of cooperation based genuinely on mutual respect as well as mutual benefit. The nature of cooperation promoted by APEC is different from 'foreign aid'—that is, transfers of funds from donors to clients, often conditional on some surrender of political sovereignty. Instead, the new model seeks to take advantage of the enormous scope for cooperation by sharing the region's richly diverse resources of information, experience, expertise and technology for the benefit all Asia Pacific economies.

The Manila Declaration stipulated that ecotech should be goal-oriented with explicit objectives, milestones and performance criteria. Furthermore, it should combine government actions, private sector projects and joint public-private activities, with the public sector playing a direct or indirect role in creating an enabling environment for private sector initiatives. Ecotech should also draw on voluntary contributions commensurate with member economies' capabilities, and generate direct and broadly-shared benefits among APEC member economies to reduce economic disparities in the region. The six priority areas identified for joint cooperative activities to be promoted by APEC were to

- develop human capital
- develop stable, safe and efficient capital markets
- strengthen economic infrastructure
- harness technologies for the future
- safeguard the quality of life through environmentally sound growth
- develop and strengthen the dynamism of small and medium enterprises.

RECENT DEVELOPMENTS AND DILEMMAS

At present, there are 274 ongoing ecotech projects. An ecotech sub-committee of the APEC SOM was established in 1997, with the aim of coordinating and managing ecotech to ensure focused outcomes. The committee has produced a set of principles and in reviewing proposals will consider those that have value added. The committee has proposed that specific members of APEC be designated to act as coordinator for each of the six priority areas. This is a significant development which could result in greater coherence in the ecotech agenda. In Vancouver in 1997, infrastructure was elevated to the attention of the leaders. In Kuala Lumpur in 1998, human resources (skill) development and industrial science and technology were brought to the highest level of policy. It remains to be seen whether these initiatives will bring concrete results in the near future.

In their 1997 Vancouver Declaration, 'Connecting the APEC Community', APEC leaders committed themselves to a balanced agenda and pointed to the indivisibility of the different pillars of the APEC agenda. However, despite the increased attention to ecotech, more needs to be done to develop a coherent and integrated view of the nature of economic and technical cooperation and its place in the overall APEC process.

There have been constructive moves, by the business/private sector as well as by governments, to turn that conceptual framework into a new operational model of development cooperation. Several hundred activities have been proposed by APEC committees and working groups, mostly involving the exchange of information and expertise. Some of these are already underway, with some being supported by the private sector as well as by existing development agencies. Nevertheless, the total number of potential activities is growing more rapidly than the small number being implemented. A sense of frustration and several misunderstandings persists.

One set of problems is that there are widely varying and incompatible expectations about the nature of the cooperative activities which could be promoted collectively by APEC governments and about how these could be financed and implemented. This is being compounded by an inadequate appreciation of the current and potential role of existing agencies—such as the Asian Development Bank (ADB)—in promoting the new ideas for economic and technical cooperation emerging from the APEC process.

In that context, Morrison (1997) suggested that APEC members should view ecotech broadly as a process by which they work together to develop the entire region in mutually agreed ways. It is in this sense that the activity is a collective action. Morrison proposed that the modality of cooperation in the ecotech area be developed along the modality adopted for TILF. Work programs should primarily be national ones. Individual member economies should make and compare their own national action plans for economic and technical cooperation to achieve regional goals—such as efficient regional transportation networks, world-class telecommunication links, human resources for economic growth, and protection of the regional environment. APEC governments, as a group, would then seek to supplement and strengthen these individual efforts by sharing information and experience as well as concerting national efforts and formulating joint endeavours involving the private sectors as well as the existing development agencies of APEC economies. Such a sense of strategy has yet to emerge.

ECOTECH VERSUS TILF?

A further serious problem for the APEC process is the unduly sharp dichotomy which has come to be drawn between work to promote TILF and other forms of cooperation. Moreover, ecotech activities are being seen as residual activities which are not part of the drive towards free and open trade and investment. This is an incorrect perception which underestimates the potential contribution of economic and technical cooperation to all of APEC's efforts to enhance the capacity for sustainable economic growth, including through trade and investment policy reforms.

The current perception of ecotech as an alternative to TILF (and even as a competitor to it), leads to unhelpful debates about their relative importance. The developing economies in APEC believe—correctly—that more open international trade and investment is just one of several ingredients for sustained growth. Accordingly, they are pressing to move the emphasis away from TILF. At the same time, the currently more wealthy APEC economies perceive less benefit to themselves from activities other than TILF. There is a risk that reluctant support for economic and technical cooperation will be seen as the 'price' the currently more developed economies have to pay to persuade the others to pursue trade and investment policy reforms. Such perceptions make it difficult to distinguish ecotech from old-style 'foreign aid'. They also tend to erode mutual respect and weaken APEC's ability to promote a sense of community in the diverse Asia Pacific.

If ecotech and TILF continue to be seen a separate strands of the APEC process, it will be hard to build a sense of shared economic interests and mutual respect. Unless ecotech is understood to be an essential ingredient of TILF as well as of other cooperative activities, TILF can be too easily viewed as an adversarial negotiating process, rather than a joint cooperative effort with all-round benefits. The frustrating experience with early 'voluntary' sectoral liberalisation (EVSL) in 1998 indicated a drift towards a perception that trade policy reforms are 'concessions' Asia Pacific governments must make to preserve the credibility of the APEC process. Such a drift will rapidly erode APEC's potential contribution towards more open global trade and investment. As a voluntary process of cooperation, APEC has no comparative advantage over the WTO as a forum for traditional trade negotiations.

AN INTEGRAL APPROACH: ECOTECH AT THE HEART OF APEC

For these reasons, this paper advocates an integrated view of the APEC process. As expressed in the 1991 Seoul Declaration, the primary objective of Asia Pacific economic cooperation is 'to sustain the growth and development of the region for the common good of its peoples and, in this way, to contribute to the growth and development of the world economy.' (APEC 1991, Clause 1(a)).

In that context, all the cooperative activities promoted by APEC can be seen as ways to strengthen the capacity of Asia Pacific economies to reach their full potential for sustainable economic growth.

The basic challenge is to enhance the capacity of all Asia Pacific economies to increase their productive resources and to allocate them in an increasingly efficient and sustainable way. Cooperation among APEC economies can help by sharing the information, experience, expertise and technology needed to design and administer a progressively more efficient set of economic policies to achieve these ends. Cooperation which improves the ability of Asia Pacific governments to reduce impediments to trade and investment through unilateral or coordinated reforms—that is, TILF—is just one important part of this overall cooperative effort.

As set out in this chapter, there are many potential cooperative arrangements among APEC governments and/or their private sectors which can help every Asia Pacific economy enhance its institutional and technological capacity. Some of these cooperative arrangements will be more directly related to international economic policy, while others will relate more to enhancing the economic environment, including the policy framework within individual Asia Pacific economies. However, progress on both fronts is complementary.

It is widely recognised that as economies become increasingly interdependent, the evolution of policies to manage and strengthen domestic economies will have increasingly significant indirect effects on the costs and risks of international as well as domestic economic transactions. Divergent ways of regulating domestic economic activity tend to increase the impediments to international commerce. Conversely, cooperative activities among Asia Pacific economies in all types of institution-building can reduce the costs and risks of international trade and investment. Cooperative policy development can improve the capacity of Asia Pacific governments to anticipate the international implications of the way their policies are formulated and administered. Enhanced communications among the region's policymakers should also lead to more compatible and, in some cases, more convergent approaches to economic management in all Asia Pacific economies. All such cooperative activities will contribute—more or less directly—to TILF.

Turning to TILF itself, efforts to reduce impediments to international economic transactions involve several stages.

- identifying particular impediments (or sets of impediments)
- identifying policy measures which cause these impediments
- understanding the policy objectives being pursued by these policy measures
- estimating the effects of these policy measures on economies, particularly on the economies which impose these measures
- identifying alternative policy combinations which can achieve the same policy objectives more efficiently, while reducing impediments to international economic transactions
- developing the expertise and institutional capacity to implement alternative policy options
- persuading Asia Pacific governments to adopt such alternative policy combinations.

APEC participants can undertake each of these steps individually. In practice, TILF was well underway before APEC was established. However, economic and technical cooperation among Asia Pacific economies can help at each of these stages. In reality, much of APEC's potential contribution to achieving free and open trade and investment is through cooperative policy development and technical cooperation.

Some impediments, such as tariffs, are deliberate policy measures intended to raise the cost of international economic transactions relative to comparable domestic transactions. In many other cases, impediments may be due simply to a lack of awareness of the costs (or risks) they impose, or a lack of attention to reducing or eliminating them.

For example, differences in commercial regulations—such as disclosure or auditing requirements—may be due to historical factors in various economies, but can add to the costs and risks of international commerce, without any direct intention of doing so. Once the nature and effects of such differences are understood, it is usually possible to find ways of amending regulations or procedures to reduce needless differences and to make them more transparent and less arbitrary. In the case of costly international transport or telecommunications links, it is often possible for trading partners to identify the policies—or absence of them—which make it difficult to link up the transport and telecommunications networks of different economies. One early form of practical technical cooperation in APEC has been to harmonise the procedures for gathering and processing customs information, thus reducing the cost of international trade. Work is also underway to build the institutional capacity needed for a successful program of mutual recognition of product and process standards.

More generally, economic and technical cooperation can encourage, then enable, Asia Pacific governments to reform policies which currently impede trade and investment. Sharing the policymaking experience of Asia Pacific economies and sharing the expertise needed to estimate the effects of alternative policy options can help change perceptions about the merits of policies. Clearer insight into the effects of policy instruments and alternative ways to achieve policy objectives can encourage governments to reduce impediments through voluntary unilateral policy reforms, including unilateral trade liberalisation.

In many cases, economic and technical cooperation taking place in APEC committees and working groups is already helping to change perceptions. It is leading to continuing improvements in the scope and depth of Individual Action Plans (IAPs) to dismantle impediments to international economic transactions. Further economic cooperation in the form of coordinated enhancement of IAPs, consistently with the principles of the Osaka Action Agenda, can also assist Asia Pacific governments to overcome short-term resistance to change within each of their economies.

Economic and technical cooperation will not always prove sufficient to change perceptions. If certain border barriers continue to be perceived of net political benefit to particular governments, they will not be reduced voluntarily. They may be reduced through negotiations, but it does not follow that APEC is an appropriate forum for such negotiations.

As a voluntary process of cooperation, APEC is not likely to provide an effective framework for negotiating and enforcing involuntary reforms of trade and investment policies. Moreover, if reforms are regarded as 'concessions' to others, it is difficult to negotiate lower border barriers to trade or investment which are in line with the principle of open regionalism. There will be continual pressure to deny the benefit of reforms to those not involved in the negotiations. Therefore, if negotiations are necessary to agree on trade or investment policy reforms, it is more sensible to conduct these negotiations in the WTO where

- all significant non-APEC trading partners are automatically involved
- the framework and procedures for negotiations are well established
- there are agreed procedures—including dispute settlement procedures—for monitoring and enforcing adherence to agreements (Bora and Findlay 1996).

Against this background, it is somewhat artificial to try to distinguish TILF from ecotech. Most opportunities for cooperation among Asia Pacific economies to promote free and open trade and investment are, in practice, opportunities for economic and technical cooperation. It may be more useful to separate APEC's facilitation and liberalisation efforts into two components, namely: TILF which is economic and technical cooperation, and TILF which is the negotiation of involuntary trade or investment liberalisation. For the latter type of TILF, the time has come for APEC to adopt a more efficient strategy.

Rather than attempting to mimic WTO negotiations within the region, it would be preferable to accept that the negotiation of involuntary reforms should be left to the WTO. At the same time, there is considerable scope for economic and technical cooperation among APEC governments to prepare the ground for successful WTO outcomes. Part of that task is to promote progressively more accurate perceptions of the economy-wide benefits of what are still regarded as 'concessions'; the other is to exercise joint leadership in the WTO to set the principles, priorities and objectives of future WTO negotiations.

To sum up, all cooperative activities promoted by APEC can be seen as enhancing the capacity of participants to devise and adopt more efficient and compatible policies for economic management and to enhance their capacity to administer them. Such cooperation for capacity-building can serve to advance all the objectives which have been set out in the Seoul, Bogor and Manila Declarations of APEC.

The APEC process provides a new means of interaction among Asia Pacific political leaders and officials which can lead to innovative ideas and opportunities for cooperative policy development and technical cooperation. That does not mean that APEC should be seen as just one more development cooperation agency. There is no project or program for enhancing the capacity of Asia Pacific economies for sustainable growth which could not, in principle, be financed and managed by the ADB, by various United Nations agencies, by the development agencies of many individual APEC participants or by the private sector.

Just as APEC should make use of and complement the WTO—not imitate it—it should motivate and steer the extensive development cooperation effort already underway, rather than compete with it. It follows that APEC should not try to assess its contribution to capacity-building in Asia Pacific economies in terms of projects directly financed or managed by any new APEC mechanism—such as APEC-funded dams, bridges or training institutes. That would certainly not be in line with comparative advantage. Nor should APEC seek to measure progress in terms of the additional amounts contributed to APEC by its member governments. At a time of tight budget constraints and 'aid fatigue', such funds would most likely be simply diverted from resources of other development agencies.

Compared to the business sector or to Asia Pacific governments, the APEC process has—and is always likely to have—very modest funds at its direct disposal. These can be used to fund, at most, a small proportion of the many economic and technical cooperation opportunities it has already identified. This need not imply a passive role for APEC, but a serious effort to concentrate on its comparative advantage and to complement the work of others.

Having built up new channels for region-wide communications, APEC leaders and officials do have comparative advantage in designing options for economic and technical cooperation which can draw on information, experience, expertise and technology from throughout the region and make it available widely to many Asia Pacific economies. The next challenge is to develop a strategy for using these ideas as a catalyst for cooperation; APEC leaders should be able to evoke a positive response to such new ideas from the business/private sector and from Asia Pacific governments. Such a strategy for encouraging their involvement can be summarised as identifying carefully selected regional public goods to create an environment in which

- more of the vast pool of private savings being generated within the region is steered, through sensible policies and market signals, into capacity-building investments to boost the growth potential of Asia Pacific economies
- the activities of all existing, as well as any new, government-sponsored programs of development cooperation come to be increasingly consistent with the shared objectives and guiding principles of a new Asia Pacific model of development cooperation.

The following sections explain how economic and technical cooperation among Asia Pacific economies is already contributing to enhancing their capacity for sustained growth and development, helping to

- strengthen domestic and international financial markets
- facilitate trade and investment
- liberalise traditional border barriers to trade
- defend and strengthen the multilateral trading system
- develop the capacity of economic infrastructure
- promote human resource development
- enhance technological capacity.

In continuing all of these efforts, it will be essential to distinguish what the APEC process itself can be expected to contribute—either directly through its committees and working groups or its own limited budget, or in terms of mobilising and/or redirecting the resources of the private sector and existing development agencies—to promote these objectives.

STRENGTHENING FINANCIAL SECTORS

APEC was slow to react as the financial crisis deepened dramatically soon after Asia Pacific leaders met in Vancouver in late 1997. Nevertheless, by November 1998, there was a worthwhile set of initiatives for economic and technical cooperation to help overcome the crisis. Economic activity has begun to recover in most of the worst-affected economies, but there is plenty of scope for further economic and technical cooperation to strengthen the recovery and to lessen the probability of future financial crises.

RESTORING CONFIDENCE—POLICY DEVELOPMENT

In the aftermath of the crises, APEC leaders have agreed to adopt internationally recognised principles for financial sector management and supervision. This will help provide a framework for more sound financial management, but further cooperative policy development is needed. Experience in many economies has shown that it is not sufficient to rely on fixed parameters to avert problems. There will be continuing scope to exchange information and experience, with gradually more sophisticated and flexible forms of financial risk management.

An important challenge for cooperative policy development by APEC governments is to build the foundations for coping with international financial movements. The Bogor objective of free and open trade and investment cannot be realised without a high degree of capital mobility. On the other hand, the experience of 1997 and 1998 demonstrated that the policy framework and/or the institutional capacity of several Asia Pacific economies was not yet able to manage international capital movements, particularly those of a short-term nature.

There is widespread agreement that 'pegged' exchange rates contributed substantially to the crises by creating unsustainable expectations of exchange rate stability. Some economies may follow the Hong Kong precedent of a permanently fixed exchange rate, which would need to be backed by the expertise to manage currency board type arrangements and to adapt all other aspects of macroeconomic management to the lack of any exchange rate flexibility. More Asia Pacific economies are likely to adopt freely floating exchange rates; these will require strong demand management and an adequate international coordination of macroeconomic policies to avoid erratic fluctuations of exchange rates. Helping to put effective macroeconomic management into practice is one of many important opportunities for ongoing economic cooperation and cooperative policy development among Asia Pacific economies; APEC finance ministers and officials have already initiated cooperative arrangements for sharing information about macroeconomic developments.

STRENGTHENING INSTITUTIONS—TECHNICAL COOPERATION

An institution-building effort is needed to back up any understandings on basic parameters and methods for financial sector risk management. A correspondingly significant program of technical cooperation can help to strengthen institutional capacity and to train the people who are going to make these systems work, both as parts of the regulatory or policymaking system and as part of the private sector institutions which will implement the new financial systems of the Asia Pacific region.

The types of information needed and the basis for decision-making will be very different in the financial systems of the future. Therefore, a massive human resource development program is needed; first to pool the wide range of experience and expertise available in the Asia Pacific; and second to provide appropriate training for those directly involved in the financial sector and for those who supervise them (Petri 1998).

Such training efforts do not need to be financed by APEC itself. The ADB has already lent money to support reform and restructuring of financial systems—it and the development cooperation agencies of APEC governments can be urged to do more along these lines. Coordination among APEC governments can increase the effectiveness of training programs by encouraging region-wide programs which can make the best expertise in the region available to all economies interested in strengthening their financial sectors. The establishment of an International Monetary Fund (IMF) Regional Training Institute in Singapore is a positive example.

RESTRUCTURING FINANCIAL SECTORS

APEC governments can also speed up the process of rescheduling or writing off the very substantial amounts of private debt which certainly cannot be serviced at anything like current exchange rates. A very large amount of capital will be needed to recapitalise the reformed and strengthened next generation of financial institutions; most estimates of the cost of 'working out' from the current debt crises are over 20 per cent of the GDP of the economies most heavily affected. The private sector will make some direct contribution by rescheduling or writing off some debt, but much of the funds will need to be raised by governments.

In late 1998, the Japanese Government announced a US$30 billion fund to support economic recovery. This was followed, in Kuala Lumpur, by an initiative announced by the United States and Japan, in conjunction with the World Bank and the ADB, to contribute a further US$10 billion. These funds have the potential to accelerate the restructuring of corporate debt and the recapitalisation of the region's banks, both of which are unavoidable and urgent in restoring growth and the return of investor confidence.

STRENGTHENING INTERNATIONAL CAPITAL MARKETS

In the wake of the events of 1997–98, there is already broad agreement on the need for a fundamental reassessment of the nature and mandate of international institutions to help prevent a recurrence of such problems. The debate has moved beyond whether international capital markets are regulated. It is becoming evident that all markets—domestic or international—are regulated; the practical issue is the nature of regulation and the means of administering it while continuing to strive to improve the markets' effectiveness (Stiglitz 1998). As noted earlier, unsustainable exchange rate regimes were partly to blame for the crisis, by encouraging excess borrowing on short-term global capital markets. But the problem of excessive lending also needs to be addressed.

It is beyond the scope of this chapter to canvass specific proposals for improving international capital markets.[2] Nor is it up to APEC governments alone to resolve the problem by themselves. These are global issues which are most efficiently addressed by global understandings and institutions, but APEC governments can cooperate to help ensure timely, constructive reforms. International consultations on future international financial architecture will continue for several years. Close consultations among APEC governments can help the nature of any new international institutions and the regulation of international capital markets reflect the needs and interests of developing, as well as already developed, economies.

FACILITATING TRADE AND INVESTMENT

Since its establishment in 1989, APEC has sought to promote closer and mutually beneficial economic integration in the Asia Pacific, consistent with the overriding interest of all participating economies in a rules-based multilateral trading system. The Osaka Action Agenda sets out the very broad scope of the challenge of free and open trade and investment by no later than 2020—thus setting the agenda for a comprehensive drive to facilitate trade and investment by dismantling obstacles to trade and investment. As described below, economic and technical cooperation—in the sense of pooling the region's diverse resources of information, experience, expertise and technology—is an essential ingredient of all aspects of facilitation, including the liberalisation of border barriers to trade and investment.

CAPACITY BUILDING AND FACILITATION

The experience of 1997 and 1998 has demonstrated the need to ensure that the foundation of institutions and the way they are managed keeps pace with the challenges of rapid economic growth and structural change. Strengthening and maintaining these foundations requires much more than a response to market signals. Individual economic agents cannot be expected to meet the needs for institution-building and human resource development, which extend well beyond the financial sector.

Massive investment is needed in what are essentially public goods, some of which are international public goods. Individual businesses cannot be expected to set up effective public regulatory institutions to meet economy-wide needs for education and training. Similarly, it will not always be efficient for Asia Pacific governments to design and administer such institutions or human resource development programs in isolation. In many cases, international economic cooperation can realise economies of scope. In some cases cooperation among governments may prove to be essential to implement options for reducing impediments to international economic transactions.

There should be scope to create mechanisms for new forms of economic cooperation among Asia Pacific governments, and new opportunities for pooling the resources and capabilities of existing development cooperation agencies to promote institution-building and human resource development. There are very positive signs that the business/private sector is willing to become involved, collectively, in the provision of some of these international public goods.

Facilitating international trade and investment by reducing transactions costs usually involves institution-building in the economies that wish to encourage closer economic integration and the establishment of effective and confident communications among parallel institutions in these economies. As illustrated by the following examples, economic and technical cooperation to share and disseminate the region's best available administrative and technical practices is an efficient way to promote such capacity-building.

Harmonisation of customs procedures. APEC governments are already well on the way to implementing a harmonised approach for the collection, electronic transmission and processing of customs information. This approach promises very significant economic returns, not only by reducing costs and delays in processing, but also by reducing the need for new investment in infrastructure at ports and airports, thus allowing existing facilities to operate more efficiently. Implementing the new system has been, essentially, an exercise in economic and technical cooperation. The policy development work of APEC working groups has led to the design and acceptance of new parameters and software for processing the vast amounts of data handled daily. That has been followed by technical cooperation to help Asia Pacific governments to develop the capacity to install, test and operate the new system. Such cooperation represents the supply of an international public good with mutual benefits, which can only be created through cooperation by several governments.

APEC-wide work has concentrated on cargo-handling, but some APEC governments have also cooperated to design and install more efficient systems for the issue and processing of business travel visas, lowering transaction costs for business people and reducing congestion at airports. 'APEC channels' are appearing in more and more customs halls and—through further technical cooperation—the experiment is likely to spread to much of the region in the next few years.

Mutual recognition of standards. Free and open trade among any group of economies requires acceptance of the principle of 'tested once, tested everywhere'. That need not rely on the creation of new, let alone uniform, product and process standards. Commercial realities are driving producers to conform to existing globally widespread standards (such as ISO standards) and placing pressure on governments to develop credible means of monitoring conformance with their national standards for quality, performance and environmental or other safeguards.

The response to these pressures is already laying the groundwork for a potentially comprehensive region-wide agreement on mutual recognition of product and process standards. For such a system to operate sustainably and efficiently—without excessive need to resort to litigation—products users will need to have a high degree of confidence in the ability and integrity of all the institutions in the region which monitor compliance with standards. Such confidence requires, in turn, a high degree of mutual respect and trust among this network of parallel institutions.

Establishing and sustaining such trust requires both policy development and technical cooperation. The legislative frameworks need to be adequate—and internationally accepted as being adequate—for effective monitoring of standards. Mutual confidence in the capacity to use such regulatory powers depends on well-trained staff. This is an ongoing technical cooperation challenge as those trained move to, or are promoted to, other occupations.

POLICY DEVELOPMENT AND TECHNICAL COOPERATION

The above are just two examples of the thousands of opportunities for cooperation among APEC governments to design compatible approaches to a wide range of commercial regulatory issues. Taking up such opportunities is a technically difficult challenge. A complex set of changes to a very wide range of domestic commercial policies is required to achieve anything like free trade in services (for example) by moving towards full national treatment of international investment, which is often an essential vehicle for trade in services (PECC 1996a).

Dealing with these issues is, once again, essentially a matter of cooperative policy development backed up by ongoing technical cooperation.

For example, a thoughtful evolutionary approach will be essential to develop competition policies within economies, let alone to deal with their international implications. Many aspects of competition policy, of which competition laws or 'anti-trust' laws are just one component, will need to be dealt with internationally. There is much more to be done than attempting to 'deal with' competition policy in the WTO, especially since the WTO deals with government actions, while many competition policy issues relate to private actions. As noted in PECC (1996a), a much clearer understanding of the linkages between trade and many aspects of competition policy is essential, starting with building consensus on the objectives of competition policy and some basic guiding principles for its evolution.[3]

More generally, a close examination of issues of trade in services and international investment demonstrates the importance of working consistently to address the current problems that have been identified as business priorities.

These problems go well beyond cross-border barriers; they are inherent in international business due to interacting sets of legislation and regulations in each economy, including competition policy, company laws and tax laws. It may prove useful to adopt a general evolutionary approach to dealing with an increasing range of issues which used to be regarded as purely 'domestic', in order to facilitate international economic transactions while respecting the autonomy of all governments over their policies. The first steps involved are to promote transparency and then to foster mutual understanding.

Mutual understanding of the issues and motives of current policies, once achieved, can lead to the mutual respect needed for governments to agree on objectives and non-binding guiding principles or norms for various aspects of economic or commercial policies. These involve the pooling of the region's resources of information, experience and expertise; it is yet another challenge for cooperative policy development.

Efficient policy norms or guiding principles for the many aspects of commercial policy are likely to incorporate, in each case, the fundamental concepts of transparency, non-discrimination and national treatment. Once desirable region-wide norms are agreed upon, they can then be the basis for

- individual governments to use such principles, if they wish, in the ongoing reform of their domestic policies
- mutual recognition
- (where considered efficient and desirable) some convergence or harmonisation of approaches.

Such an evolutionary approach is already being applied by APEC to facilitate trade and investment by improving the efficiency of customs procedures, and by its work on product and process standards and conformance. A similar approach can also be used to encourage the acceptance of shared principles for the conduct of other commercial policy.

Promoting gradually more compatible and potentially convergent approaches to a wide range of commercial policies and regulations will need extensive cooperative policy development. That challenge is already being tackled by APEC's working groups. They can draw on the international cooperative policy development work of others including the Pacific Economic Cooperation Council (PECC) who, in turn, can draw on research and experience from the rest of the world, for example by the Organisation for Economic Cooperation and Development (OECD), adapting it to the realities of a diverse Asia Pacific.

Once new principles and policies are accepted by some Asia Pacific economies, they will need to be backed by efforts to strengthen relevant institutional capacity, then by ongoing training. Communications among APEC leaders can create opportunities for region-wide training efforts. Such cooperative activities can capture economies of scale and scope as well as create a sense of mutual respect and trust among the region's administrators. This is essential for such new policies and institutions to be effective in terms of facilitating international trade and investment.

The preceding examples of options for facilitating trade and investment demonstrate that their implementation relies on building the capacity of institutions and strengthening human resources through economic and technical cooperation. In other words, ecotech is an essential ingredient of—not an alternative to—facilitation. As discussed below, ecotech is also an essential ingredient of serious efforts to promote trade liberalisation by APEC governments.

TRADE LIBERALISATION

Cooperative policy development work by officials—particularly in the Committee for Trade and Investment (CTI)—has underpinned APEC's progress towards trade liberalisation to date and will be needed to sustain progress. The Bogor Declaration and its vision for free and open trade and investment would have remained no more than a vision in the absence of valuable work by the CTI and senior officials to define the guiding principles of tangible progress towards dismantling border barriers, consistent with the principles of open regionalism and voluntary cooperation. The concepts of concerted unilateral liberalisation and voluntary collective action to facilitate trade and investment were developed jointly through consensus-building among APEC officials, then endorsed by Ministers in the 1995 Osaka Action Agenda. This was followed by intensive work to draw up IAPs for market-opening and deregulation as set out in the Manila Action Plan for APEC, and subsequently updated.

Trade liberalisation is technically easy to implement; unlike the extensive capacity-building needed for facilitation, it does not require much technical expertise to abolish or change tariffs and non-tariff barriers to trade. On the other hand, concerted unilateral liberalisation relies on APEC governments continuing to perceive that further voluntary liberalisation is in their self-interest. The challenge for cooperative policy development and analysis is to build, then to sustain, political support for liberalisation, by demonstrating the advantages of 'opening to the outside world' and of doing so in concert with other APEC participants.

ENHANCING POLITICAL SUPPORT FOR TRADE LIBERALISATION

The greatest gains from liberalisation flow to those undertaking the reforms. That has been demonstrated by the experience of recent decades. In the three decades from 1965 to 1995, those economies which have opened to international competition and taken advantage of opportunities to specialise in line with their evolving comparative advantage spectacularly outperformed those which sought to follow an inward-looking strategy concentrating on import substitution and

175

sheltered domestic markets. This remains true despite the very severe setbacks of 1997 and 1998. However, the crisis has shaken confidence about the long-term gains from further market-opening and strengthened the hand of protectionists in uncompetitive sectors that would lose from further liberalisation.

Under these circumstances, it would be useful for APEC officials to commission economic analysis which puts the long-term net gains of liberalisation into perspective, under different assumptions about the length and severity of the current downturn. Moreover, the increased questioning of the costs of exposure to global competition points to the ongoing need for economic and technical cooperation among Asia Pacific economies to share their experience in liberalisation, particularly the experience of coping with the short-term strains of adjustment to wider competition in a somewhat unpredictable international economic environment.

Future voluntary liberalisation can also be promoted by sharing information and experience gained, either in terms of the benefits of past policy reforms, or the long-term problems of inefficiency caused by decisions to shield particular sectors from competition. The region-wide dissemination of expertise and technology can also foster mutual trust and confidence that the drive towards free and open trade and investment is designed to enhance.

Political support for concerted unilateral liberalisation can also be enhanced by confidence that all APEC governments are committed to progressive elimination of border barriers to trade since 'home economy' gains from liberalisation can be magnified if an economy's main trading partners are also opening their markets. Correspondingly, both forms of gain will be foregone if the failure of some APEC participants to meet their commitments induces other governments to follow suit by slowing down, or turning away from, liberalisation. Moreover, arguments against liberalisation are easier to counter if other APEC governments are also reducing the protection given to their producers.

Economic cooperation among APEC participants to sponsor objective and independent assessment of progress is vital to sustaining region-wide confidence in continuing commitment to the process of concerted unilateral liberalisation. Independent studies by the PECC served to lay the foundation for concerted unilateral liberalisation. One of these (PECC 1995a) documented the substantial progress most Asia Pacific economies had already made in terms of unilateral liberalisation even before their Bogor commitment, providing confidence that such a trend can be expected to continue, especially if all APEC governments act in concert. The other study, (PECC 1995a) documented the barriers which remain, especially in terms of border barriers to trade, setting a basis for monitoring progress. A subsequent analysis (PECC 1996b) of the Manila Action Plan for APEC indicated that, at that time, individual APEC economies were well on track towards their Bogor goals and that their actual, or committed, tariff reductions were mostly faster or deeper than their commitments under the Uruguay Round.

On the other hand, there have been only very modest commitments to trade liberalisation since then. As Bogor target dates loom closer and the sectors which remain to be tackled are increasingly sensitive, it is becoming increasingly evident that voluntary cooperation alone will not achieve free and open trade and investment by 2010/2020. Nor does the 1998 experience with EVSL provide grounds for confidence about the prospects for WTO-style negotiations among APEC governments.

DEALING WITH SENSITIVE SECTORS

An urgent challenge for cooperative policy development among APEC governments is to develop a credible strategy for sustained progress towards dismantling traditional border barriers to trade, not just in the region, but globally.

Having learnt the lessons of 1998, it would not be helpful for APEC to simply try even harder to convert itself into a negotiating forum. As already emphasised, a voluntary process of economic cooperation has no comparative advantage over the WTO in terms of negotiations in which trade liberalisation is regarded as a 'concession' to others. Any attempt to change the basic principles of APEC to make it a treaty-based process which could enforce reforms would place the 2010/2020 targets for trade liberalisation well beyond reach.

A possible compromise might be to seek a restructuring of APEC so that while most cooperative arrangements and activities remained voluntary, traditional trade liberalisation would no longer be voluntary. Instead, trade liberalisation within APEC would proceed by means of negotiating binding commitments. Even if that were acceptable to all participants (which is doubtful) and could be agreed upon quickly (also doubtful), it would still not change APEC's lack of comparative advantage over WTO-based negotiations on border barriers to trade. More importantly, such an attempt would also be likely to undercut any current comparative advantage in terms of other options to facilitate trade and investment.

As demonstrated by earlier examples, facilitating trade and investment essentially involves a patient search for more compatible and/or convergent approaches to often complex matters of commercial policy. Moreover, it is more than a matter of adopting new regulations, it also requires the capacity to implement them and the willingness to do so in good faith. Cooperative arrangements for mutual recognition of standards or harmonised customs procedures will not deliver anything like their potential benefit if there is frequent need for litigation about the way these arrangements are being implemented. Sustained progress in terms of facilitation to reduce many of the costs and risks of international commerce requires a high degree of mutual respect and mutual trust. These crucial ingredients cannot be expected to be nurtured in the shadow of high profile negotiations and disagreements about a few traditional trade barriers.

CHANGING PERCEPTIONS

A more effective strategy is to accept that there are some sectors—such as parts of agriculture and some labour-intensive manufacturing in different Asia Pacific economies—where protection has become deeply entrenched. In most of these cases, governments are aware of the long-term advantages of dismantling protection—both to their own economies and the credibility of their commitment to APEC—but these potential gains are perceived to be outweighed by the short-term political risks of reform. In these cases, there is some room for changing public perceptions over time, but free and open trade and investment in these sectors by 2010/2020 is most unlikely to be achieved, except through negotiations. This points to the need for APEC governments to cooperate to increase the prospects of dealing with these sectors in the WTO. Enhancing the likelihood of success in the WTO involves far more than accumulating either leverage or bargaining chips.

In some other sectors of certain Asia Pacific economies, there are genuine concerns about the risk of reliance on international markets. There are some products—such as foodgrains, fertilisers, steel and energy—where concern with the security of supply (and/or the capacity to pay for them) can outweigh the potential benefits of international specialisation. Free trade in such products, which would allow all economies to benefit from the efficient location of production, will not be achieved until these concerns are dealt with.

Much work is needed to create an environment in which economies which are potentially large net consumers can be confident about regular supplies being available on international markets at reasonably stable prices. Correspondingly, potentially large net suppliers will not risk long-term investment to supply unstable or unreliable international markets; these problems are likely to be acute for sectors with strong economies of scale and long investment lead times. Despite the obvious complementarity of Asia Pacific economies due to very different resource endowments, long-term decisions for efficient location of production will only be possible if these underlying problems are addressed and there is good reason to be confident about stable demand and supply conditions. There is ample scope for APEC officials and policy-oriented researchers around the region—for example in PECC—to engage in cooperative policy development to create the confident international market environments necessary for serious commitment to free trade in some of these vital commodities.

Steel products provide an example. For large potential net importers to consider free trade, they would need comprehensive assurance, not only of secure supplies, but also that potential suppliers are not seeking to retard either the technological capacity of domestic steel industries in general, or defence capabilities in particular. For sustained success in exporting, potential exporters will need to be seen to be willing to bolster—not undermine—the domestic capacity of potential importers. That could be demonstrated by willingness to transfer technology and to invest in production in the net importing economy. Without such assurances of cooperation as well as competition, potential suppliers will continue to face the risk of disruption of their markets due to policy changes by importers. They will be aware that appeals to peer pressure by APEC governments, or even recourse to time-consuming WTO dispute settlement mechanisms, cannot assure the commercial survival of large-scale export-oriented investments.

Some essential ingredients of an understanding which might pave the way for confident agreement on promoting the growth of mutually beneficial large scale international trade in steel and steel products in the Asia Pacific region, have been outlined by Drysdale (1992:13) as follows

… recognising the central importance of the steel industry in the continuing industrialisation and development of East Asia, participants in such an agreement could be required to

1. Encourage the expansion of production and efficient use of resources in all facets of steel production so as to contribute to raising standards of living in the region and in other countries.

2. Assure stable and continuing supplies of raw materials and open access to markets for raw materials on a commercial basis.

3. Promote free trade in steel products among participants on terms which in no way disadvantage third parties.

4. Facilitate the flow of investment into the steel industry on a commercial basis, including the flow of foreign investment through provision for national treatment of foreign investors and exemption from such national laws and regulations as inhibit foreign investment.

5. Foster internationally acceptable safety and related conditions of labour in the steel industry and related raw materials industries in the region and encourage schemes for exchange and training.

6. Promote the continuing development and transfer of new technologies on commercial terms in all aspects of production, environmental impact of the production and use of steel products.

7. Have regular consultations for the purpose of reviewing developments in regional steel trade and production and providing an opportunity for comment on any measures taken by governments or international agencies to assist the industry or its adjustment and, if appropriate, make proposals for such assistance, from the viewpoint of their consistency with the objectives of the agreement.

8. Encourage research and development on both technical and economic aspects of the development of the steel industry in the region.

9. Insure, collectively, private investors against loss from breach of the steel community agreement by one or more governments.

Most of these ingredients can only be 'supplied' by joint policy development and technical cooperation among potential participants in such an understanding, while the last point emphasises the potential need for financial cooperation to facilitate the growth of trade.

Similar types of confidence-building policy development and technical cooperation will also be needed to permit serious consideration of free trade in other vital commodities. Garnaut and Ma (1992) and Garnaut (1993) set out some similar issues relating to the prospects for substantial growth in international trade in wool, textiles and grains. Such issues need to be addressed constructively to avoid the prospect of substantially reduced potential for economic growth and trade in the region—and globally—if large and densely populated East Asian economies consider it necessary to be largely self-sufficient in basic agricultural products like foodgrains.

Based on an assessment of resource endowments and likely comparative advantage, China could quickly emerge as the largest trader in many commodities. Large-scale imports of many raw materials and foodgrains would permit a more efficient allocation of China's resources and create huge opportunities for potential suppliers. However, these opportunities will be severely restricted unless China becomes a member of the WTO. While accession continues to be blocked, China cannot have the level of confidence in the international economic environment for it to take full advantage of global export opportunities and, in turn, create correspondingly large new market opportunities for others. A very important short-term option for economic cooperation among most APEC participants is to make it clear to the United States that it is the only member which is opposed to the immediate membership of China in the WTO, based on its already demonstrated record of outward-looking policy reform.[4]

CAPACITY-BUILDING AND TRADE LIBERALISATION

To sum up, much of APEC's potential contribution to trade liberalisation is cooperative policy development, backed by support of objective economic analysis to

- improve the understanding of currently distorted markets
- find ways of reducing uncertainties
- estimate the potential effects of trade liberalisation
- monitor the progress towards free and open trade and investment achieved and expected from the progressive enhancement of IAPs.

Each of these is a form of economic and technical cooperation. Once the important role of ecotech as a necessary ingredient of trade liberalisation is accepted, that should resolve the past difficulties in integrating ecotech into the

APEC agenda, where it has tended to be seen as separate from, and competing with TILF.

The recently introduced APEC Joint Fora Meetings can be seen as a positive step. It is important, however, that the meetings not only help coordinate the various activities in APEC but also contribute to their effective integration. This means that the ecotech agenda must be relevant for TILF and vice versa. An attempt at integration was made in the EVSL initiative in which the reduction of impediments to trade in specific sectors calls for facilitation measures and ecotech cooperation. It is unfortunate that the EVSL framework has been misguided, lapsing into adversarial trade negotiations, which has meant that the various sectoral initiatives could not be implemented successfully.

APEC's contribution to trade liberalisation will be to help governments increase their capacity to reduce barriers, either unilaterally or in the course of WTO negotiations. Once efforts to liberalise border barriers to trade go beyond such capacity-building to attempt formal negotiation of 'concessions' within the APEC process, APEC no longer has comparative advantage. The region's scarce resources of policymaking capacity and goodwill can be allocated more productively to strengthening, rather than duplicating, the WTO-based multilateral trading system.

STRENGTHENING THE MULTILATERAL TRADING SYSTEM

The recent financial crisis has demonstrated that the potential benefits of highly mobile international capital will only be realised in an appropriate policy environment. In the absence of adequately managed and supervised domestic banking systems and international institutions able to respond to emerging signs of instability, short-term capital movements can be greatly destabilising and detrimental to economic growth.

Correspondingly, the potential benefits of free trade in goods and services can only be realised in the context of a rules-based and non-discriminatory multilateral trading system. The examples discussed above indicate that, in the absence of confidence about the likely behaviour of trading partners, the risks of interdependence can sometimes outweigh the potential benefits of international specialisation along lines of underlying comparative advantage. Hence the overriding shared economic interest of Asia Pacific economies to sustain and defend the WTO-based rules for international trade. Free and open trade will only be achieved if the integrity of the WTO-based system is respected by all significant economies.

In that context, the resurgence of new and serious trade disputes between the United States and the European Union (EU) is a cause for serious concern. The refusal of the EU to abide by recent WTO rulings threatens to weaken the usefulness of the dispute settlement mechanism adopted by the WTO. If that mechanism is not respected, there is a high probability that the United States will, once again, resort increasingly to unilateral judgments about the appropriateness of the trade policies of other governments, backed by threats of trade retaliation inconsistent with WTO disciplines. The potential erosion of adherence to WTO disciplines and determinations poses a far more serious threat to the prospects of continued outward-oriented rapid development in the Asia Pacific than the remnants of protection provided to some sectors of steadily declining relative importance.

The growing complexity of international economic transactions and of WTO articles, coupled with political pressures, makes it inevitable that there will be problems in meeting all WTO commitments. Disputes will continue to arise, pointing to the need for an effective dispute settlement mechanism. To defend the new dispute settlement mechanism of the WTO, a worthwhile option for cooperation among APEC leaders would be for them to make an unequivocal commitment to abide fully and promptly with any determinations by WTO dispute settlement panels. To add weight to such commitment, it would be desirable to set a timetable for enacting domestic legislation to provide for such compliance. Such commitments would form a valuable new component of IAPs aimed at achieving free and open trade and investment.

In addition to defending the current form of the WTO, there are many opportunities for economic cooperation among APEC participants, to deepen, broaden and widen the capacity of the organisation. The need for widening membership has already been discussed. Even if China is admitted in the near future, there will be some APEC participants who are not members of the WTO and such a situation may persist as APEC admits new participants. An important contribution of economic cooperation within APEC would be for their governments to undertake that all other APEC participants will be treated no less favourably in terms of trade policy than WTO trading partners.

Since the end of the Uruguay Round, increased attention has been given to the links between trade and other policy areas, including investment, competition policy, environmental management and labour standards. These will need to be addressed, but it does not always follow that they should all be dealt with in the WTO; otherwise that organisation would also stray from its comparative advantage. There are opportunities for Asia Pacific governments to set positive WTO-consistent examples for others to follow, though not necessarily within the explicit context of the WTO.

It should be possible to adopt gradually more precise guiding principles for the conduct of policies, such as competition policies, which have implications for trade policy. In each case these guiding principles can incorporate the fundamental WTO principles of transparency, non-discriminatory and national treatment. At the outset, cooperative policy development can encourage the adoption of non-binding principles; once such principles prove useful, APEC governments can be encouraged to incorporate them in relevant domestic legislation. Cooperative development of approaches to new policy areas can also help ensure that appropriate account is given to the diverse needs of economies at different stages of development.

There is also scope for deepening, by dismantling the remaining border barriers to trade in areas already covered by the WTO. APEC governments can contribute to that effort most effectively by setting positive examples. A strong political commitment to the full liberalisation of information technology products by APEC leaders in November 1996 led to swift agreement on binding schedules for the WTO-wide dismantling of protection in a sector where free trade can help boost economic development and where several APEC economies are highly competitive. However, the information technology precedent has not proved easy to follow.

EARLY VOLUNTARY SECTORAL LIBERALISATION

In November 1997, APEC leaders agreed to the early voluntary sectoral liberalisation of nine sectors.[5] By early 1998, the 'V' had disappeared from EVSL and the process turned into a GATT-style trade negotiation to establish a balance of the short-term political costs of trade liberalisation among participants. By November, 16 out of the then 18 APEC participants had agreed on concerted action in terms of trade liberalisation, facilitation and technical cooperation for 7 out of the 9 nominated sectors.[6] Despite this progress, almost all the reporting about trade liberalisation at the Kuala Lumpur meeting focused on the refusal by Japan—already a large importer of fisheries and forest products—to open these particular markets to a greater extent.

Much less attention was given to the reality that the United States administration has no legal authority to deliver on any EVSL commitments. EVSL cannot remain viable without such authority, but that is only likely to be granted if the EU is willing to match such commitment. APEC governments have agreed to table the agreements they have reached on EVSL as an 'offer' in the WTO; these offers should be sufficient to test the willingness of the EU to respond by comparable offers. If there is such a response—as there was in the case of information technology products—all APEC and EU governments could bind their reductions in protection in the WTO. This would be an extremely significant step towards global free and open trade and investment.

EVSL has led to some progress, but transforming part of the APEC process into a negotiating forum carries risks. With widening membership, it will be increasingly difficult to set up 'package deals' to balance an ever-wider range of diverse sectoral interests and it would be counter-productive to recreate a false perception that 'opening to the outside world' is a concession to others, rather than of intrinsic benefit to the economies which undertake these reforms. Nevertheless, it may be possible to identify, cooperatively, some sectors where a significant number of APEC participants can see a shared interest in early, and genuinely voluntary, liberalisation.

This approach would accept that EVSL is not the vehicle for attempting to negotiate involuntary liberalisation of sensitive sectors. Instead, it would be more productive to concentrate on sectors where protection has not yet become entrenched, as was the case for information technology. While the immediate economic gains would not be large, it would help ensure that these do not evolve into the sensitive sectors of the future and would also help APEC governments to show joint leadership in the WTO. It may also be possible to identify some sectors—especially energy-intensive sectors—where the original reasons for protection have been weakened by changes in circumstances.

STRENGTHENING ECONOMIC INFRASTRUCTURE

Border barriers to trade and investment, and costs imposed by divergent approaches to commercial regulation are not the only transaction costs on international economic transactions. There are also natural barriers of distance and poor communications. Shortages of economic infrastructure, or inefficient operation of existing capacity, can also impose heavy costs on international trade and investment.

A recent estimate by the World Bank (1995) indicated that the developing East Asian economies alone would need between US$1.2 trillion and US$1.5 trillion for infrastructure investment in the decade ending in 2004. Additions to infrastructure—ranging from ports, telecommunications, power generation to sewerage facilities and enhancing the efficiency of their operations—will be vital for sustained economic growth in general and for TILF in particular. An important component of any program to facilitate trade and investment is to reduce the costs currently imposed by transport and communications bottlenecks.

The current slump in activity might reduce, temporarily, the urgency of investment in economic infrastructure, but trillions of dollars will still need to be found and spent on infrastructure projects in the near future. It is widely accepted that such amounts are far beyond the capacity of Asia Pacific governments' savings, let alone their 'windows' for concessional financing. The bulk of these essential infrastructure investments will need to be financed with private risk capital.[7]

Nevertheless, there is a great deal that governments can do to help ensure that the necessary private investment occurs at the time it is needed, rather than after costly bottlenecks develop. Policy development is also necessary to try to minimise the costs and risks of such investment, which are ultimately passed on to users. Moreover, the design and implementation of sound policies towards infrastructure can be enhanced through economic and technical cooperation.

The customs procedures and passport control examples discussed above illustrate how the need for new physical investment can be reduced by the more efficient operation of existing facilities based on policy development and technical cooperation among Asia Pacific governments. Technical cooperation can also help attract, on reasonable terms, the risk capital which will still be needed on a large scale to build new economic infrastructure.

Cooperative policy development work by APEC officials, combined with technical cooperation, can improve the framework for attracting commercial investment, including by strengthening financial markets, or by creating the policy environment needed in cases where several Asia Pacific economies may need to cooperate in order to facilitate investment in infrastructure—for example, in sub-regional power or irrigation schemes.

APEC is already seeking ways to enhance the prospects for large-scale private investment in economic infrastructure. In November 1997, APEC leaders endorsed the 'Vancouver Framework for Enhanced Public-Private Partnerships in Infrastructure Development'. Such partnerships will be essential to finance and manage the enhancement of economic infrastructure needed in the Asia Pacific region in order to meet its economic, environmental and social goals.

Within this framework, multilateral financial institutions are to catalyse and support efforts by each APEC economy to enhance their policy environment for facilitating flows of private capital while continuing to raise private capital on their own account to finance infrastructure development. Several export credit agencies and export financing institutions have signed a protocol for mutual cooperation in order to enhance the attractiveness of private sector investment in infrastructure. There is also scope for redesigning the lending rules of multilateral development cooperation agencies to make it simpler for them to raise funds for activities in several neighbouring economies.

Region-wide technical cooperation can also help to gather and disseminate information on best practices for policies to facilitate large-scale private investment in economic infrastructure. A lot of information has been gained about the design of effective and transparent tendering procedures and about options for sharing risks between investors and users—for example, through combinations of performance guarantees, pricing and risk sharing. Potential investors would also welcome the establishment of a region-wide database describing current policies of Asia Pacific governments which are relevant to their commercial assessments. Following a Canadian initiative, an APEC Infrastructure Facilitation Center is expected to be established in future (Potter 1998).

Economic cooperation can also contribute on the demand side. The present slump in East Asian economic activity provides the breathing space to ease some severe infrastructure bottlenecks, but the financial sector problems make it relatively less likely that investors will be attracted to new infrastructure projects.However, even on very pessimistic estimates of the time taken for rapid growth to recommence, many infrastructure projects with long lead times remain potentially commercially viable. Credible economic forecasting work by APEC committees and working groups can foreshadow the need for further timely investments in economic infrastructure.

ENHANCING INSTITUTIONAL AND TECHNOLOGICAL CAPACITY

The preceding sections have sought to demonstrate the many ways in which economic and technical cooperation among Asia Pacific economies can contribute to financial recovery, to economic infrastructure and to continued progress in terms of TILF. Many of these activities are already underway; these as well as potential opportunities for cooperation are essentially exercises in capacity-building by means of cooperative policy development and technical cooperation. The opportunities for technical cooperation involve pooling the information, experience and best available expertise and technology in the Asia Pacific, then disseminating it throughout the region in order to enhance institutional and technological capacity.

Such cooperative policy development and technical cooperation, with considerable emphasis on human resource development, are also the main ingredients of cooperative efforts to enhance the management of all sectors. Cooperative policy development has been carried out by APEC's committees and working groups since 1990, contributing to progress in cooperation in many sectoral activities to improve information and reduce transactions costs. The work performed by these groups is reasonably similar to the sectoral policy analysis and development work of the OECD, but requires far fewer resources and carries far fewer bureaucratic overheads.

APEC governments are financing, and should continue to finance, the bulk of the costs of policy development, partly by sending relevant officials to working meetings, but also by devoting resources to substantial preparations for these meetings. They can, and do, make use of relevant policy development work by others, such as PECC task forces. In addition, APEC committees have drawn on APEC's modest 'central' budget to commission specialised tasks of data gathering or policy-oriented research, especially when there is a need for evaluation and interpretation of options of achievements by independent analysts.

TECHNOLOGICAL CAPACITY

There is considerable scope for technical cooperation to reduce the environmental costs of rapid economic development by helping to ensure that all of the region has both access and the ability to make use of the least-polluting technology for a wide range of industries. Yamazawa (1997) lists a series of 'model projects' to encourage fast-growing Asia Pacific economies to adopt clean coal and efficient energy use technology. These projects are designed to adapt an environmentally-friendly technology developed in one Asia Pacific economy, install it in a plant of another economy and provide the training needed to use it.

Typically such products transfer technology between a pair of economies. APEC can provide a framework in which industry managers from anywhere in the Asia Pacific can be familiarised with and trained in the use of the most efficient technology available in the region. Compared to a proliferation of bilateral projects, such a regional approach can create efficiencies of both scale and scope.

There are many other ways in which Asia Pacific governments can cooperate to enhance the capacity of their researchers and producers to absorb and adapt and disseminate new technologies as well as to begin to build the capacity for basic research. Governments can also contribute to technological development by creating a competitive environment which encourages innovation. Those in the region can also draw, to some extent, on the relevant experience of European governments. Several Asia Pacific governments—including Korea, Singapore and Taiwan—have already set up centres for promoting technological capacity-building. There is scope for linking such initiatives through a network of National Innovation Systems, which can share the technology and experience gained by each centre in terms of developing and disseminating new technologies.

HUMAN RESOURCE DEVELOPMENT

Technical cooperation relies very heavily on the design and delivery of human resource development programs. The success of many options to facilitate trade and investment—such as the mutual recognition of standards—depends on confidence in the willingness as well as the capacity of each APEC economy to ensure compliance with their own domestic standards. That, in turn, requires a massive training effort.

The need for enhanced institutional capacity to support sustained economic growth goes well beyond cooperative activities to support TILF. For example, the financial crisis highlighted the desirability of well-structured bankruptcy procedures to sort out the after-effects of financial shocks. Cooperative policy development can help each economy identify the type of bankruptcy legislation and procedures suited to each Asia Pacific economies, drawing on the experience of others. But once new procedures are legislated, there is an even greater human resource development challenge to ensure that new institutions are staffed by competent people.

Similar institution-building and training needs arise in all sectors. In many Asia Pacific economies, there is an urgent need to upgrade the ability to administer, as well as update, commercial legislation and regulations. This needs to be supported by training in the administration of sectoral policies—for example to provide and manage a policy environment which can encourage private sector investment in economic infrastructure.

As noted earlier, the need for training for managing new institutions and implementing new policies is an ongoing task as those trained move to, or are promoted to, other occupations. Meeting these needs provides an excellent opportunity for region-wide cooperation. Each Asia Pacific economy could implement its own training programs. However, there are significant economies of scope to be gained by having staff with potentially similar future responsibilities undergoing their training together as a way of fostering mutual respect and trust in eachothers' competence.

IMPLEMENTING TECHNICAL COOPERATION

Cooperative policy development can be implemented using the existing structure and modest financial resources of APEC committees and working groups, drawing on (and perhaps commissioning) policy research by others, such as the PECC. By contrast, widespread benefits to Asia Pacific economies from technical cooperation will need substantially greater resources than the funds at the joint disposal of APEC Ministers. The very large number of ongoing training programs that could be usefully established on a region-wide basis will all need resources such as buildings, training materials, payments for the design and updating of curriculae and for trainers. Such costs are in addition to the direct and opportunity costs of the time of those being trained.

All APEC governments can benefit from financing such activities. But that should not lead to the establishment of a new regional ecotech bureaucracy with a large central budget. There is now widespread agreement that APEC should play a catalytic, rather than direct role in implementing projects which APEC leaders jointly identify to be of region-wide benefit. The challenge is to forge partnerships with existing development cooperation agencies as well as with the business/private sector to turn ideas into tangible cooperative activities.[8]

Re-orienting development cooperation agencies. Many APEC governments already manage development cooperation agencies which provide resources for institution-building, human resource development and upgrading technological capability. In most cases, these are carried out on a bilateral basis. As already explained, there are large economies of scope as well as scale to be gained by cooperation among several governments to set up regional, rather than economy-specific activities. Such a cooperative approach can ensure the dissemination of the best expertise and techniques available anywhere in the region. Moreover, as discussed above, human resource development activities to support the implementation of cooperative arrangements for trade or investment facilitation will be most effective if regional administrators receive at least some of their training together.

To take advantage of such opportunities and potential gains from coordination, APEC governments will need to review the priorities of their own international development agencies. This may involve some diversion of resources from bilateral activities to regional projects which are designed to benefit several (ideally all) Asia Pacific economies and which are more consistent with the principles of the 1996 Manila Declaration on economic cooperation and development. Some existing agencies have already taken responsibility for implementing activities proposed by APEC working groups, and more agencies can be encouraged to consider shifting their emphasis to supporting projects of region-wide significance emerging from APEC, rather than projects with a narrower, bilateral focus. The recent Australian Government initiative for enhancing the capacity for economic governance in the region provides a positive example.

Once APEC governments have set priorities for technical cooperation, they will have considerable potential collective influence over the priorities and activities of multilateral development agencies, particularly the ADB. Such development agencies have the institutional capacity to raise the funds required and to select firms best qualified to construct physical facilities, and for the day-to-day management of technical cooperation projects.

Engaging the business/private sector—Partnership for Equitable Growth. In its 1997 report to APEC leaders, ABAC confirmed the willingness of the business sector to give direct support to APEC's economic cooperation and development agenda by establishing a 'Partnership for Equitable Growth' (PEG). PEG is to serve as a new framework to encourage business participation in economic and technical cooperation activities, noting that the private sector can add value by undertaking projects in areas where neither the market nor governments currently meet regional needs. This initiative by ABAC was welcomed and endorsed by APEC leaders in Vancouver and should commence in 1999.

PEG is expected to facilitate project funding by coordinating partnerships and/or joint ventures involving private capital, multilateral development cooperation agencies, and foundations. Activities for potential support through PEG would be selected in accordance with the objectives, guiding principles and priorities expressed in the 'Manila Declaration on an Asia Pacific Economic Cooperation Framework for Strengthening Economic Cooperation and Development'. In selecting cooperative activities for support, PEG intends to focus on activities that

- will benefit at least two Asia Pacific economies in order to reflect the community-building goal of APEC and ecotech
- can be financially self-sustaining and business/private sector led in execution
- are endorsed by governments of APEC economies, in order to underline the importance of forging partnerships between governments and the business/private sector.

PEG itself is to be a business/private sector-oriented organisation, designed to act as a 'merchant bank of ideas' by forming partnerships or joint ventures to implement particular ecotech projects. These are likely to include activities to promote human resource development, technological capacity, and education in information technology. Each activity is expected to be implemented initially on a small scale, then possibly be expanded if it proves successful and financially self-sustaining.

SUMMARY AND RECOMMENDATIONS

The financial crisis has clarified both the limitations and the potential of APEC. While trade and investment issues are important, it has become evident that economic cooperation needs to be far more broadly based in order to nurture a sense of community.

There are some welcome signs of recovery from the crisis, but much remains to be done to shore up the foundations for resumed rapid growth and to limit the risks of similar crises of confidence. Cooperation among Asia Pacific economies can help to accelerate and facilitate the costly, short-term effort of restructuring and the multi-year capacity-building effort needed to create better-managed and more robust financial sectors. It has been recognised that these are essentially tasks of economic and technical cooperation among Asia Pacific governments, in either a regional or global context. This perception will help to convince the region's leaders that ecotech is at the heart of the APEC process.

Since the signing of the 'Manila Declaration on an Asia Pacific Economic Cooperation Framework for Strengthening Economic Cooperation and Development' there have been constructive moves, by the business/private sector as well as by governments, to turn that conceptual framework into a new operational model of development cooperation. Several hundred projects are under way, but a sense of frustration and several misunderstandings persists.

There remains a wide range of incompatible expectations about the nature of the cooperative activities which could be promoted collectively by APEC governments and how these could be financed and implemented. That is being compounded by an inadequate appreciation of the current and potential role of existing agencies in promoting the new ideas for ecotech emerging from the APEC process.

A further serious problem is the unduly sharp dichotomy which has come to be drawn between work to promote TILF and other forms of cooperation. Moreover, ecotech activities are often seen as residual, and not part of the drive towards free and open trade and investment.

If ecotech and TILF continue to be seen as separate, competing strands of the APEC process, it will be hard to build a sense of shared economic interests and mutual respect. The difficult experience with EVSL in 1998 showed that TILF can quickly come to be perceived as an adversarial negotiating process, rather than a joint cooperative effort with all-round benefits. To avoid such problems, this chapter advocates an integrated view of the APEC process within which all cooperative activities are seen as ways to strengthen the capacity of Asia Pacific economies to reach their full potential for sustainable economic growth.

The basic challenge is to improve the capacity of all Asia Pacific economies to enhance their productive resources and to allocate them in an increasingly efficient and sustainable way. Cooperation among APEC economies can help by sharing the information, experience, expertise and technology needed to design and administer a progressively more efficient set of economic policies to achieve these ends. The PECC Competition Principles provide a valuable reference point for cooperation to encourage and enable all Asia Pacific economies to adopt more efficient policies for all markets. Economic and technical cooperation which improves the ability of Asia Pacific governments to reduce impediments to trade and investment through unilateral or co-ordinated reforms—that is, TILF—is an important part, but only one part, of this overall cooperative effort.

The paper sets out the opportunities for cooperative policy development and technical cooperation to
- strengthen domestic and international financial markets
- facilitate trade and investment
- liberalise traditional border barriers to trade
- defend and strengthen the multilateral trading system
- develop the capacity of economic infrastructure.

Many of the challenges in these areas—including those recommended by other papers to PAFTAD 25—are, in large part, challenges of capacity-building through economic and technical cooperation.

RECOMMENDATIONS FOR IMPLEMENTING ECOTECH

The general objective should be to encourage and enable Asia Pacific economies to continue to strengthen their economic policy framework in order to enhance their available productive resources and promote their efficient allocation. This can be achieved by means of a combination of cooperative policy development and technical cooperation, with particular emphasis on human resource development and institution-building.

Cooperative policy development among APEC economies parallels what the OECD is seeking to promote in a very different context. In the Asia Pacific, an evolutionary approach which is less bureaucratic, less expensive and less centralised should continue to be followed. APEC committees and working groups, which are already engaged in such work, should be encouraged to draw more intensively on existing networks such as the PECC and APEC Study Centres. There is no need for a large new bureaucracy.

Technical cooperation should focus on a small number of well-defined priorities, such as

- strengthening financial sectors
- promoting progressively closer adherence to principles based on the PECC Competition Principles, which are likely to be endorsed by APEC leaders
- sectoral analysis to help demonstrate the significant long-term net benefits of reducing impediments to trade in key sectors such as financial services, air and maritime transport, iron and steel products and foodgrains.

Long-term programs for technical cooperation should be developed in each of these areas, focusing on human resource development and institution-building. Once such programs are endorsed by APEC leaders, they should invite APEC governments, regional and multilateral development banks and the business/ private sector to mobilise resources to finance the technical cooperation programs jointly identified by APEC, and to make arrangements for their ongoing implementation.

ABAC has already indicated how the business sector can support APEC's ecotech agenda by establishing PEG. PEG is to serve as a new framework to encourage business participation in technical cooperation activities. APEC leaders should continue to encourage such innovative contributions.

APEC governments should be encouraged to include their commitment to promote specific aspects of the priority technical cooperation programs endorsed by APEC leaders as a significant part of their IAPs. This would emphasise the natural link between the policy reform aspects and ecotech aspects of promoting progress towards the Bogor vision of free and open trade and investment. Where possible, APEC governments should be encouraged to promote technical cooperation projects jointly; their contributions to such cooperative activities could be included as part of APEC's Collective Action Plans (CAPs).

It is also important to note that APEC governments, collectively, are well placed to direct regional and multilateral development banks to take up significant components of long-term human resource development and institution-building programs endorsed by APEC leaders.

REFERENCES

Asia Pacific Economic Cooperation (APEC), 1991. 'Seoul APEC Declaration', Ministerial Declaration, Seoul, November.

——, 1994. 'Bogor Declaration of Common Resolve', 2nd APEC leaders meeting, Bogor, November.

——, 1995. 'Osaka Action Agenda', Ministerial Declaration, Osaka, November.

——, 1996a. 'Manila Declaration on an Asia Pacific Economic Cooperation Framework for Strengthening Economic Cooperation and Development', Ministerial Declaration, Manila, November.

——, 1996b. 'Manila Action Plan for APEC', Manila, November.

——, 1997. 'Vancouver Framework for Enhanced Public-Private Partnerships in Infrastructure Development', Vancouver, November.

APEC Business Advisory Council (ABAC), 1997. 'APEC Means Business: ABAC's Call to Action', 1997 report to APEC leaders, APEC Secretariat, Singapore, November.

Bora, B. and Findlay, C., 1996. 'Introduction and overview', in B. Bora and C. Findlay (eds), *Regional Integration and the Asia Pacific*, Oxford University Press, Melbourne.

Drysdale, P., 1992. 'Next steps in Asia Pacific Economic Cooperation: an East Asian steel community', in P. Drysdale (ed.), *in East Asia, the East Asia Steel Industry*, Research School of Pacific and Asian Studies, The Australian National University, Canberra.

Elek, A. and Wilson, D., 1999. 'The East Asian crisis and international capital markets', *Asian-Pacific Economic Literature*, 13(1):1–21.

Elek, A. (ed.), 1997. *Building an Asia Pacific Economic Community: development cooperation within APEC*, The Foundation for Development Cooperation, Brisbane.

Foundation for Development Cooperation (FDC), 1998. 'Forging new partnerships: economic and technical cooperation and the APEC process',

Report of meetings and recommendations to APEC and ABAC, Kuala Lumpur, 2 December 1997 and 10 August 1998, FDC, Brisbane, December.

Garnaut, R. and Ma, G., 1992. *Grain in China*, East Asia Analytical Unit, Department of Foreign Affairs and Trade, Canberra.

Garnaut, R., 1993. 'Strategies for growth in the Chinese wool textile industry and the role of Sino-Australian cooperation, Keynote address to the Symposium Wool—Australia and China: the natural partners, Beijing.

Intal, P., 1997. 'Towards strengthening development cooperation in the Asia Pacific: hardware vs software', in A. Elek (ed.), *Building an Asia-Pacific Economic Community: development cooperation within APEC*, FDC, Brisbane.

Japan International Cooperation Agency (JICA), 1995. APEC Partners for Progress (PFP), research report, Tokyo.

Morrison, C.E., 1997. 'Development cooperation in the 21st century: implications for APEC', in A. Elek (ed.), *Building an Asia-Pacific Economic Community: development cooperation within APEC*, FDC, Brisbane.

Petri, P., 1998. 'Role of Asia Pacific governments in supporting ecotech activities identified by APEC', remarks to the *Second APEC Dialogue on Economic and Technical Cooperation*, Kuala Lumpur, 10 August.

Pacific Economic Cooperation Council (PECC), 1995a. *Milestones in APEC Liberalisation: a map of market opening measures by APEC economies*, PECC Secretariat, Singapore.

——, 1995b. *Survey of Impediments to Trade and Investment in the APEC region*, PECC Secretariat, Singapore.

——, 1996a. 'Road Map for APEC and the WTO: business priorities and policy leadership', report of Trade Policy Forum IX, Seoul, PECC Secretariat, Singapore.

——, 1996b. *Perspectives on the Manila Action Plan for APEC*, PECC Secretariat, Singapore.

——, 1999. 'Principles for guiding the development of a competition-driven policy framework for APEC economies', report of Trade Policy Forum Competition Principles Project, Singapore.

Pomfret, R., 1998. 'Regionalism in Europe and the Asia Pacific economy', in P. Drysdale and D. Vines (eds), *Europe, East Asia and APEC: a shared global agenda?*, Cambridge, University Press, Cambridge.

Potter, P., 1988. 'APEC infrastructure facilitation center: a mediating structure for interdependent nonconvergent political economy', paper to the

Conference Regionalism, and Global Affairs in the Post-Cold War Era: the European Union, APEC and the new international political economy, International Institute for Asian Studies, Leiden University and the APEC Studies Center, University of Washington, held in Brussels, March.

Stiglitz, J., 1998. 'Must financial crises be this frequent and this painful', McKay Lecture, Pittsburgh, Pennsylvania, 23 September. Available online at <http://www.worldbank.org/html/extdr/extme/js-092398/index.htm>.

World Bank, 1995. *Infrastructure Development in East Asia and the Pacific: towards a new public-private partnership*, The World Bank, Washington, DC.

Yamazawa, I., Nakayama, S. and Kitamura, H., 1996. 'Asia Pacific cooperation in energy and environment', in I. Yamazawa and A. Hirata (eds), *APEC: Cooperation from Diversity*, Institute of Developing Economies, Tokyo.

Yamazawa, I., 1997. 'APEC's economic and technical cooperation: evolution and tasks ahead', in A. Elek (ed.), *Building an Asia-Pacific Economic Community: development cooperation within APEC*, FDC, Brisbane.

NOTES

This paper was originally prepared for the 25th annual conference of the Pacific Trade and Development (PAFTAD) Conference held in Osaka, Japan, 16–18 June 1999.

[1] The authors would like to acknowledge the contribution of The Foundation for Development Cooperation, based in Brisbane Australia. With its support, a group of Asia Pacific researchers (including the authors) and officials in their private capacity met several times between 1995 and 1998 to consider opportunities for economic and technical cooperation to be promoted by APEC, as well as to design a conceptual framework which helped to shape the 1996 'Manila Declaration on an Asia Pacific Economic Cooperation Framework for Strengthening Economic Cooperationand Development'. A previous version of this paper was presented to an international conference on 'APEC liberalisation and the Chinese economy' in Beijing, in October 1998. The authors are grateful for the comments received at that time and subsequently from Ippei Yamazawa.

[2] Some of many recent proposals, including for 'bailing-in' lenders in the event of financial crises, are reviewed in Elek and Wilson (1999).

[3] PECC (1999) proposes a set of competition policy principles for consideration and adoption by APEC governments.

4   In the longer term, the United States will also need to be persuaded to repeal current legislation (the Jackson-Vanek amendment) which prevents an assurance of unconditional most-favoured-nation (MFN) treatment of imports from China.

5   The nine sectors were environmental goods and services, fish and fish products, toys, forest products, gems and jewellery, chemicals, the energy sector, medical equipment and instruments and telecommunications mutual recognition arrangements.

6   Mexico and Chile did not participate in the EVSL exercise as they were already committed to a schedule for elimination of border barriers across the board.

7   See Intal, in Elek (1997).

8   The following remarks on technical cooperation draw on FDC (1998).

11

PROMOTING APEC'S ECOTECH INITIATIVE

CHEN LUZHI

The Bogor Declaration was adopted by the APEC in 1994 to make trade and investment liberalisation and development cooperation the two wheels of the APEC process. The Action Agenda adopted by the APEC Osaka meeting in 1995 was accordingly divided into two major parts: trade and investment liberalisation, and economic and technical cooperation (the equivalent of development cooperation). The Manila meeting in 1996 adopted the Action Plan which also included these two parts and the 'Declaration on an Asia Pacific Economic Cooperation Framework for Strengthening Economic Cooperation and Development', which lay down the guiding principles and priorities of economic and technical cooperation (ecotech). At the 1997 Vancouver meeting, APEC decided to establish an Ecotech Subcommittee of APEC Senior Officials (SOM). Their role was to review ecotech proposals from various APEC working groups, set priorities and promote implementation, and draw on the resources of the business sector and existing development agencies. Over the past four years, APEC has done a lot to promote economic and technical cooperation. Despite this, and repeated calls from APEC leaders to strengthen ecotech, it still lags far behind trade and investment liberalisation. This is mainly because a big gap exists between the goal of economic and technical cooperation set out in the Bogor Declaration, and the measures taken thereafter.

The Bogor Declaration states that '[m]embers are...committed to intensifying development cooperation to enhance the capacity for sustainable growth and equitable development while reducing economic disparities among APEC economies and improving economic and social wellbeing'. Accelerating development, reducing disparities, alleviating poverty and enhancing wellbeing have been the objectives and functions of numerous multilateral institutions. In the United Nations there is the United Nations Development Programme; in the

197

Asia Pacific region there is the Asian Development Bank. Developed countries provide official development assistance bilaterally—more or less—for the same purpose. As a regional, multilateral and governmental forum, APEC has been committed to promoting regional economic cooperation since its establishment in 1989. Seven work projects were designated then, three more were added at the 1991 APEC Seoul meeting, and thus ten working groups were established. When the Bogor Declaration was adopted in 1994, the ten working groups undertook roughly 200 projects. Why, then, did the Bogor Declaration put forward the new concept of 'development cooperation'?

First, because the developing economies of APEC held that trade and investment liberalisation alone cannot solve all the problems of their further development. The financial crisis that began in Southeast Asia in July 1997 has proved this. Within the APEC framework, there exist differences not only between developed and developing economies, but also differences between developing economies. As a result of rapid development over the past two decades, some developing economies have become newly industrialising economies and others 'new' newly industrialising economies. They need and can provide mutual support among themselves without rendering their relationship into the conventional pattern of donor and recipient.

Second, due to the financial constraints of developed economies, developing economies can no longer rely on their assistance in infrastructure development and instead must mobilise the resources of the private sector through the market. Furthermore, they need an institution such as APEC to act as a catalyst in exchanging information, promoting policy dialogue, and helping members with related interests carry out practical cooperation. Therefore, the Bogor Declaration established a new path for development cooperation which differs from traditional development assistance.

The 1995 Osaka Action Agenda was actually a compilation of the projects undertaken by various working groups. Economic and technical cooperation was dealt with separately in part of the Action Agenda, and included 13 areas, consisting of the 10 areas covered by the original 10 working groups and 3 new areas. At the same time there was emphasis on departure from the conventional modality of donor-recipient relationships. However, it did not include specific measures to meet the requirements of the Bogor Declaration. The Manila Declaration of 1996 set 4 goals, 4 guiding principles and 6 priority areas for APEC's ecotech, and clearly defined a way to assess cooperation achievements. It was that ecotech must be goal-oriented, with explicit objectives, milestones and performance criteria. It also called on the public sector to create a suitable environment for private sector initiative. Thus the ecotech activities would combine government actions, private sector projects and joint public-private activities, and should draw on voluntary contributions commensurate with member economies' capabilities and generate direct and broadly-shared benefits among member economies to reduce economic disparities. Ecotech can be said to have made a big step forward with the adoption of the Manila Declaration. But the problem of implementation for ecotech activities remains to be solved.

The Manila Action Plan for APEC (MAPA), adopted in 1996, contained a progress report on joint ecotech activities, giving an overview of 320 joint activities and 151 sub-activities. The action plan for trade and investment liberalisation consists of the individual action plans submitted by each of the member economies. Each activity in ecotech is coordinated by its lead 'shepherd'— generally the original proponent of the activity—and participated in by other members on a voluntary basis. Classified by type, almost two-thirds of the activities are survey/research and seminars, which are followed up by publications, data, compilation and training. The activity is usually a 'pet project' of a member economy and is coordinated and mainly financed by it with a certain amount of support from APEC Central Funds.

The total budget of APEC for 1997, approved at the Manila Ministerial Meeting, was only US$809,000 which severely limited its contribution to ecotech. Against this background the APEC SOM Subcommittee on ecotech made an evaluation report in April 1998 on 238 activities underway in APEC which appeared to support one or more of the six priority areas set by the Manila Declaration. The report found a high incidence of duplication of effort and some activities appeared to fall short of the Manila Declaration's injunction that they be 'goal oriented with explicit objectives, milestones and performance criteria'. Most project outcomes are oriented more towards process than easily measurable results such as studies, training for APEC officials, and new databases. The extent of economies' interest and participation varies widely from one activity to another. The East Asian financial crisis has had a negative impact on members' participation in activities. Business relevance and participation also vary widely among priorities. Business interest appears to be higher in cases where it has been included in work program design compared to the various roundtables soliciting business views on general topics.

On the whole, ecotech remains within the original framework of working groups, despite great efforts to bring about a change. There is little doubt that the activities of the working groups have achieved a lot. But generally speaking, this kind of economic and technical cooperation falls well short of the requirements of the Bogor Declaration and the Manila Declaration.

THE CONCEPT OF ECOTECH

From 'development cooperation' in the Bogor Declaration to 'economic and technical cooperation' in the Osaka Action Agenda, the change is evidence that there are different views on the concept among APEC members. What is crucial is the word 'development'. The conceptual squabbling during the past several APEC annual meetings has helped to develop a series of principles, priorities and requirements. Yet economic and technical cooperation is still in a difficult position to go beyond the original framework of working groups mainly because it lacks a driving mechanism. The reason for the continuous progress of trade and investment liberalisation lies in the fact that its mechanism—that is, 'concerted unilateral actions'—was formulated at the Osaka meeting. Economic and technical cooperation has to follow the way of working groups because it has failed to find a driving mechanism and this failure is the result of a conceptual barrier. Developing countries consider development as their top priority, just as developed countries value the removal of trade and investment barriers through liberalisation most highly. Development and liberalisation are of course not contradictory to one another. APEC is trying to prove this through its deeds. Developed economies in APEC consider development and development assistance as one and the same. They see development as one way to transfer capital and technology from developed to developing economies. Replacing 'development cooperation' with the term 'economic and technical cooperation' is aimed at clarifying the point that cooperation means pooling resources, and yields-shared benefits, making it different from development assistance. It is generally accepted that APEC cannot become another assistance agency. But it is not clear how and where to pool resources and what APEC can do to promote this process. Hence the difficulty in progress. Developed economies are not enthusiastic about economic and technical cooperation because they want the APEC process to benefit them more. How to define the concept of economic and technical cooperation still creates debate.

Some APEC developed economies indicate that they are not opposed to economic and technical cooperation *per se*. However, they see the following as problematic

- if capital flow is involved, it is beyond the control of the government because money is in the hands of businessmen
- their governments provide development assistance in varying amounts, but it is somewhat complicated to divert some of the money to APEC programs because both the donors and the recipients have to be consulted
- APEC is an institution of cooperation based on voluntarism, in which the principles of equality and mutual benefit must be strictly observed.

With respect to the first point, APEC leaders have stated that a partnership between government and the business sector can be established. At the Vancouver meeting, APEC leaders endorsed the 'Vancouver Framework for Enhanced Public-Private Partnership in Infrastructure Development'. The APEC Business Advisory Council has decided to establish a 'Partnership for Equitable Growth' to encourage business participation in economic and technical cooperation. This has been endorsed by APEC leaders.

On the second point, it has been agreed that APEC should bring the existing development assistance agencies into play and selectively channel the bilateral development assistance of developed member economies and multilateral assistance into APEC cooperation projects. Some projects under APEC working groups have already received help from multilateral assistance agencies. Regarding the third point, the 'conflict between the North and the South' should be avoided on the understanding that the North and the South should become partners without insisting that the North is in debt to the South.

But this is easier said than done. Public-private partnership is one example. The business sector requests suitable conditions for their participation first, such as maintaining a healthy macroeconomic environment, ensuring a stable and transparent legal system exists, providing efficient infrastructure services and strengthening the domestic capital market.

In order to use the existing assistance agencies, an effective channel needs to be in place. Within APEC, donors of bilateral and multilateral assistance are just a few. It is said that international multilateral assistance agencies generally find APEC projects insufficiently attractive. Suggestions have been made to cancel those projects. It is not so easy.

According to Yamazawa, individual ecotech activities are proposed voluntarily by individual member governments as their 'pet projects'. Nobody in APEC oversees all ecotech activities. When the APEC Economic Committee was in charge of ecotech, its report only gave a long-term perspective on the ecotech activities, and no comments on existing problems. Most activites are small technical cooperation projects with small budgets, so there is peer pressure on member governments to refrain from proposing big, significant projects. The progress report on MAPA gives sufficient justification for individual ecotech activities so that one can hardly reject any of them as inadequate or having little impact on the Bogor goal. 'Goal oriented', 'explicit milestones', and 'explicit performance criteria' sound good but they are abstract. Yamazawa's critical view cannot be simply taken as Japanese prejudice. But the activities of working groups constitute the mainstay of the current economic and technical cooperation. Although the SOM Subcommittee on ecotech has been instructed by APEC leaders to review working group activities according to the Manila Declaration, what concrete action can be taken is still under question because the coverage of the six priority areas set by the Declaration is so broad that 238 project activities undertaken or proposed by various working groups have been included. If the working group framework remains the mainstay, ecotech will basically remain at the level of roundtable-type cooperation, with exchanges of information and views the main activities.

This mode of operation was designed to be based on the principle of mutual benefit, taking into account differences in the stages of economic development and in socio-political systems, and giving due consideration to the needs of developing economies as well as a commitment to open dialogue and consensus building, with equal respect for the views of all participants. This type of cooperation, judged by the 17 year experience of the Pacific Economic Cooperation Council (PECC)—the forerunner of APEC—usually takes the preference of individual members as a guide. A project proposed by a member, once accepted, generally is not to be rejected by other members. APEC wishes to take over this practice, not only for the purpose of balancing trade and investment liberalisation but also to counter the inadequacy of 'development cooperation' put forward by the Bogor Declaration, which aimed to replace roundtable cooperation with action-oriented cooperation having explicit objectives, tasks and measures. It is not clear how to make the adjustment. Hence the old practice continues. Even after the adoption of the Manila Declaration, the proposal of new activities in accordance with the six priority areas still occurs in the old way. The old way cannot be easily replaced because the old idea has not been displaced.

Obviously the concept of ecotech has to be further clarified if the principles of the Bogor Declaration are to be upheld and development cooperation— 'economic and technical cooperation' essentially has the same meaning—is to be pursued in earnest to achieve the goal of 2020, promoting development, reducing disparities and enhancing well-being. It is not conventional development assistance. It is also not economic and technical cooperation in its literal sense. Ecotech is an extension of APEC's original roundtable-style cooperation.

THE MECHANISM OF ECOTECH

Ecotech as a special term has been in use since the Osaka meeting. But because the meaning of the term has not been clarified, the actual cooperation process is affected. Now ecotech is defined as a kind of action-oriented cooperation for development with explicit objectives, tasks, measures and results.

The nature of APEC certainly will not allow it to follow the way of other multilateral development institutions, that is, to raise funds from members and distribute them to selected projects. Obviously, relying on individual members to propose activity projects and to raise money for them—including allocations for approved projects from Central Funds—on a voluntary basis with other members participating at their own will, is also not adequate to fulfil the objectives of the Bogor Declaration. Ecotech needs a mechanism which suits the nature of APEC.

It has been suggested that the mechanism of 'concerted unilateral action' adopted for trade and investment liberalisation represents a kind of motivation based on members' self-interests. Could it also be used for ecotech? The APEC members draw up their individual liberalisation plans according to the time limits set by the Bogor Declaration—2010 for developed economies and 2020 for developing economies—on a voluntary basis because reducing tariff and non-tariff barriers is in every country's interests. However, the Bogor Declaration did not set a time limit or numeral target for ecotech. In fact such a target is difficult to set. Individual plans for reducing tariff and non-tariff barriers can be coordinated by time limit and numeral targets, but the areas of action for economic and technical cooperation have to be coordinated before any meaningful action can be taken. Furthermore, reducing tariff and non-tariff barriers is basically government action while ecotech relies on the involvement of the business sector. Finally, trade and investment liberalisation has no funding problem, but economic and technical cooperation requires the pooling of resources. An effective mechanism for ecotech has not yet been found over the past four years. The conclusion seems to be that the mechanism of 'concerted unilateral action' for trade and investment liberalisation cannot be used for economic and technical cooperation.

Judging by the nature of APEC, the practice inherited by APEC working groups from PECC—that is, where individual members propose activity projects and raise funds on a voluntary basis—seems reasonable and practical. However, the projects proposed should not become 'pets' of the proponents, only or mainly serving their trade and investment interests. Here the views on the need to create a 'new partnership', included in the communique of the G7 Lyon meeting on 28 June 1996 may be taken as a reference. The meeting reviewed the official development assistance of developed countries, but the real focus was on economic relations between developed and developing countries. The meeting suggested a new partnership be established to reflect changing realities. The major point was that the donor-recipient relationship should change, development assistance should not be used for market expansion, and the new development partnership should be mutually beneficial and based on a spirit of solidarity and burden-sharing of all those involved. But the meeting also stressed that promoting development should be the primary responsibility of developing countries themselves. No one can act on their behalf. Developed countries must support the efforts of developing countries in a spirit of common purpose and efficiency. Essentially, it is identical to the spirit of the Bogor Declaration.

At the time of the Osaka meeting, a survey was published of 201 project activities of the APEC working groups. According to the so-called 'overseers' (actually sponsors) of the activities, the majority of activities were overseen by developed economies: 38 by Australia, 36 by the United States, 24 by Japan, and

17 by Canada, a total of 115 activities. The 13 developing economies that constitute the majority of APEC oversaw only 86 activities, of which Korea topped the list at 15 and Thailand followed with 11. Developed economies voluntarily proposed and oversaw so many activities because it served their own interests. More importantly, they could raise the money. According to the evaluation made by the SOM Subcommittee on ecotech, the situation has not changed much following the Manila and Vancouver meetings. It is quite understandable that cooperation arranged in such a way has failed to meet the requirements of the Bogor Declaration. It has also shown that the views of the G7 are to the point. Hence, in order to push cooperation forward in the direction of the Bogor Declaration, not only should the existing activities be streamlined, measures should also be taken to encourage developing economies to take initiative and play a more active role, as they do in the field of trade and investment liberalisation.

Under ecotech, developing economies cannot rely on developed economies' voluntary transfer of resources and technology to support their development efforts. In the same vein, it is but empty talk when developed economies say they will support the development efforts of developing economies if the necessary conditions are created. To establish a real partnership, a mechanism is needed that will ensure all members take concrete steps in implementing economic and technical cooperation just as in the field of trade and investment liberalisation. The goals, principles, and priorities of economic and technical cooperation all are ready. Conditions for adopting the 'concerted unilateral action' mechanism in ecotech have been put in place. The differences between trade and investment liberalisation, and economic and technical cooperation are not absolute. With proper arrangements, problems can be solved. The following practical steps should be taken into consideration.

- Indexation of activities included in each priority area. The Manila Declaration set six priorities: developing human capital; developing stable, safe, and efficient capital markets; strengthening economic infrastructure; harnessing technologies for the future; safeguarding the quality of life through environmentally sound growth; and, developing and strengthening the dynamism of small and medium enterprises. They are all important. Therefore, only focusing on one or two areas each year is not enough. But all these areas are very broad. Within each area, how much should be done to reduce disparities is not clear. Areas requiring immediate attention—for example, training programs in human capital development, banking system reform in capital markets, institutional arrangements for absorbing foreign investment, the removal of obstacles for technology exchanges in harnessing technology for the future—should be highlighted. Targets should be established so that for each step taken, the results of activities can be measured.

- Phased implementation plans for each priority area. Just as in trade and investment liberalisation, the tasks within the six priority areas can only be fulfilled over a long period. In addition to highlighting tasks requiring immediate attention, a phased program with clear objectives for each stage must be worked out in detail. The whole program can then be implemented stage by stage within a timeframe. There should be a focus for each stage, with the work highlighted for immediate attention integrated so that the cooperation will be grasped in concrete terms and will not become a mere formality. The phased program can roughly be divided into short, medium and long-term activities.

- Individual action plans for all members drawn up in accordance with the abovementioned arrangements. These individual action plans will constitute the substantive part of ecotech. Just as with trade and investment liberalisation, individual action plans for ecotech should be formulated in accordance with norms worked out and agreed upon for developed and developing economies respectively. By way of illustration, in technology exchanges, developing economies may concentrate their individual action plans on measures and steps for creating conditions to absorb technology, hi-tech items they urgently need to import, and the capital and technical arrangements to match those imports. Developed economies may concentrate their individual action plans on the areas they are seeking for technology export and the preferential treatment they want to secure from importing economies.

- Collective action plans to facilitate and ensure the implementation of the individual action plans. These include information exchange, policy dialogue, enterprise consultation and business contacts. Collective plans of course constitute a part of APEC's ecotech action plan. In line with the individual action plans, collective action plans should also have foci. For example, establishing information infrastructure may be the focus at present.

- The SOM Subcommittee on Ecotech to take responsibility for ecotech activities. This includes helping members select priority areas and draw up phased plans, formulating plan requirements and norms, coordinating relations between government and the business sector, and between APEC and other bilateral or multilateral development institutions, carrying out the decisions of ministerial meetings and leaders' informal meetings, and regularly reviewing and reporting on the progress of ecotech.

These steps aim to push ecotech forward in the spirit of the Bogor Declaration and on the basis of what has been done so far. If it is workable, the goal of promoting development, reducing disparities and enhancing well-being will be realised step by step, and APEC's new partnership will be forged.

Following the financial crisis, there have been suggestions that APEC should assist in financial technology cooperation. While APEC's role in financial cooperation is limited, it can play an important role in developing financial technology. APEC's ecotech program will be soundly based if it adheres to the following principles

- joint action of all the APEC members through 'concerted unilateral action', rather than separate actions based on members' individual initiative for their own purposes
- shared benefits derived from multilateral efforts and motivated by common interests, rather than benefits split between the proponent and the participants of activities due to differing degrees of interest in involvement
- action-oriented programs for each ecotech activity with explicit objectives, measures and results, instead of process-related projects which yield no measurable achievements
- public-private partnership in specific ecotech activities, in which both government and business sector have particular roles to play instead of a general idea of combining the efforts of the two without concrete measures and requirements
- using exchanges between market and technology in early voluntary sectoral liberalisation for integrating ecotech with liberalisation instead of separating the two by stressing only liberalisation without sectoral arrangements for ecotech
- making the SOM Subcommittee on Ecotech the effective coordinator of ecotech activities instead of allowing it to become an institution subservient to working groups which was the old practice.

If these principles can be made effective ecotech will be established as a crucial part of the APEC process.

12

(APEC)

ECONOMIC AND TECHNICAL COOPERATION: CREATING THE ENVIRONMENT TO REMOVE THE BARRIERS

ZHOU XIAOBING & ZHAO JIANGLIN

With the ongoing process of economic integration in the Asia Pacific region, APEC members have made many positive contributions to realising sustainable economic development in the region. However, integration has failed to narrow the gaps in economic development among members. Indeed, the disparity has widened in some respects. Enhancing technical cooperation and improving the capacity for technical renewal is one means of promoting sustainable development in the region. In the words of the Eminent Persons Group (EPG), the flow of new and high technology accelerates economic development and enhances scientific and technological capability, promotes trade and investment liberalisation and reduces disparities in the level of economic development.

PROGRESS IN APEC ECONOMIC AND TECHNICAL COOPERATION

Economic and technical cooperation helps speed the pace of trade and investment liberalisation and facilitation (TILF). A common understanding has been reached among APEC members that economic and technical cooperation and TILF are complementary wheels driving the development of APEC. Any activity in economic and technical cooperation among APEC members is certain to have a positive impact—direct or indirect—on TILF. Such cooperation also helps promote long-term sustainable development in the Asia Pacific region.

The capability of APEC members for technical progress is of key importance to sustainable development in the Asia Pacific region, and technical cooperation among members is an integral part of this process. Developing members need to enhance technical cooperation with developed members to meet the increasing demand for high technology products because improving the knowledge and technology components of economic growth not only promotes sustainable development in their own economies but also helps promote efficiency of resource

207

allocation in the entire Asia Pacific region. Promoting technology transfer to developing members and helping them develop their economies is also in the interests of developed members because economic development among developing members will provide larger markets for developed members. In the meantime, technology transfer to developing members presents an opportunity to enhance the profit-earning capacity of developed members because the transfer also helps them to speed the pace of technological development. Technical progress among APEC members spurs economic growth—particularly of developing members—and helps improve the efficiency of resource allocation in the region. Moreover, some technical cooperation projects—in fields such as environmental protection, industrial production and agricultural production—directly promote sustainable development in the region. Strengthening technical cooperation is also an important safeguard for the continued existence of APEC, and makes APEC a more vibrant institution.

Since APEC's establishment in 1989, economic and technical cooperation has undergone three stages.

INITIAL STAGE, 1989· 92

During the initial years of APEC, there was much talk about APEC organisations. When talking about the concrete activities of APEC, people also discussed issues concerning the liberalisation of trade and investment. Although some cooperative activities have been conducted—in fields such as economic research, trade liberalisation, investment, technology transfer, human resources development and infrastructure industries—most activities focused on consultation and had few concrete outcomes.

ESTABLISHING THE BASIC PRINCIPLES OF ECOTECH, 1993· 95

Although the Seattle Summit in 1993 failed to make significant contributions to economic and technical cooperation, it established an approach to future economic and technical cooperation. The concept was to launch the Asia Pacific community through TILF. This notion of community spirit later became the foundation for economic and technical cooperation (ecotech). Economic and technical cooperation was listed as one of the three pillars of APEC activities in the Bogor Declaration at the informal meeting of APEC leaders held in 1994. The importance of economic and technical cooperation was reiterated in the Osaka Program of Action at the informal Osaka APEC leaders' meeting in 1995. The program also used the concept of economic and technical cooperation to replace the concept of development cooperation in a bid to distinguish it from the traditional notion of development assistance. It also laid down the principles of mutual respect, mutual benefit and voluntary participation in economic and technical cooperation and defined three basic aspects of ecotech: common policy concepts, joint activities and policy dialogue. Activities included research, data and information sharing, surveys, training programs, seminars, technical demonstrations, exchange of experts and establishment of research and business networks. In addition, it listed 13 fields for cooperation: human resources development, trade and investment data, trade promotion, industrial knowledge and technology, energy, ocean resources protection, fishery, telecommunications, transportation, tourism, small and medium-sized enterprises, economic infrastructure and agricultural technologies. All these represented constructive steps towards boosting technical cooperation.

Meanwhile, a new mode of cooperation, different from the traditional donor–recipient relationship system, was established, based on economic and technical cooperation. Private enterprises and other related organisations were to be encouraged to take part in cooperative activities while the market mechanism was to play a role in providing an activity system for technical cooperation.

Japan proposed the establishment of 'Partners for Progress' (PFP) and provided 10 billion yen to fund economic and technical cooperation. However, the money was used mainly to support TILF. As pointed out in the Osaka Ministerial Meeting Joint Statement, 'PFP will cover all aspects of economic and technical cooperation with an emphasis on directly supporting TILF cooperation'. This indicated that although developed members would like to provide more technical support and assistance to promote the opening up of the Asia Pacific market, the extent of economic and technical cooperation they advocated still fell short of the type of cooperation required by developing members.

IMPLEMENTATION STAGE, 1996·

It became clear that APEC members could benefit much more from the sustainable development of the Asia Pacific economy than simply through trade and investment liberalisation in the region. In 1996, for the first time, economic and technical cooperation was listed on the agenda of the APEC ministerial meeting held in Manila. 'The Framework Declaration on Enhancing Economic and Technical Cooperation'—a key document guiding APEC economic and technical cooperation—was passed at the meeting. This declaration pointed out that the targets of APEC technical cooperation were to realise sustainable and equal development in the Asia Pacific region, to narrow disparities in economic development among members, and to improve people's economic and social life. Cooperation would adhere to the principles of equality, mutual respect, mutual benefit and consensus. In addition, constructive partnerships would be established. The declaration also listed six priority fields: human resources development; developing stable, safe and effective capital markets; strengthening economic infrastructure facilities; utilising future technologies; protecting the environment; and enhancing the vitality of medium and small-sized enterprises. The Manila meeting made important progress in economic and technical cooperation.

FEATURES OF ECONOMIC AND TECHNICAL COOPERATION

Diversity is the most important feature of APEC's membership, which is characterised by relatively large gaps in technical development levels. Developed members have more advanced production technologies while developing members lack, or have not yet developed, appropriate new technologies for industrial transformation. Such a gap is the basis for technical cooperation, but it also presents a challenge. Disparities in technological development among APEC members are the motivation for cooperation. Through technology transfer, the exporter can recover most of the capital required to fund research, development or the introduction of more advanced technologies and produce products with more added value, while importers can save on the cost of technology development and market exploration. Moreover, they only need to make a small investment in training because of the relatively low level of the introduced technologies. Such technical cooperation benefits both parties. Traditional technical cooperation mode no longer meets the demands of economic development in the Asia Pacific region. Although the essence of cooperation—the transfer of technologies from developed members to developing members—has not changed, the traditional mode is a one-way flow of financial resources whereby wealthy countries offer aid to poorer countries. Such cooperation, aimed at narrowing the income gap, and mainly funded by government, does not narrow the development gap. An additional difficulty in reaching cooperation targets is reductions in government input. Reform is required, although APEC technical cooperation does not rule out the possibility of adopting the traditional approaches to cooperation. This is what is known as the APEC-style ecotech system, which has several defining characteristics.

A REASSESSMENT: FROM INEQUALITY TO RELATIVE EQUALITY

APEC demonstrated a spirit of openness, equality and progress in the Seoul Declaration. It first cast off the closed organisational style that had been adopted by traditional regional organisations, opening its door not only to members but also to non-member countries. Members are required to be as impartial as possible. APEC respects the diversity of its members, arising from economic and technical disparities. In addition, consultation and voluntary participation are the effective principles propelling APEC progress and providing new guidelines for APEC economic and technical cooperation. Cooperation among members must be based on equality and voluntary participation. APEC members respect each other in their cooperation and contribute to the cooperative process according to their own capacities. Such cooperative partnerships are rare in traditional forms of economic cooperation. In the past, partners in cooperation were not equal, as the side with the technological advantage usually attached many provisos to the cooperation.

This restricted the development of mutual interests and made it hard for cooperation to be lasting. Today, although the levels of technological development remain unequal in APEC cooperation, cooperative partners are of equal status. Developing members enjoy ownership in cooperative ventures while developed members also benefit from cooperation. The new cooperative mode takes into consideration the needs and interests of both parties. The establishment of equal relationships enables both sides to benefit from APEC technical cooperation and leads to the establishment of sincere friendship, which helps to make the cooperation enduring.

A REASSESSMENT: FROM ODA TO ECOTECH

The basic model for traditional cooperation is that developed members (wealthy countries) offer official development assistance (ODA) to developing members (poor countries) and the relationship between the two is that of donor and recipient. This model played a role in boosting the economic development of recipient countries. However, this cooperation model stresses the demands and interests of one side only and projects usually included non-economic or indirect economic goals. Such a model is inappropriate to APEC member development. The traditional model must be reformed in the context of APEC economic and technical cooperation and a new model of co-investment of resources needs to be adopted, under which cooperation is a matter of common willingness, requiring joint efforts, while cooperative targets are reached through sharing specialised knowledge and experience. For example, when dealing with environmental protection problems, although they possess the relevant technologies, developed members still require assistance from developing members in fields such as information, capital and qualified personnel. The APEC economic and technical cooperation model stresses the co-investment of both parties' resources—including knowledge, technology, human resources, capital and experience—to improve the benefits of technical cooperation. Ecotech is a complement to, rather than substitute for, ODA (Manzano and Villacorta 1996) because there is no way for ecotech to replace ODA, either in the scale of capital or in the mode of cooperation. Perhaps the most important contribution of ecotech is not direct financing but the establishment of networks and cooperative systems within APEC.

A REASSESSMENT: FROM GOVERNMENT BEHAVIOUR TO NON-GOVERNMENT BEHAVIOUR

Most traditional technical cooperation projects are conducted by governments with little private sector involvement. Changes in government foreign assistance policies—including financial cutbacks by donor countries, reductions in foreign assistance budgets and new policies—might offset the effect of such aid and affect the scale, level and achievement of technical cooperation. They also lead to a lack of long-term systematic safeguards in cooperation. As well as fluctuations in the market mechanism, government administrative behaviour can also affect cooperation. The scope of cooperation will be limited if governments act as the principal players in cooperation. For example, most assistance is directed towards public utilities, but most recipient countries in fact need cooperation in a range of other sectors. Sole reliance on government input no longer meets the demands of APEC members in cooperation. It has become imperative to attract the involvement of the private sector and improve cooperative efficiency through the market mechanism. In fact, given its possession of both technologies and capital, the private sector—as long as it is interested in cooperative projects—should be encouraged to participate in cooperation while governments concentrate on facilitating private sector cooperation. Such a model would not only expand the scale, deepen the level, and add vigour to cooperation among APEC members, it would also have a far-reaching impact on common economic development in the Asia Pacific region. In addition, introduction of the market mechanism would enable the selection, investment and use of projects to be more efficient, thereby reducing waste and making the projects truly mutually beneficial.

MAJOR ACHIEVEMENTS IN TECHNICAL COOPERATION IN THE ASIA PACIFIC REGION

BILATERAL AND MULTILATERAL COOPERATION UNDER THE APEC FRAMEWORK

After a start-up period, APEC has defined 13 fields for economic and technical cooperation while 13 corresponding workshops have been established and 320 cooperative projects (including 151 subsidiary projects) have been launched (Table 12.1). The cooperative projects were proposed by the governments of APEC economies, based on the principle of voluntary participation, while cooperative funding was mainly provided by project initiators with some assistance from APEC central funds.

Cooperation in the 13 fields has helped to improve the fundamentals of sustainable economic development in such fields as human resources development, infrastructure construction, small and medium-sized enterprises and science and technology. It has facilitated economic cooperation in areas such as the establishment of information networks that issue regular economic information. It has reduced the trading costs of economic activities and increased economic efficiency through efforts to promote standardisation, and has strengthened consultation on policy issues among economic bodies through policy dialogues in the 13 sectors.

Under the general framework of economic and technical cooperation, the priority theme that encompasses the largest of the APEC activities in the area of science and technology is 'harnessing technologies for the future'. At present, there are 45 activities identified under this area (Table 12.2). Among them, 31 activities are designed mainly to help absorb existing industrial science and technology, while 14 activities focus on developing new technologies for the future.

The role of workshops in promoting technical cooperation includes
- promoting the upgrading of the technological capability of members, such as the work undertaken by the Human Resources Development (HRD) workshop in improving the quality of human resources, research work by the Industrial Science and Technology (IST) workshop on personnel exchange and technical personnel training, and industrial knowledge education seminars undertaken by IST and HRD
- promoting the infrastructure for environmental technical transfer, such as the trans-cultural technical transfer research and property rights training carried out by the HRD workshop, research on trans-cultural technical transfer carried out by the IST, the collective action plan made by the CTI on improving transparency in the field of property rights, and the work on foreign direct investment (FDI) and Market Framework Policies carried out by the European Community (EC)
- strengthening the establishment of information networks on technical proliferation among members, such as the APEC technology internet carried out by the IST workshop and technology exchange and training in small and medium-size enterprises undertaken by the APEC centres
- solving technical problems in specific departments, such as work done by the telecom, energy and agricultural technological cooperation workshops.

Table 12.1 Activities in the 13 ecotech areas, November 1996

Area	Total number	Completed
Trade and investment data (TID)	5	2
Trade promotion (TP)	13	8
Industrial science and technology (IST)	41	20
Human resource development (HRD)	86	29
Regional energy cooperation (Energy)	43	30
Marine resource conservation (Marine)	7	4
Fisheries (Fisheries)	12	6
Telecommunications (Telecom)	26	7
Transportation (Trans)	13	1
Tourism	10	7
Small and medium enterprises (SME)	20	10
Economic infrastructure (Infra)	9	1
Agricultural technology (Agr. Tech)	35	3
Total	320	120

Source: Yamazawa, I., 1997. 'APEC's economic and technical cooperation: evolution and tasks ahead', in Andrew Elek (ed.), *Building an Asia Pacific Community: development cooperation within APEC*, Foundation for Development Cooperation, Brisbane:45.

ECONOMIC AND TECHNICAL COOPERATION AMONG APEC MEMBERS OUTSIDE THE APEC FRAMEWORK

There had been extensive technical cooperation in the Asia Pacific region encompassing almost all economic sectors prior to the establishment of APEC; its role in the economic development of APEC members was not negligible.

The principal components of cooperation outside the APEC framework included: international or regional multilateral economic organisations such as the United Nations Development Program and its specialised organisation, the United Nations Industrial Development Organisation (UNIDO), the World Bank, the International Monetary Fund, the Development Assistance Council of the OECD and the Asian Development Bank; bilateral development assistance organisations such as American International Development, Japan's Overseas Economic Cooperation Fund, and Canada's International Development Association; international multilateral or bilateral non-governmental organisations (NGOs) such as private funds, research institutions and non-governmental development institutions; and, private activities such as FDI undertaken by multinational companies.

The position and role of these cooperation agencies are changing in line with changes in the world economic structure. The changes include the gradually decreasing role of government in cooperation, and the growing role of private organisations. In the 1990s, great changes have taken place in the structure of

Table 12.2   Types of and priorities for harnessing technologies for the future

		Number
Types	Total	45
	Seminar/conference/workshop	8
	Survey/research/publication	14
	Network/database	6
	Policy reform activities	6
	Mixed/other	11
Priorities	Total	45
	Improved infrastructure	22
	Improved business climate	7
	Enhanced policy dialogue	5
	Networking and partnership	11
Status	Total	45
	To be completed in 1998	15
	To be completed after 1998	13
	Ongoing/annual	9
	In preparation	8

Source: APEC Secretariat 1998.

external capital flowing to developing countries. The ratio of private capital has risen from 44 per cent in 1990 to 86 per cent in 1996, while the ratio of official development capital has continued to fall. The flow of foreign investment increased 5.5 times, accounting for 54 per cent of the total private capital flow to developing economies. Second, the ratio of governmental assistance in developed countries' GDP is gradually declining. The OCED's DAC noted in its report that the overseas aid budgets of donor countries continued to fall. ODA dropped 14 per cent between 1992 and 1995, and the type of assistance has also changed. Some of the aid for long-term development is now devoted to peace-keeping and emergency assistance. At the same time, new donors have emerged, such as the newly industrialising countries in Asia. Third, the distribution model for capital assistance is also changing. The achievements and efficiency of recipient countries have become the major standards for determining their eligibility for loan renewals. The World Bank International Development Assistance now lists indices of achievements and efficiency in the distribution system for its shrinking assistance funds. Major indices to assess recipient countries include economic stability and structural reform, poverty reduction efforts and the quality of the loan portfolio under implementation.

Economic and technical cooperation outside the APEC framework has several distinguishing features. The partners in cooperation tend to have strong fund-raising capability, are able to undertake large-scale cooperative projects and guarantee capital resources, and have well-developed specialised functions that enable them to accomplish definition, management, examination and evaluation of the projects. The partners, having been engaged in technical work over long periods of time, have accumulated significant experience and knowledge. Finally, the partners have won the trust of APEC member governments— especially developing members— which makes it easy for projects to be conducted among members. As for the capital scale of cooperation projects, non-APEC ecotech projects have established a much better track record than that of APEC economic development. This is of great importance to sustainable economic development in the Asia Pacific region. Of course, the two kinds of cooperation are not comparable because APEC's role is not principally one of cooperation; it has limited fund-raising ability and it has just begun to engage in ecotech. The purpose of this discussion of the achievements of non-APEC cooperation is to explore ways to incorporate such forms of cooperation into APEC's ecotech process.

MAJOR PROBLEMS IN APEC ECONOMIC AND TECHNICAL COOPERATION

APEC has made great strides in economic and technical cooperation. The major problem now is how to give more scope to technical cooperation in promoting sustainable economic development. To date, APEC has not made enough progress in facilitating technical cooperation.

It took a long time to reach unanimity on technical cooperation and this hindered the process. In the initial stages, economic and technical cooperation was organised as a complement to TILF, with targets set in line with the common development of APEC members. Generally, these projects were not very practical. In a report made by the APEC Economic Committee, only long-term targets for economic and technical cooperation were set, and no concrete measures to strengthen short-term cooperation were mentioned. Meanwhile, the criteria for evaluating activities—such as goal-orientation and explicit performance criteria— were very abstract, making it difficult to direct cooperative activities.

Second, although many economic and technical activities have been discussed, few have been put into action. At present, most APEC economic and technical cooperation activities are preparatory in nature—chiefly information collection, research and discussion. Although such activities help to improve the environment for economic activity, they have little direct economic impact. For example, environmental protection has become a severe problem and a hot topic in the Asia Pacific region. However, a lot of barriers must be overcome before environmental protection projects can be implemented in this area. Few cooperation projects concerning environmental protection have been finalised between developing and developed members, especially in the technology sector. More cooperation among APEC members is needed to solve environmental problems. Such cooperation should be based on the overall interests of the region.

Third, cooperation projects lack sufficient start-up capital. At present, most APEC cooperation projects are selected and funded by APEC members with part of the capital coming from APEC's central fund. Implementation of economic and technical cooperative projects is restricted by the limited capital provided by APEC member governments and the limited capital raised by APEC itself. Budgeted expenditure for economic and technical cooperation was a mere US$809,000 under the 1997 APEC budget approved by the Manila meeting. In sharp contrast, the scale of projects funded by ODA is much larger. Although no average budget scale for bilateral economic and technical cooperation is available, it is estimated to be 10 to 20 times the scale of APEC economic and technical cooperation. Yamazawa (1996) estimates that APEC funding for economic and technical cooperation comprises no more than 0.1 per cent of total ODA.

Fourth, there remains a paucity of successful examples and operating models to assess project implementation. Most ongoing technical cooperative projects are small in scale and urgently needed; large-scale projects are few.

There is a simple explanation for APEC's failure to achieve the expected results. The diversity of its members is the basis for cooperation. At the same time, however, such diversity exacerbates the difficulties of cooperation.

Some developed members believe that technical cooperation mainly refers to technical assistance from developed to developing members, without recognising the mutual benefits. Some developed members also feel that they gain less than they expend. In the process of promoting the mobilisation of technology and knowledge, developed members are reluctant to embark on technology trade in the same liberalised manner as commodity and capital trade. Instead, they often adopt conservative or even restrictive technology trade and prefer to maximise the sale of products while minimising the sale of technologies. When they do transfer technology, they often attach harsh terms to it. The technology monopoly of developed members and the restrictive measures they adopt in technology trade are the major reasons for difficulties in conducting technical cooperation among APEC members.

Developing members must strive to create better preconditions for bilateral cooperation. Cooperation requires developing members to improve the quality of their labour force, attract more domestic reserves to increase cooperative funding, reform domestic systems to establish efficient and convenient cooperative institutions in order to reduce the unnecessary spending caused by blockages in the system, readjust relevant domestic policies to provide criteria for the selection of cooperative projects, and make APEC technical cooperation more efficient by reducing their own internal barriers.

APEC has failed to fulfil its unique role in technical cooperation. Just as was the case with the realisation of TILF, APEC needs to create the conditions necessary to enable the free mobilisation of knowledge and technology among its members. APEC is not a funding entity; it cannot fund specific technical cooperation projects as the main form of its participation in cooperation. This aspect distinguishes it from other multilateral organisations. However, APEC has the ability to influence member governments and to encourage members to speed up the mobilisation of knowledge and technology through implementing some of its decisions to abolish restrictions. In addition, it can create a more accommodating and efficient environment for technical cooperation. Virtually no other multilateral organisation can fulfil these functions. APEC should do more in the following regard: strengthen information collection to avoid duplication of cooperative projects, help member governments coordinate and communicate their technical policies, and stimulate the interest of private organisations in participating in technical cooperation and gradually enable private organisations to engage in meaningful and large-scale technical cooperation. At present, few cooperation projects directly involve private organisations, mainly due to the disparity between technical cooperation projects and the areas of private interests. Meanwhile, private organisations are becoming more cautious about technology transfer, creating a further restriction on their participation in cooperation. In addition, APEC has not yet created enough stimulus to encourage the participation of the private sector. Strengthening coordination between APEC and other cooperation organisations is essential. Other multilateral organisations have a greater capacity to raise funds and have accumulated much experience over the years. Some multilateral organisations continue to be heavily involved in technical cooperation projects. By coordinating these projects, APEC cannot only avoid duplication of and competition between projects, but also give full play to the potential for cooperative funding.

CREATING AN ENVIRONMENT CONDUCIVE TO ECONOMIC AND TECHNOLOGICAL COOPERATION

Strengthening economic and technological cooperation and promoting sustainable development in the Asia Pacific region requires a joint effort by government and the private sector. Such efforts will enable the creation of an environment conducive to the free flow of knowledge and technologies so that economic and technological cooperation can achieve their full potential.

ROLE OF GOVERNMENT

Governments of member economies play an extremely important role in APEC economic and technological cooperation. They can determine the orientation of the cooperation on the basis of their own national interests and with regard to the interests of other member states. The role of government is multi-faceted.

INFLUENCING ECONOMIC AND TECHNOLOGICAL COOPERATION THROUGH APEC

As participants in APEC's various working teams and committees are all representatives of the corresponding organisations of member states' governments, the activities of APEC's working organisations at different levels can be regarded as an extension of the work of those corresponding organisations. According to APEC's principle of consensus, APEC has neither the ability nor any mechanism to influence the governments of member states directly. Governments of member states can influence the formulation of APEC's policy frameworks through the participation of their corresponding organisations in APEC's activities; they can influence the selection and determination of APEC's stated objectives through APEC working teams; they can influence the selection and determination of multilateral organisations' stated objectives through APEC's stated objectives; and they can influence the direction of the private sector's economic activities through the stated objectives of APEC and multilateral organisations.

IMPROVING THE DOMESTIC POLICY ENVIRONMENT

Governments of member states can formulate policies and legislation in accordance with APEC's regional policy frameworks in a bid to encourage and support technological cooperation both within and outside APEC. They can also make efforts to improve their policymaking processes by making them more transparent. This will aid in the opening-up of market systems, which will in turn encourage technological cooperation among member states. It is suggested that developed member states could emphasise the adjustment of their domestic technological policies and coordination between their technological and other policies—such as trade policies—so as to minimise the restrictions on and obstacles to technological cooperation. The efforts of governments should centre on reform of their domestic economic structures and policies, with a view to reducing unnecessary transaction costs, thereby enhancing the effective flow of knowledge and technologies and encouraging private sector participation. At the same time, there should be sustained policy dialogue between developed and developing members to consolidate policy consistency.

SPEEDING UP INFRASTRUCTURE DEVELOPMENT

Governments of member states can create an environment conducive to technological cooperation by accelerating the construction of infrastructure in the region. Emphasis should be placed on the construction, rejuvenation and refining of energy, transportation and communication installations. Equally important is improvement in the management of financial systems and development of information networks.

Governments should give priority to the establishment of an information network, installing hardware and including relevant information about their respective countries on the network. The information should include: government policies and legislation, which constitute an important step in enhancing the transparency of government policies; government statements on the objectives of technological cooperation, which can be used to guide the direction of economic and technological cooperation; and the present status of economic development, which can be used to assess economic development trends and the prospects for cooperation.

RESOURCES AND PARTICIPATION IN ECONOMIC AND TECHNOLOGICAL COOPERATION

In view of the diminishing capacity of governments of member states to contribute to economic and technological cooperation, there is a need to emphasise the orientation and 'demonstration by example' effect of technological cooperation and to support or guide input from other sources, especially the private sector. Government input can be directed inward or outward. Inwardly-directed input centres on guiding industry and embarking on structural adjustments. Outwardly-directed input takes two different forms. The first is bilateral participation, such as ODA, a form that has been widely used and one through which governments can support the transfer of enhanced technological content in ODA projects. The other form is multilateral participation. Under this type of cooperation, all parties can participate as multilateral cooperating partners without encountering the kind of friction that often emerges in bilateral participation. This form of input not only decreases the risks faced by participants, but also enlarges the scope of the recipient parties, and it is now attracting increasing interest from APEC member economies.

ROLE OF NGOS

NGOs include private foundations, research institutions and non-governmental development institutions. Most NGOs in the developing member states of APEC lag far behind their counterparts in the developed member states both in terms of the number of organisations and their activities. The principal NGOs in APEC are PBEC, PECC and ABAC. Through their commitment to assisting APEC in research work for the formulation of APEC policy frameworks, they have become one of the links between governmental organisations and the business community. They tend to be strongly directed towards technological cooperation. Their functions mainly include: (for those with fund-raising ability) supporting policy research work and cooperation projects such as small and medium-scale technological and personnel exchanges and training; undertaking or managing cooperation projects (regardless of the source of the funds); enhancing the public's understanding of and support for APEC's cooperative mechanisms; and, helping APEC evaluate and supervise the progress, impact and effects of its economic and technological cooperation projects from a relatively objective and independent standpoint.

ROLE OF THE PRIVATE SECTOR

The private sector will gradually replace governments as the leading player in APEC's ecotech programs and become the main conduit for economic and technological cooperation. It will play an increasingly important role in fund-raising and technological development and transfers.

Participation of private businesses in technological cooperation is clearly and directly motivated by self-interest and so is easily affected by market principles. The basic functions of private business are to act as the major funding source for economic and technological cooperation; to take a major role in or directly undertake economic and technological cooperation projects in the APEC region; and to undertake or manage economic and technological cooperation projects financed by funds from non-free capital sources. Under certain conditions—characterised by clearcut policies, a stable economic environment and favourable prospects for the project—the private sector also undertakes or manages large-scale long-term infrastructure projects.

ROLE OF APEC

To promote economic and technological cooperation in the region, APEC needs to speed up the creation of a favourable and accommodating environment for such cooperation. Its main functions are collection of information and coordination of projects.

COLLECTION OF INFORMATION

Sharing information is an important precondition for strengthening economic and technological cooperation in APEC. Of most importance is sharing information about ways to create and preserve highly efficient manpower resources, and information about infrastructures and technological capabilities. Accelerating the creation of a good information environment for APEC will lower the transaction costs of collecting and using information and reduce research and development (R&D) expenses. Emphasis should be placed on comprehensive information processing and establishing storehouses for collecting information about technological capabilities and information networks.

Policy-collecting storehouses can help to enhance the policy transparency of member states and can play a role in indirect policy coordination because they enable member states' governments to consult directly on policy issues and make comparisons between them. Information processing and analysis provide governments with the contents of their respective stated objectives, and furnish forecasts on economic development trends and potential input directions. The limited resources available should be utilised selectively to carry out information cooperation projects of an appropriate scale, mainly to conduct exchanges of personnel and technologies. These exchanges may take two forms. The first involves setting up APEC training centres that focus on projects requiring more specialised installations. The second concerns the organisation of APEC mobile training groups in charge of projects requiring less specialised installations. The latter may incorporate lectures by professionals in the fields concerned and the recruitment of local trainees by the governments of member states.

COORDINATION OF PROJECTS

Within APEC, there are already several organisations capable of supporting economic and technological cooperation. In particular, there are specialised financial institutions with well-established systems, substantial experience and competence in the areas of multilateral fund-raising, investment and management. The fact that systems are in place means that the costs of technological cooperation should be minimal. APEC has several coordination functions, including

- strengthening ties between and among the governments of member states, multilateral governmental organisations, NGOs and the private sector within the APEC region; arranging projects around the objectives of cooperation so as to avoid duplication of projects or excessive competition between various projects; and, increasing the efficiency of fund utilisation
- attaching significance to the multilateral input provided by non-multilateral institutions and to projects with multilateral beneficiaries, with the aim of reducing the friction often present in traditional forms of bilateral cooperation. When multilateral institutions select projects, they should

make more use of market forces to determine their stated objectives and enhance the projects' ability to give private capital clear objectives to guide their actions. This is of great significance if private capital is to undertake follow-up investments in projects in accordance with specific stated objectives

- allowing non-members to participate in APEC-related projects so as to enlarge the scope of economic and technological cooperation in the region. It is suggested that to make use of the limited resources for technological projects at the regional level, the whole region needs to undertake R&D and to set up common R&D institutions at the APEC level to promote technological cooperation.

REFERENCES

APEC, The Economics Committee, 1996. *The State of Economic and Technical Cooperation in APEC*, Economic Committee APEC, Singapore.

Australian APEC Study Centre, 1997. The Ecotech Agenda—APEC's other side.

Arayama, Y., Yoshino, F. and Miyanaga, T., 1996. Economic Growth and Environment in APEC Countries: the effects of technological progress on consumption, capital and environment, GSID, Nagoya University, APEC Discussion Paper series, March.

Elek, A. (ed.), 1997. 'Building an Asia-Pacific Economic Community: development cooperation within APEC', The Foundation for Development Cooperation, Brisbane.

Manzano, G. and Villacorta, W., 1996. The APEC Approach to Development Cooperation: equal partnership for unequal partners.

Plummer, M.A. and Abe, S., 1997. 'An Aid Crisis? The New ODA Environment and the Role of APEC', Working Paper Series No. 10, Institute of Developing Economies, Japan.

Yamashita, S., 1996. 'Technology Transfer for Upgrading the National Capabilities of Technology Absorption', IDEC Research Paper Series, Hiroshima.

Yamazawa, I., 1997. 'APEC's economic and technical cooperation: evolution and tasks ahead', in Andrew Elek (ed.), *Building an Asia Pacific Community: development cooperation within APEC*, Foundation for Development Cooperation, Brisbane.

CAPITAL FLOWS, TECHNOLOGY AND TRADE LIBERALISATION

P33 P34   2 25-42
(China) 033 019
F32 F23

13

IMPACT OF CAPITAL INFLOWS AND TECHNOLOGY TRANSFER ON THE CHINESE ECONOMY

ZHOU XIAOBING

THE TREND IN FOREIGN CAPITAL INFLOWS

Since 1978, China has increasingly been making use of overseas capital for the development of its domestic economy. In retrospect, China has gone through four distinct stages.

THE INITIAL STAGE, 1979–87

During the initial stage, China began to utilise foreign direct investment (FDI). But as China's overall framework for attracting overseas capital, such as legislation, policy and infrastructure was still rather backward, overseas investors generally adopted an exploratory attitude, making only minimal direct investments in the country. During this stage, the total amount of actually utilised overseas direct investment was US$10.6 billion—only US$1.18 billion a year on average.

THE DEVELOPMENT STAGE, 1988–91

During the development stage, China made great progress in utilising FDI. After the mid 1980s, China quickened its pace in enacting laws concerning FDI. The government promulgated regulations for encouraging foreign investment in October 1986, and various departments under the supervision of the State Council took steps towards implementation of the new regulations. Simultaneously, China increased its investment in the construction of infrastructure. As these measures initially improved the investment environment in China and as a consequence gained the confidence of overseas investors, direct investment in China increased rapidly. The amount of actually utilised FDI in these four years totalled US$14.44 billion—an annual rate of US$3.61 billion, or more than three times the prevailing annual rate during the initial stage.

225

During the period 1979–91, actually utilised foreign capital mainly took the form of loans and credits which accounted for 60 per cent of foreign capital investment. In spite of a steady increase in direct investment, this form of financing only accounted for 38 per cent of the total overseas capital actually utilised up to 1991. Other forms of foreign investment accounted for the remaining 2 per cent over the same period.

THE PERIOD OF RAPID GROWTH, 1992–95

During the rapid growth stage, the amount of overseas capital utilised by China increased dramatically. After Deng Xiaoping defined the establishment of a socialist market economy as the objective of China's economic reforms at the beginning of 1992, China picked up the pace of opening up to the outside world. From initially opening up the coastal regions, the Chinese government swiftly extended its liberalising reforms to the entire country. As a result, FDI registered tremendous growth during the period. In 1992, the amount of utilised foreign capital in China came to US$11 billion, up by a factor of 1.5 from the previous year; and in 1993, the figure further rose to US$27.5 billion, up again by a factor of 1.5 from the amount in 1992. China was ranked first among the developing countries and second among all countries for its growth in foreign capital uptake. In 1994 and 1995, there was a decline in the number of foreign investment projects ratified by the Chinese government and also the amount of overseas investment agreed upon. Nonetheless, the amount of actually utilised foreign capital continued to increase to US$33.8 billion in 1994 and to US$37.5 billion in 1995.

During this stage, foreign capital utilisation in China displayed several features.
- direct investment grew rapidly
- foreign-investment projects expanded in scale
- overseas investors paid more attention to obtaining control of the projects they invested in, and so there was a strong move towards sole ownership by overseas investors in newly built enterprises, and there was also a trend to expanding capital and shareholding in existing enterprises
- big transnational corporations began to enter China in large numbers, making a powerful impact on Chinese state-owned enterprises in certain industries, and securing monopolies in those industries to a certain extent
- new forms of foreign capital utilisation emerged, such as BOT, and raising funds in the securities market
- FDI became the main form of overseas capital utilised by China, surpassing overseas loans and credit in 1992 and accounting for 78 per cent of the total actually utilised overseas capital in 1995.

THE ADJUSTMENT PERIOD, 1996 ONWARDS

During this stage, China has been adjusting its policy towards the utilisation of overseas capital and trying to raise economic efficiency. In June 1995, China promulgated the provisional regulations for guiding the direction of overseas investment and published a catalogue of industries for guiding overseas investment. This indicates that China began to make appropriate adjustments to its policy of overseas capital utilisation—shifting the focus from the quantity of foreign capital utilised to the quality of overseas capital utilised. In fact, it was the first time that China publicly published statutes to clarify the industrial areas in which foreign investment was encouraged and permitted, and where foreign investment was restricted or even prohibited. This guide helped overseas investors to choose the right direction when making investment decisions in China.

In 1996, there was another major adjustment to China's policy towards foreign capital that concerned the reduction or remission of some of the preferential taxation arrangements enjoyed by overseas investors. A decision was made to gradually abolish the preferential taxation treatment enjoyed by foreign-invested enterprises importing capital goods. To take effect from April 1996, the decision was made with the aim of placing domestically-funded enterprises and foreign-invested enterprises on an equal and competitive footing. Following enforcement of the new policy, the number of foreign-invested projects and the amount of foreign investment agreed upon suffered decline, but the amount of actually utilised foreign capital increased steadily, rising to US$42.35 billion in 1996. This indicates that the scale of foreign investment and the ratio of actually paid principal have both grown. In addition, foreign investment in new and high technology industries and infrastructure has greatly increased. In 1997, FDI continued to rise rapidly, with the actually utilised amount reaching US$51.9 billion, and accounting for 83.7 per cent of the total amount of foreign capital that year.

Over the last 20 years, the grand total of foreign capital utilised by China has accumulated to more than US$380 billion, of which direct investment accounts for about 60.1 per cent (US$228.5 billion), loans and credit for 36.5 per cent (US$139 billion), and securities financing for 3.4 per cent (or US$13 billion).

The steady decline in the number of foreign-invested projects and in the amount of agreed foreign investment in recent years will have harmful effects on the actual utilisation of foreign capital in the future. In addition, the East Asian currency crisis that appeared in the second half of 1997, resulted in a drastic devaluation of affected currencies and their weakened ability to invest abroad will have a negative impact on China's endeavours to attract overseas capital. The Chinese government has a view to maintaining the steady inflow of overseas capital, enhancing foreign capital utilisation and encouraging the importation of advanced technologies and equipment to promote China's industrial restructuring and technological progress. Hence, the Chinese government decided that from the beginning of 1998, customs duties and taxes on imports of value-adding equipment should be remitted for the equipment imported by foreign-

Table 13.1 Utilisation of foreign capital by China, 1979–96 (US$ billion)

Year	Item (number)	Agreed investment	Utilised investment
1979–82	920	49.58	17.69
1983	638	19.17	9.16
1984	2166	28.75	14.19
1985	3073	63.33	19.56
1986	1498	33.30	22.44
1987	2233	37.09	23.14
1988	5945	52.97	31.94
1989	5779	56.00	33.93
1990	7273	65.96	34.87
1991	12978	119.77	43.66
1992	48764	581.24	110.07
1993	83437	1114.36	275.15
1994	47548	826.80	337.67
1995	37011	912.82	375.21
1996	24529	732.13	423.50
Total	283820	4693.90	1765.95

Source: Ministry of Foreign Trade and Economic Cooperation, China.

invested and domestically-funded projects, as a sign of encouragement and support from the government.

THE STRUCTURE AND ROLE OF OVERSEAS DIRECT INVESTMENT IN CHINA

Overseas investment in China has generally taken the form of joint ventures, but the proportion of solely foreign-owned enterprises has been on the rise in recent years. Until the end of 1996, joint ventures accounted for 51 per cent of the total of actually utilised foreign capital. Solely foreign-owned enterprises and Chinese-foreign cooperative enterprises accounted for 24 and 22 per cent, respectively (Table 13.2).

The majority of FDI in China originates from Hong Kong, Macao and Taiwan, with the remainder coming from the United States, Japan, Singapore, the Republic of Korea, Britain, Germany and France. To the end of 1996, 59.1 per cent of the total actually utilised foreign investment in China came from Hong Kong and Macao, with 12 per cent coming from Taiwan and 8 per cent from the United States (Table 13.3).

Foreign investment in China is mostly concentrated in secondary industries. While the tertiary sector ranks second for foreign investment, primary industry

Table 13.2   FDI by form, 1979–96 (US$ billion)

	Item (number)	Share (%)	Agreed investment	Share (%)	Utilised investment	Share (%)
Joint ventures	174014	61	2174.42	46	907.26	51
Cooperation	41992	15	1101.60	24	380.34	22
Overseas-owned	67677	24	1378.58	29	425.51	24
Co-development	137	..	39.29	1	52.81	3
Total	283820	100	4693.90	100	1765.95	100

Source: Ministry of Foreign Trade and Economic Cooperation, China.

Table13.3   FDI by source area, 1979–96 (US$billion)

Country	Item (number)	Share (%)	Agreed investment	Share (%)	Utilised investment	Share (%)
Hong Kong & Macao	167681	59.08	272.992	58.16	103.497	59.12
Taiwan	35033	12.33	34.608	7.37	15.061	8.53
America	22227	7.83	35.569	7.58	14.176	8.03
Japan	15036	5.30	25.632	5.46	14.011	7.93
Korea	7757	2.73	11.014	2.35	3.616	2.05
ASEAN	12325	4.34	23.359	4.98	9.388	5.32
EU	7194	2.53	25.291	5.39	8.497	4.81

Source: Ministry of Foreign Trade and Economic Cooperation, China.

Table 13.4   FDI by industry, 1979–95 (US$billion)

	Enter-prises	Share (%)	Total investment	Share (%)	Regist'd capital	Share (%)	Overseas paid	Share (%)
Primary industry	5661	2	8.0	1	6.0	2	4.0	2
Secondary industry	175744	76	386.5	61	258.2	64	159.0	62
Tertiary sector	51159	22	244.5	38	134.9	34	93.9	36
Total	233564	100	639.0	100	399.1	100	256.9	100

Source: Wang Loulin (ed.), 1997. *Report on Foreign Direct Investment in China*, Economy and Management Publishing House, Beijing.

Table 13.5   FDI by region in China, 1990–94 (per cent)

Region	1990	1991	1992	1993	1994
Eastern	93.2	92.5	91.3	87.4	87.8
Central	4.0	4.5	6.8	8.9	7.9
Western	2.8	3.0	1.9	3.7	4.3

Source: Institute of Industrial Economics, Chinese Academy of Social Sciences, 1997. *China's Industrial Development Report 1996*, China Economy and Management Publishing House, Beijing.

accounts for only a very small percentage of total foreign investment in China. The industrial sector accounted for 62 per cent of the total actually utilised foreign capital at the end of 1996, while primary industry accounted for only 2 per cent. But since the beginning of the 1990s, the share of foreign capital invested in the industrial sector has gradually declined while the share of foreign investment in the tertiary sector has rapidly increased (Table 13.4).

Foreign investment in China is overwhelmingly concentrated in China's eastern coastal region, but the central regions have increased their share in recent years. Until 1994, China's 12 eastern provinces and regions accounted for 88 per cent of total foreign investment, but the percentage accounted for by the 9 central provinces and regions rose from 4 per cent in 1990 to 8 per cent in 1994 (Table 13.5).

The scale of foreign-invested enterprises in China has expanded on average since the beginning of the 1990s. Prior to 1990, the scale of foreign-invested projects was generally small. However, the amount of investment agreed upon for an average foreign-invested project has increased to US$2.86 million from US$0.92 million in 1991. An important reason for the expansion in scale has been that the ratio of actually paid principal was raised from 18.9 per cent in 1992 to 47.1 per cent in 1995.

A majority of foreign-invested enterprises have incurred losses, but not critical losses. In 1995, of all the foreign-invested enterprises already in operation, 32.6 per cent earned profits of US$400,000 on average for an individual enterprise, but 58.7 per cent incurred losses of on average US$160,000 for an individual enterprise. A majority of foreign-invested enterprises incurred losses, their losses were not heavy. In fact, most foreign-invested enterprises only incurred slight losses. Moreover, it should be noted that some of the foreign-invested enterprises have managed to evade taxes by transferring their profits to subsidiaries overseas. In such cases, the enterprises appeared to have incurred losses but were profitable in reality. It can therefore be assumed that there is exaggeration of the publicly declared losses reported by foreign-invested enterprises.

Table 13.6   FDI by amount of average program and the ratio of actually paid principal, 1991–95

	1991	1992	1993	1994	1995
Item (number)	12978	48764	83437	47549	28000
Agreed investment (US$ billion)	11.98	58.12	111.44	82.68	80.00
Amount of average item(US$'000)	923	1192	1336	1739	2857
Ratio of actually paid principal (%)	36.5	18.9	24.7	40.8	47.1

Source: Institute of Industrial Economics, Chinese Academy of Social Sciences, 1997. *China's Industrial Development Report 1996*, China Economy and Management Publishing House, Beijing.

Table 13.7   FDI enterprises' performance during 8ᵗʰ Five-year Plan (US$ billion)

	1991	1992	1993	1994	1995
Operated (number)	...	39551	66988	93453	108955
Profits (number)	...	...	27658	31229	35530
Losses (number)	...	...	34150	56111	63922
Profits after tax paid	1.27	4.19	8.15	8.35	14.26
Losses	...	2.67	13.75	8.59	10.27
Taxation	8.2	33.8	65.6	67.0	88.7
Domestic sales	...	39.7	72.9	162.0	158.1
Export	3.6	38.0	61.6	59.3	120.5

Source: Wang Loulin (ed.), 1997. *Report on Foreign Direct Investment in China*, Economy and Management Publishing House, Beijing.

THE IMPACT OF FOREIGN-INVESTED ENTERPRISES ON CHINA'S NATIONAL ECONOMY

As a result of its rising share in China's GDP and as against China's own investment in fixed assets, foreign direct investment has become an important force in China's national economy. Since the early 1990s, foreign direct investment has been growing rapidly. It is estimated that from 1994 onwards, the amount of actually utilised foreign direct investment has risen to over 5 per cent of the country's GDP and more than 10 per cent of the country's investment in fixed assets.

Foreign-owned firms now accounts for half of China's total export trade and are playing a leading role in import trade. In 1996, the proportion of import-export trade operated by foreign-invested enterprises accounted for 47.3 per cent of China's total external trade (40.7 per cent of export and 54.5 per cent of import trade respectively).

Foreign-invested enterprises have become an important source of growth in China's foreign exchange reserves. In 1995, foreign direct investment led to an inflow of US$33.74 billion into China. In the same year, foreign-invested enterprises incurred a deficit of US$16.06 billion in their external trade and remitted profits of US$9.95 billion abroad. On balance, they helped China to increase its foreign exchange reserves by US$7.72 billion, accounting for 34.4 per cent of the total increase of China's foreign exchange reserves in that year. In addition, since the early 1990s, the foreign exchange balance of foreign-invested enterprises indicates that their yearly foreign exchange payment has consistently surpassed their foreign exchange income.

Foreign-invested enterprises have also provided jobs for a portion of China's large labour force. According to statistics, foreign-invested enterprises accounted for 10.8 per cent of China's total number of employees. By November 1997,

Table 13.8   FDI as a ratio of China's GDP and investment in fixed assets

	1990	1991	1992	1993	1994	1995	1996
Investment in fixed assets (billion yuan)	451.70	559.45	808.01	1307.23	1704.21	2001.93	1366.00
GDP (billion yuan)	1854.79	2161.78	2663.81	3463.44	4675.94	5847.81	6779.50
Utilised FDI (US$ billion)	3.49	4.37	11.01	27.52	33.77	37.52	42.35
Exchange rate (yuan/US$)	4.78	5.32	5.51	5.76	8.62	8.35	8.31
FDI as ratio of GDP (per cent)	0.9	1.1	2.3	4.6	6.2	5.4	5.2
FDI as ratio of investment in fixed assets (per cent)	2.6	2.9	5.3	8.5	12	11	10.4

Note: According to statistics, about 70 per cent of FDI represents investment in fixed assets.

Source: Wang Loulin (ed.), 1997. *Report on Foreign Direct Investment in China*, Economy and Management Publishing House, Beijing.

Table 13.9   Imports and exports of FDI enterprises as a share of China's total foreign trade

	1991	1992	1993	1994	1995	1996
Total trade of FDI firms (1)	28.96	43.76	67.07	87.65	109.82	137.11
China's total foreign trade (2)	135.63	166.53	195.71	236.90	280.86	289.91
(1)/(2) per cent	21.4	26.3	34.3	37.0	39.1	47.3
FDI export trade (3)	12.05	17.38	25.24	34.71	46.88	61.51
China's export trade (4)	71.84	84.94	91.74	121.01	148.78	151.07
(3)/(4) per cent	16.8	20.5	27.5	28.7	31.5	40.7
FDI import trade (5)	16.91	26.38	41.83	52.94	62.94	75.60
China's import trade (6)	63.79	80.59	103.96	115.61	132.08	138.84
(5)/(6) per cent	26.5	32.7	40.2	45.8	47.7	54.5

Source: State Statistical Bureau, 1997. *China Statistics Yearbook 1997*, China Statistical Publishing House, Beijing.

Table 13.10   The foreign exchange balance of FDI enterprises (US$ billion)

	1990	1991	1992	1993	1994.4-12	1995
Foreign exchange outflow	2.24	3.84	5.94	10.07	7.13	14.14
Foreign exchange inflow	1.24	2.19	3.54	4.01	4.01	9.22
Foreign exchange balance	1.01	1.65	2.42	6.06	3.12	4.92

Source: Ministry of Foreign Trade and Economic Cooperation, China.

145,000 foreign-invested enterprises existed in China with a total payroll of US$17.5 million.

Taxes paid by foreign-invested enterprises have increased rapidly. Taxes paid by foreign-invested enterprises accounted for 2.3 per cent of China's total tax revenue in 1991. The figure increased to 7.6 per cent in 1994 at 39 billion yuan.

Overseas capital has played a considerable role in promoting the development of China's economy (Table 13.11). Since the early 1990s particularly, foreign-invested enterprises have become a significant force that affects China's overall performance in terms of investment, foreign trade, foreign exchange, employment, and taxation revenue.

Foreign-invested enterprises have also played a positive role in promoting restructuring and the internationalisation of the Chinese economy in several ways.

*   They have introduced China to the mechanisms of market and competition and have brought competition to bear upon Chinese national enterprises, helping raise awareness of competition and its place in the market.
*   They have helped China's state-owned enterprises to transform their management practices. Joint ventures combining foreign-invested enterprises and the Chinese state-owned enterprises have compelled the state-owned enterprises to transform their existing management practices. In addition, foreign-owned enterprises have led the way in management innovation, showing the way for Chinese state-owned enterprises to transform their own management strategies.
*   Foreign-invested enterprises have also promoted China's reform of the institutional framework in order to conform with international best practice. Production and management in foreign-invest enterprises are all conducted according to international best practice, which is incompatible with China's traditional economic structure. Now that the Chinese government is keen to be the host for vast amounts of overseas capital, the traditional economic structure must be transformed so that laws and institutions enforce international best practice.
*   Foreign-invested enterprises have helped to strengthen relations between the Chinese economy and the world economy. Foreign-invested enterprises are familiar with the world market and are much more outward-looking than Chinese state enterprises. They have not only helped the Chinese authorities develop contacts in the world market, but have also helped Chinese state enterprises to develop a more outward-oriented focus.

CHALLENGES AND PROBLEMS CAUSED BY THE MASSIVE INFLOW OF OVERSEAS CAPITAL

Foreign-invested enterprises have brought competitive pressures to bear upon China's domestic enterprises. Brisk expansion in inflows of overseas capital has

Table 13.11 Taxes paid by FDI enterprises as a proportion of China's total tax revenue (billion yuan)

	1991	1992	1993	1994
Taxes paid by FDI (1)	6.9	10.7	20.6	39.0
Total tax revenue (2)	299.0	329.7	425.5	512.7
(1)/(2)　per cent	2.3	3.2	4.8	7.6

Source: Institute of Industrial Economics, Chinese Academy of Social Sciences, 1997. *China's Industrial Development Report 1996*, China Economy and Management Publishing House, Beijing.

made a substantial impact on China's domestic economy. Even in the home market, a number of local Chinese enterprises are confronted with competitive pressures similar to those found in the world market. On the one hand, foreign-invested enterprises enjoy preferential treatment which local firms cannot access. On the other hand, foreign-invested enterprises have a number of competitive advantages with respect to technology, sales, and branding in addition to capital and management techniques; in all of which Chinese enterprises are disadvantaged.

In certain industries, foreign-invested enterprises maintain a dominant or controlling position. Overseas investors have managed to dominate certain industries by establishing entirely foreign-owned enterprises or by acquiring majority share ownership in joint ventures. In selecting avenues for investment, overseas investors have concentrated their investment in industries with high rates of profit. More specifically, they tend to invest in downstream industries that produce end products. In this way, most industries with high costs and low profits are left to Chinese enterprises. Overseas capital has maintained a dominant position in certain highly profitable industries, and has constituted a high proportion of the exclusive investment and holding companies.

The Chinese government has paid much attention to the quantity of the overseas capital imported but is not good at managing it. This has resulted in a number of problems.

- There is no accurate asset appraisal; the Chinese government's assets are often under-valued or even partially neglected.
- Since overseas capital is concentrated in certain industries and certain regions, there is a tendency towards foreign dominance in those industries and regions.
- There are no enforced regulations on the transfer of pollution in certain industries.
- In foreign-invested enterprises, there is often insufficient social insurance for Chinese employees whose working conditions are generally poor.

Much of the overseas capital flowing into China was unaccompanied by new and advanced foreign technologies. Most joint ventures have been small scale and have utilised existing technologies, generally engaged in the processing and trade industries that have had little to do with advanced technologies. The technologies brought to China by big transnational corporations have not been advanced, and have generally been imported for standardising production and processing. Moreover, the governments of many industrial countries restrict transfer of new and advanced technologies to foreign countries. In addition, when transnational corporations make investments in China, they often refuse to establish research and development programs, sometimes cancelling existing programs in order to use the technologies developed by their parent companies. As a result, the ability of Chinese firms to develop technologies in conjunction with foreign enterprises in joint ventures is weakened.

PROSPECTS FOR FOREIGN CAPITAL

In the near future, the Chinese government will direct efforts at maintaining the level of capital inflow, because foreign capital has become an important factor for China's economic stability in the short term. First, since the massive inflows of foreign capital have occupied a significant position in China's national economy, a sudden decrease may have a great impact on the country's domestic economy. Second, owing to the depreciation of currencies in neighbouring countries following the East Asian financial crisis of 1997, China has had to bear reduced demand for exports for a period of time. As a consequence, export trade can no longer be the driving force for economic growth and overseas investment will have to take its place. Hence there is a need to maintain stability in foreign capital inflows. Third, a decline in exports could cause deficits in the current account, which would have to be offset by a surplus in the capital account to balance international payments, again highlighting the need to maintain foreign capital inflows.

In the long term, the importation of overseas capital should shift in emphasis from quantity to quality. As properly functioning markets are established in China, market forces should attract overseas capital as opposed to the preferential treatment that foreign investment now receives such as reductions in or the remission of tax payments. The benefits associated with fully-functioning markets are obvious. First, they will enable Chinese enterprises to compete with foreign-invested enterprises on an equal footing. Second, market forces will prompt foreign-invested enterprises to increase their sales in the Chinese domestic market, which may lighten China's dependence on foreign trade, and may also help overseas investors to turn their eyes to China's interior regions. A shift to more indirect forms of foreign investment, such as foreign loans and credits will enable China to take the initiative in regard to promoting industrial adjustment and the importation of technology. International indirect investment presents no difficulty as far as possible conflicts over the objectives of the investment are concerned, as recipient countries are free to purchase technology and equipment in the world market according to their industrial and technological requirements.

TECHNOLOGICAL TRANSFER AND ITS IMPACT

A GENERAL SURVEY OF TECHNOLOGICAL TRANSFER TO CHINA

In the early 1980s, China changed the emphasis on technological importation from the importing of technology for new large-scale projects to the importing advanced technologies for transforming existing enterprises. During the Sixth Five-year Plan (1981–85) and the Seventh Five-year Plan (1986–90), 30,000 technological items were imported for the light and textile industries, in addition to the machinery and electronic industries. During the Eight Five-year Plan (1991–95), and apart from the continued importation of technologies for transforming old enterprises, China imported a number of technologies destined for major projects in energy, petrochemistry, metallurgy, aviation, machinery and electronics.

The Chinese government tended to import technologies for major projects and large and medium-scale enterprises. The technological transformation of medium and small-scale enterprises was basically dependent upon foreign direct investment.

IMPACT OF TECHNOLOGICAL TRANSFER ON CHINA'S ECONOMIC DEVELOPMENT

The importation of technology and equipment has significantly raised the technological standard among Chinese enterprises. An important form of China's importation of technology has been to sign contracts to import equipment. In this way both the machinery and advanced technology are purchased simultaneously. During the Eighth Five-year Plan, expenditure on the importation of technology was US$23 billion, registering an increase of 48 per cent as compared with that during the Seventh Five-year Plan. Following the massive inflow of overseas capital into China, the importation of equipment grew rapidly and began to occupy a considerable proportion of China's total imports. It is estimated that during the Eighth Five-year Plan, expenditure on imported machinery and transport equipment accounted for nearly 40 per cent of the country's total expenditure on imports.

Advanced or fairly advanced equipment accounted for about one-third of total equipment imported during the Eighth Five-year Plan, at a value of around US$150 billion. Imported equipment included textile machinery, machine tools for metal processing, machinery for rubber and plastics processing, instruments, and machinery for loading and unloading. By the end of the Eighth Five-year Plan about half of the large and medium-scale state-owned enterprises had gone through considerable technological transformation with the aid of imported advanced technologies and equipment. Among the state-owned enterprises, those engaged in producing goods for export underwent the most comprehensive technological transformation.

Imports of technology and equipment have expanded the productive capacity and technical level of China's export processing industry. As a result, there has been a considerable increase in the production of export goods. At present, manufactured goods are in a dominant position relative to other export goods. During the Eighth Five-year Plan, the proportion of imports and exports of manufactured industrial products in China's total foreign trade increased from 77.7 per cent in 1991 to 83.7 per cent in 1995. The growth in exports of machinery and electrical products and textiles was the most dramatic. In 1985, exports of

Table 13.12 Technology import projects and contracted value by type of import (contract numbers, value in US$ million)

| | 1991 | | 1992 | | 1993 | |
	Contract	Value	Contract	Value	Contract	Value
Total	359	3459	504	6590	493	6109
Whole set equipment	86	2570	166	4308	194	5112
Technology permission	116	478	166	604	200	448
Technology consult	8	4	18	31	12	17
Technology service	10	13	18	118	17	79
Co-production	8	53	11	1108	12	186
Key equipment	124	333	116	393	54	264
Others	7	7	9	29	4	4

| | 1994 | | 1995 | | 1996 | |
	Contract	Value	Contract	Value	Contract	Value
Total	444	4106	3629	13033	6074	15257
Whole set equipment	195	3519	1355	9089	1028	6626
Technology permission	169	390	677	1474	97	1675
Technology consult	22	22	15	112	35	52
Technology service	14	66	22	199	70	506
Co-production	5	3	2	1	75*	376*
Key equipment	38	106	1558	2159	4637	5812
Others	...	...	...	...	132	210

Note: * Technological transfer.

Sources: Statistical Bureau, State Science and Technology Commission, 1996. *China Statistical Yearbook on Science and Technology 1996*, China Statistical Publishing House, Beijing; *Almanac of China's Economy 1997*, Almanac of China's Economy Publishing House, Beijing:7.

Table 13.13 Technology import projects and contracted value by type of import (US$ million)

	1991	1992	1993	1994	1995	1996
Total	3459	6590	6109	4106	13033	15257
Energy	1547	1464	1138	682	3593	1361
Machinery, electronics	384	1909	546	248	3965	2331
Petro-chemistry	1121	2045	2600	605	1104	3068
Communication and traffic	162	120	427	1348	1814	3236
Metallurgy	86	602	709	726	1282	1356
Construction materials	5	1	49	47	473	438
Light Industry and textiles	105	328	355	405	473	1022
Others	50	119	285	47	329	2445

Source: Statistical Bureau, State Science and Technology Commission, 1996. *China Statistical Yearbook on Science and Technology 1996*, China Statistical Publishing House, Beijing; *Almanac of China's Economy 1997*, Almanac of China's Economy Publishing House, Beijing:7.

machinery and electrical products only accounted for 6.5 per cent of China's total export trade. The figure leapt to 29.5 per cent in 1995, surpassing that of the textiles for the first time. Currently, mechanical and electrical products rank as the most important export goods. As for textiles, the proportion of medium and low-grade products in China's total textile trade decreased from 50 per cent in the 1980s to less than 20 per cent in the latter years of the Eighth Five-year Plan. In contrast, the proportion of end products like garments rose from 50 per cent to over 80 per cent during the same period.

The electronic and machinery industries have benefited most from using overseas investment to raise their technological levels. According to a survey of the electronic industry in 1995, the aggregate quantity of equipment owned by an individual Chinese enterprise surpassed that owned by foreign-invested enterprises by 44.9 per cent on average, but the quantity of imported equipment, automatic production lines and computers owned by foreign-invested firms greatly surpassed that of Chinese enterprises. Moreover, a portion of the advanced equipment owned by Chinese enterprises was acquired with the help of overseas capital. It is clear that overseas investment has played a large role in promoting technological progress of the Chinese electronic industry. According to a survey conducted in 1995 investigating foreign-invested enterprises in the machinery industry, their technological level overall reached the international standard of the 1980s, while some individual enterprises reached the international standard of the early 1990s.

The importation of technology has prompted domestic enterprises to raise their management performance and the quality of their human capital. To equip Chinese enterprises with advanced technology and equipment inevitably demands a corresponding rise in the quality of management practices, workers and staff in order to make the most of the advanced technology and equipment. Moreover, the importation of technology generally includes support services such as technical training and technical guidance. In addition, the nature of imported technologies has changed from operational technologies to mainly manufacturing technologies.

PROBLEMS IN THE TRANSFER OF TECHNOLOGY

Among the technologies imported with foreign direct investment, there are not many genuinely advanced technologies. The technologies imported by medium and small-scale enterprises are technically low grade. Especially in the case of enterprises engaged in processing industries, the Chinese party can only earn processing rebates without acquiring much technology. Small and medium-scale enterprises are great in number, and produce goods that account for about half of the total value of China's export trade. In particular, processing firms in 1994 produced 71 per cent of total exports of mechanical and electrical products.

Table 13.14 Exports and imports of high-tech products, manufactured industrial products and primary products (US$ billion)

	1987	1988	1990	1993	1994	1995
I. Total foreign trade	82.65	102.79	115.41	195.71	236.73	280.85
Manufactured prod.	62.51	78.29	89.70	164.82	200.56	234.95
share (per cent)	75.6	76.2	77.7	84.2	84.7	83.7
High-tech prod.	6.31	9.42	9.65	20.58	26.94	31.92
share (per cent)	7.6	9.2	8.4	10.5	11.4	11.4
Primary prod.	20.15	24.50	25.71	30.89	36.18	45.90
share (per cent)	24.4	23.8	22.3	15.8	15.3	16.3
II. Export	39.44	47.54	62.06	91.76	121.04	148.77
Manufactured prod.	26.21	33.11	46.21	75.09	101.33	127.28
share (per cent)	66.4	69.6	74.5	81.8	83.7	85.6
High-tech prod.	0.92	1.29	2.69	4.68	6.34	10.09
share (per cent)	2.3	2.7	4.3	5.1	5.2	6.8
Primary prod.	13.23	14.43	15.86	16.68	19.71	21.49
share (per cent)	33.6	30.4	25.5	18.2	16.3	14.4
III. Import	43.21	55.25	53.35	103.95	115.69	132.08
Manufactured prod.	36.30	45.18	43.50	89.73	99.22	107.67
share (per cent)	84.0	81.8	81.5	86.3	85.8	81.5
High-tech prod.	5.32	8.13	6.97	15.91	20.60	21.83
share (per cent)	12.5	14.7	13.1	15.3	17.8	16.5
Primary prod.	6.92	10.7	9.85	14.22	16.47	24.41
share (per cent)	16.0	18.2	18.5	13.7	14.2	18.5

Source: Statistical Bureau, State Science and Technology Commission, 1996. *China Statistical Yearbook on Science and Technology 1996*, China Statistical Publishing House, Beijing.

The transfer of technology from big transnational corporations has tended to be more basic technology used in the standardisation of production and processing. Moreover, foreign governments often restrict the transfer of new and advanced technology to other countries.

China's ability to assimilate advanced technology is still limited. China's scientific research institutions and enterprises are relatively independent of each other, but relations between the two have become closer since the start of economic restructuring. Nonetheless, the research and development capabilities of Chinese enterprises are rather poor. Although there is a policy of markets for technology there are still many difficulties in its implementation. The process of technological transfer is stepwise and overseas parties tend to impose conditions. The pace of technology transfer is controlled within the limits of China's technological development. For Chinese parties, if the imported technology exceeds the firms' ability to assimilate it, the technology is useless in raising the firms' efficiency. In the worst case, imported equipment may be left unused or damaged. This kind of problem was prevalent in the 1980s. Since the 1990s, large-scale enterprises have paid attention to raising their ability to assimilate advanced technologies, but the medium and small-scale enterprises still have a weakness in this regard.

THE TREND OF TECHNOLOGY TRANSFER

The aggregate quantity of technology transferred will remain at a high level. At present, China has accumulated substantial foreign exchange reserves and Chinese enterprises have gone from strength to strength. The Chinese government also has encouraged domestic enterprises to engage in technological transformation by utilising advanced technologies from overseas. Moreover, many enterprises in coastal regions are under pressure to upgrade their capital equipment, and

Table 13.15   Scientific and technological research institutions (numbers)

	1990	1994	1995	1996
Total	18772	23613	24259	23610
In research institutions	8990	7805	7721	7636
In large and medium industrial enterprises	8116	12499	13107	12033
In institutions of higher education	1666	3309	3431	3398

Source: State Statistical Bureau, 1997. *China Statistical Yearbook 1997*, China Statistical Publishing House, Beijing.

Table 13.16 Technology import projects and contracted value by region of import (number; US$ million).

	1991		1992		1993	
	Contract	Value	Contract	Value	Contract	Value
Total	359	3459	504	6590	493	6109
Japan	63	269	136	1376	101	1746
USA	54	135	85	1432	104	507
Germany	54	265	70	733	83	748
Italy	28	353	44	1444	53	922
Russia	9	1374	6	245	14	383
France	35	194	22	383	17	175
Spain	9	246	5	388	6	442
UK	21	344	25	22	10	116
Canada	7	67	13	181	14	188
Hong Kong	28	20	35	76	21	42
Austria	10	25	9	67	9	120
Korea			3	17	8	304
Switzerland	9	14	17	62	13	128
Finland			6	89	7	152
Sweden	6	18	3	10	8	11
Australia						
Others	26	135	25	66	25	125

	1994		1995		1996	
	Contract	Value	Contract	Value	Contract	Value
Total	444	4106	3629	13033	6074	15257
Japan	94	769	533	2249	925	2404
USA	75	594	798	2272	1744	2130
Germany	67	1232	398	1892	705	4907
Italy	31	311	153	977	196	470
Russia	2	4	285	759	194	1177
France	26	195	78	1706	220	614
Spain	4	95	28	275	30	177
UK	12	75	82	718	134	201
Canada	12	268	62	204	115	384
Hong Kong	34	134	674	586	1021	922
Austria	8	34	45	303	69	300
Korea	7	84	38	103	56	150
Switzerland	8	10	86	188	136	194
Finland	4	17	22	101	37	199
Sweden	35	105	72	210	115	326
Australia	5	84	24	74	49	208
Others	20	95	251	416	264	385

Source: Statistical Bureau, State Science and Technology Commission, 1996. *China Statistical Yearbook on Science and Technology 1996*, China Statistical Publishing House, Beijing; *Almanac of China's Economy 1997*, Almanac of China's Economy Publishing House, Beijing:7.

need to import advanced foreign technologies and equipment to do so. These factors will give an added impetus to the transfer of technology.

The ability of Chinese enterprises to assimilate advanced technologies will gradually increase, and the mode of technology transfer will shift from predominantly importing entire plants to importing key pieces of equipment and acquiring technological licenses. As a result, the average scale of technological equipment imported will gradually become smaller and more medium and small-scale enterprises will be able to import the advanced technology required to increase their productivity and efficiency.

The sources of China's technology will remain diverse and relatively balanced. In the early 1990s, China imported technology mainly from Europe due to international political concerns. Since 1992, and owing to the gradual normalisation of Sino-US relations, China's technological imports from the United States and Japan have increased rapidly. Now that the configuration of China's political and economic relations with the outside world have fundamentally been settled, it is expected that the sources of China's technology will retain the present balance among Europe, the United States and Japan.

Progress in economic and technological cooperation within the APEC framework will play an important role in promoting the transfer of technology to China and technological cooperation with China. Economic and technological cooperation is one of the APEC's two aims, the other aim being the liberalisation of investment and trade. APEC member countries have responded to these aims, taking action to cooperate and liberalise to various degrees. China has proposed that a network for high-tech cooperation among APEC member countries be established, and has listed its 53 new and high technological development zones as the first batch of sci-tec industrial parks to be opened to APEC members. China's initiatives have received a positive response from some countries. In sum, the strengthening of technological cooperation among APEC members will not only facilitate the transfer of advanced technologies to China from overseas, but will also enhance the ability of Chinese enterprises to assimilate and develop that technology, empowering China to import more advanced foreign technology.

14

EXCHANGE RATE CHANGES, TRADE DEVELOPMENT AND STRUCTURAL ADJUSTMENT IN THE EAST ASIAN ECONOMIES

ZHOU XIAOBING & LIGANG SONG

Discussion of the relationship between exchange rate movements and the growth of trade in the East Asian economies has drawn renewed attention among economists and policymakers alike since the Asian financial crisis broke out in mid-1997. Understanding the pattern of this relationship may partly explain the occurrence of the financial crisis in these export-oriented economies. Exchange rate movements (large scale depreciations), directly caused by the financial crisis, will shape the way in which the regional economy recovers from the crisis. Discussion of exchange rate policies in the regional economy can be put into the broader context of trade reform and liberalisation. Much can be learned from the experiences of the East Asian economies as they emerge from financial crisis.

The key to understanding the relationship between exchange rate and trade is that changes in exchange rates—not only regional currencies against major currencies such as the US dollar and Japanese yen, but also major currencies such as the US dollar vis-à-vis the Japanese yen—have a direct impact on the international competitivenes of developing economies. An understanding of this relationship has important implications for these export-oriented economies with respect to ongoing structural change and adjustment and their economic recovery.

What follows is some preliminary evidence of how the trade performance of the East Asian economies has been related to changes in their exchange rates in the past—particularly in relation to major currencies such as the US dollar and Japanese yen. Some policy implications with respect to the necessity for and direction of structural adjustments in the East Asian economies is discussed, highlighting the relationship between China and other East Asian economies. The East Asia economies are treated as an entity in discussing the

243

overall trade performance and changes in exchange rates of the regional economies over the past two to three decades.

EXCHANGE RATE MOVEMENTS, TRADE AND ECONOMIC GROWTH

The defining characteristic of the East Asian economy in the past is that the rapid development and growth of the regional economies has largely been driven by trade. The trade structure in the economy has been constantly upgraded in order to implement the so-called export-oriented development strategy, presumably because of the pressure from market competition. The past experience of the regional economy shows that changes in exchange rates affect both trade development and shifts in trade structure. Figure 14.1 illustrates that trade growth of the East Asian economy has closely followed the trend of the composite exchange rate—with slight time lags—over the past 30 years.

Exchange rate misalignments can trigger structural changes. Most East Asian developing economies pegged their currencies to the US dollar in recent years, even though their trade with the United States accounted for only a proportion of their total trade. Consequently, changes in the nominal and real value of the US dollar relative to the Japanese yen may have affected the real exchange rate of those Asian currencies pegged to the US dollar. For example, when the yen was strong against the US dollar, Asian currencies pegged to the US dollar tended to depreciate relative to the yen. There are two effects. First, a strong yen against the US dollar tended to increase the international competitiveness of East Asian exports, especially in the US market. Second, a strong yen forced Japan to shift production facilities offshore in the form of foreign direct investments, benefiting other East Asian economies in their production upgrading. Consequently, the period under study can be divided into two phases: one associated with a strong yen and the other with a weak yen. The impact on competitiveness and capital flows in the regional economy can be discussed accordingly.

A large-scale exchange rate misalignment, coupled with factors such as inappropriate macroeconomic policies, can provoke a financial crisis such as the East Asian crisis. In the case of a weak yen, a real exchange rate appreciation tends to reduce the competitiveness of the regional economy, worsening the current accounts of the individual economies and endangering export-oriented development strategy, necessitating drastic policy measures to restore the external balance.

Due to a financial deregulation and liberalisation program aimed at opening up capital markets, a pegged system could provoke capital inflows because of the low exchange rate risk associated with a policy of stable currency value. Such inflows prevent currency depreciation, causing large and growing current account imbalances.

The changes in East Asian exchange rates against the US dollar in nominal terms are depicted for the period 1971 to 1995 in Figure 14.2. For convenience, the NIEs and ASEAN countries are grouped together. There were four major appreciations of the yen against the US dollar during the period under study, beginning in 1971, 1975, 1985 and 1991, respectively. Each swing lasted for at least 3 years. Such medium-term swings in nominal exchange rates—referred to as misalignments—can lead to changes in real exchange rates (Marston 1991:125).

As argued earlier, from the perspective of other East Asian economies, there are some benefits associated with a strong yen, such as improved competitiveness and large capital inflows, mainly from Japan. These effects, along with others such as a more favourable international economic climate in the early years, became the driving force for structural change and adjustment in these economies.

The first appreciation of the yen in 1971 was associated with a shift of production facilities—especially those which produced labour-intensive products—from Japan to other economies in East Asia, particularly Korea and Taiwan. Imports of capital-intensive products from Japan by ASEAN and the NIEs peaked during this period (41.8 and 47.5 per cent respectively), laying a

Figure 14.1   Changes in East Asian exchange rate (composite) and trade growth, 1966–96 (per cent)

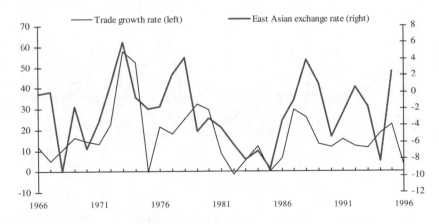

Notes: East Asian economy includes Japan, China, Hong Kong, Taiwan, Korea and ASEAN countries (5). Trade growth rate is calculated based on these economies as a whole. The composite exchange rate was formed by calculating the average changes of the respective exchange rates against the US dollar (nominal) using total trade of each as weights.

Source: United Nations' COMTRADE International Trade Data, October 1997, International Economic Databank, The Australian National University, Canberra; authors' calculations.

foundation for carrying out the export-oriented development strategy in these economies.[1] Exports had become an important source of economic growth, and a major goal of governments with respect to exchange rate policy had been to prevent their currencies from appreciating since appreciation would be detrimental to the export-oriented growth.

Exchange rate misalignment of the yen/dollar continued into the 1980s. Beginning in 1985, the yen began a sharp appreciation against other currencies, particularly the US dollar. As pointed out by Petri (1991:51), this round of appreciation was roughly twice as large as that in 1971–73 (Figure 14.2), and therefore had an even stronger effect on the structural changes associated with capital flows and changing competitiveness of the regional economy.

As the relative cost of production in Japan increased with protectionist measures directed against exports from Japan, there were massive flows of capital from Japan to the East Asian economies, particularly the NIEs and ASEAN. Through these, Japan built stronger economic and trade relationships first with the NIEs, then ASEAN and later China, and accelerated the pace of structural changes in the regional economy. The trade relationship was characterised by Japan's export of advanced consumer goods and—especially in the case of

Figure 14.2 Changes in the East Asian exchange rate against the US dollar (per cent)

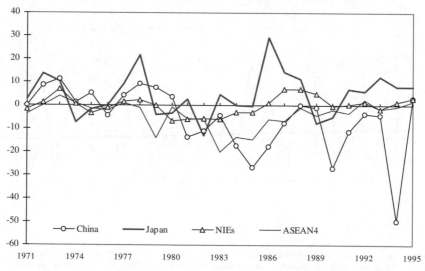

Source: The World Bank; United Nations' COMTRADE International Trade Data, October 1997, International Economic Databank, The Australian National University, Canberra and authors' calculations.

NIEs—capital goods and sophisticated components, and its imports of consumer goods—at both ends of the quality spectrum—and industrial supplies (Petri 1991:77).

There were also periods in which a weak yen relative to the US dollar, negatively affected the process of East Asian structural transformation. For example, from the late 1970s to mid-1980s, the yen consistently depreciated against the dollar. Since most East Asian exports at that time went to destinations outside the region, other East Asian economies were forced to depreciate their currencies to maintain international competitiveness.[2]

A weak yen combined with the forced depreciation of other regional currencies restrained these economies' imports. This slowed the progress of their industrial upgrading, offseting the gains in competitiveness resulting from currency depreciation. After the loss of export momentum of the East Asian economies, the regional economy was dragged into recession in the early 1980s.[3]

There is a unique relationship between economic growth of the East Asian economies and the yen/dollar exchange rate in that there is a high correlation (0.68) between GDP growth of the East Asian economies (excluding Japan) and changes in the exchange rate between the yen and US dollar. A simple Granger causality test indicates that the exchange rate Granger-causes' GDP growth and the reverse does not hold for this case.[4] This is consistent with the story that exchange rate movements—not only regional currencies against major currencies such as US dollar and Japanese yen, but especially between major currencies such as the US dollar vis-à-vis the yen—do have a significant impact on economic growth through their influence on both capital flows and export competitiveness.

EAST ASIAN COMPETITIVENESS AND BALANCE OF TRADE

The extent to which exchange rate changes affect a country's export competitiveness depends on how its real exchange rate is affected. It is the real exchange rate that affects the allocation of productive resources in the economy. Faced with a strong yen since the mid 1980s, most East Asian economies adopted a strategy of pegging their currencies to the US dollar in order to maintain currency stability.

Unfortunately, from 1995 the US dollar appreciated sharply against the yen (the yen/dollar exchange rate rose from 80 in 1995 to approximately 125 in 1997). As a result, East Asian currencies that were tied in nominal terms to the dollar also experienced a very rapid real appreciation, causing a substantial loss of export competitiveness, especially for Thailand, Malaysia, Indonesia and the Philippines (Figure 14.4).

Some of the Northeast Asian economies—such as Hong Kong, Korea and Taiwan—also experienced a decline in export competitiveness after 1995 (Figure 14.5). China stands out in comparison with other East Asian economies in that its competitiveness took several jumps (Figure 14.5) after a number of depreciations during the previous 15 years (Figure 14.2). But after peaking in 1994 due to the large-scale depreciation resulting from the exchange rate system reform of that year, China's competitiveness began to decline.

The declining trend of East Asian economies' export competitiveness in the mid 1990s is reflected in East Asia's balance of trade (Table 14.1). The figures reveal that the trade balance of the East Asian economies as a whole witnessed a structural change during the decade 1986–96. First, there was a widening trade imbalance (deficits) within the East Asian economies (first column), reflecting the rapid development of intraregional trade on the one hand and unbalanced trading relations among themselves, on the other.

Second and more significantly, in 1996, the East Asian economies—for the first time—incurred trade deficits with countries outside the region (second column), confirming that the region's overall competitiveness had deteriorated.

Figure 14.3 Changes in yen/US dollar exchange rate and East Asian GDP growth, 1970–98 (per cent)

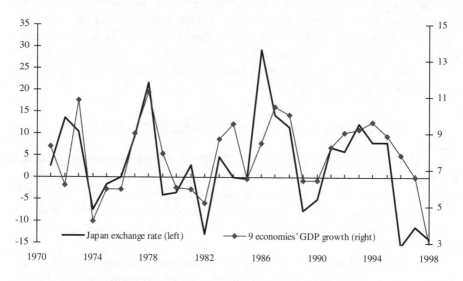

Note: GDP figures for nine East Asian economies are calculated based on the constant price of US dollar of 1987.

Source: The World Bank; World Tables, International Economic Databank, The Australian National University, Canberra; authors' calculations.

This drastic shift in the trade balance of the regional economy may underly the causes of the financial crisis that began in 1997.

The slowdown in export revenue led to expectations of reduced corporate profits and to a decline in equity prices (Noland 1998). First domestic residents, then foreign investors, began moving money offshore in search of higher returns, contributing to exchange rate depreciation (in countries with a floating currency), or alternatively, putting pressure on the exchange rate peg (in countries that pegged to a foreign currency such as the dollar). The rest of the story is well known.

Third, while the East Asian economies still enjoyed a trade surplus—albeit a declining one—with the United States, trade with the Western European countries and the world as a whole created emerging deficits in 1993 and 1994, when both NIEs' and ASEAN's nominal exchange rates showed signs of appreciation against the US dollar (Figure 14.2) and their export competitiveness began to decline (Figures 14.4 and 14.5).

Finally, large deficits for trade within the East Asian region, and the surplus with the United States reveal an interesting triangular trade relationship between the East Asian economies, Japan and the United States. Park and Park (1991) describe this relationship by examining the case for NIEs. These economies depended on the US market for their exports of manufactured products and relied heavily on Japan as a major supplier of capital goods, intermediate inputs, technology and management know-how. These patterns of trade led to a growing trade surplus with the United States and a large and persistent deficit with Japan, both of which began in the early 1970s (Park and Park 1991:85).

More importantly, this pattern of trade is often identified as one of the structural rigidities hindering adjustment of the trade imbalance between the NIEs and the United States on the one hand, and between the NIEs and Japan on the other (Park and Park 1991:85). These rigidities have been perpetuated and complicated by constant changes in the product composition of exports of the East Asian economies, driven by their underlying comparative advantage.

TRADE COMPOSITION AND STRUCTURAL CHANGE

The structural changes which have been taking place in East Asia are clearly reflected in the changing pattern of their exports of labour-intensive products. Figure 14.6 reports the shares of East Asian economies' total exports of labour-intensive products to the United States during the past three decades (1965–95), which can roughly be divided into three sub-periods.

From the mid-1960s to the mid-1970s, exports of labour-intensive products from Japan were predominant in the United States import market. Hong Kong was also a big player during this period. Other economies as a whole had a very small—though increasing—share in the US market for labour-intensive products, particularly Taiwan and Korea.

Figure 14.4   Real exchange rate for Southeast Asian economies, 1975–98

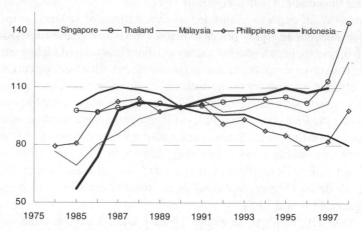

Note: 1990 = 100.

Source: *International Monetary Fund* various issues, *International Financial Statistics, International Economic Databank, Asia Pacific Economics Group, Asia Pacific Profiles 1998*, The Australian National University, Canberra.

Figure 14.5   Real exchange rate for Northeast Asian economies, 1975–98

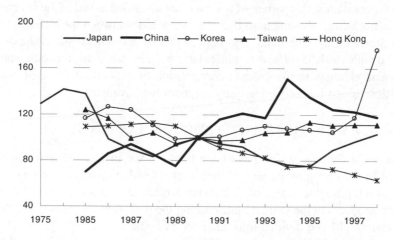

Note: 1990 = 100.

Source: *International Monetary Fund* various issues, *International Financial Statistics, International Economic Databank, Asia Pacific Economics Group, Asia Pacific Profiles 1998*, The Australian National University, Canberra.

Table 14.1   East Asian balance of trade, 1986–96 (US$ billion)

Year	Within East Asia	Outside East Asia	With the United States	With West Europe	With the World
1986	-10.10	104.81	86.88	20.62	94.71
1987	-17.06	102.22	87.92	24.31	85.16
1988	-22.89	85.15	76.40	27.43	62.26
1989	-27.55	56.60	68.15	19.85	29.05
1990	-28.05	29.95	54.93	17.28	1.90
1991	-38.80	41.95	49.00	26.27	3.15
1992	-48.97	58.95	57.38	24.06	9.98
1993	-68.35	58.13	69.82	9.75	-10.22
1994	-63.45	45.15	76.14	-4.36	-18.30
1995	-69.93	6.80	58.81	-12.10	-63.13
1996	-80.22	-39.49	41.61	-23.46	-119.71

Notes: East Asia consists of 10 economies; outside East Asia includes the United States and West Europe. Trade deficits within East Asia also include Hong Kong's trade deficit with China.

Source: UN trade data, International Economic Databank, The Australian National University, Canberra.

From the mid-1970s to the late 1980s, Japan's share of labour-intensive products in the US market shrank rapidly, while the shares of Taiwan and Korea expanded substantially. Hong Kong's share also expanded, but showed signs of declining from the early 1980s. This declining trend occurred in Hong Kong earlier than in Taiwan and Korea, presumably because of Hong Kong's closer integration with mainland China.

Singapore also enjoyed an enlarged share compared with the previous period, but still much lower than that of Japan, Hong Kong and China. ASEAN's shares started picking up, though from a very low base.

From the end of the 1980s to the mid-1990s, the Asian NIEs—following in the footsteps of Japan—reduced their shares of labour-intensive exports in the US market. ASEAN countries increased their shares rapidly in the early period and maintained a relatively constant share from the beginning of the 1990s. Among these East Asian economies, China became a predominant player in exporting labour-intensive products to the US market.

Finally, East Asia's share of labour-intensive exports to the United States peaked by the early 1980s, reaching nearly 70 per cent of total imports of labour-intensive products by the United States. Its share declined steadily through the mid 1990s. By 1995, the overall share was almost equivalent to that in 1965, implying that the product composition of exports of the East Asian economies as a whole has shifted from predominantly labour-intensive products to capital and even human-capital intensive products over the period.

Figure 14.6   East Asian share of labour-intensive products in US market, 1965–95 (per cent)

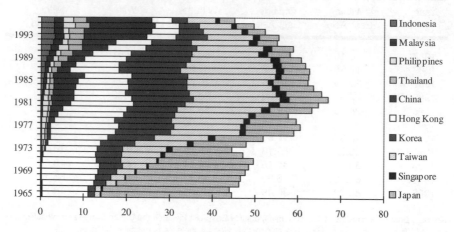

Source: STARS: UN COMTRADE International Trade Data, October 1997, International Economic Databank, The Australian National University, Canberra.

Figure 14.7   Product structure of East Asian exports to the United States, 1965–95 (per cent)

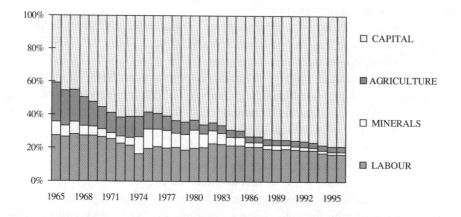

Source: STARS: UN COMTRADE International Trade Data, October 1997, International Economic Databank, The Australian National University, Canberra.

However, the pressure from competition has not been lessened by the shifts of product composition of exports, particularly among those economies with similar factor endowments and who are at similar stages of development. For example, since traded goods from China and ASEAN countries are highly homogenous, competition between them in third country markets is inevitable.

Growth rates of exports of labour-intensive products of the ASEAN 4 over the period 1986–96 peaked from the mid 1980s to the early 1990s (Table 14.2). By 1996, two economies—Thailand and the Philippines—even recorded negative growth. At the same time, China has become a large exporter of labour-intensive products.

A solution to this competition problem seems to be that the East Asian economies need to be constantly upgrading their production to raise the product sophistication of their exports. This is what Japan did in the 1960s and 1970s, the NIEs did in the 1970s and 1980s, and what ASEAN and China have been doing since the late 1980s and early 1990s (Figure 14.7).

The share of capital-intensive products in the East Asian economies' total exports to the US market increased substantially, while the shares of agriculture, minerals and labour-intensive products were falling over this period. However, in order to see how industrial transformation (upgrading) was taking place in the regional economy, we need to look at how trade structures—for example, with respect to capital-intensive products—of the regional economies with different levels of development evolve over time. The ASEAN 4 and NIEs are chosen here to see how their trade orientation of capital-intensive products with

Table 14.2 Growth rates of exports of labour-intensive products of ASEAN 4, 1986–96 (per cent)

Year	Indonesia	Malaysia	Philippines	Thailand
1986	45.47	15.34	10.40	37.00
1987	34.38	44.76	30.85	64.63
1988	51.23	20.38	24.85	36.57
1989	44.40	32.49	24.64	28.08
1990	58.28	35.98	12.12	20.95
1991	46.12	29.75	98.55	27.40
1992	42.46	19.87	-37.32	9.42
1993	9.53	1.80	5.88	16.86
1994	-1.72	16.48	13.76	11.55
1995	10.43	18.31	93.22	21.78
1996	7.73	10.88	-1.26	-36.72

Source: STARS: UN COMTRADE International Trade Data, October 1997, International Economic Databank, The Australian National University, Canberra.

other groups of the East Asian economy and the United States has changed over the past decade (Table 14.3).

First, while their dependence on capital-intensive imports from the East Asian region was similar, ASEAN's dependence on capital-intensive exports to the East Asian market was higher than that for NIEs.

Second, both ASEAN and NIEs' export dependence on capital-intensive products to the East Asian region increased substantially, while their dependence on the US market dropped over the period. This may indicate that both groups suffered a reduction in US market share similar to the situation for labour-intensive products in previous periods (Figure 14.6).

Third, both groups continued to rely heavily on imports of capital-intensive products from Japan. Although the dependence ratio was declining over this period—particularly for NIEs—it is still much higher than that of imports from the United States. It is also noted that ASEAN countries are rapidly depending on NIEs to provide capital-intensive products. This may reflect that NIEs are catching up quickly in producing more sophisticated capital-intensive products.

Fourth, for exports of capital-intensive products, both groups depend more on the United States; for imports, they both rely more on Japan. This confirms that the pattern of a triangular trade relationship between the East Asian economies, Japan and the United States identified earlier still exists. This also means that future East Asian trade will continue to be affected by the movement of the yen/US dollar exchange rate.

Table 14.3 Trade orientation of capital-intensive products by ASEAN 4 and NIEs, 1986 and 1996 (per cent)

		Exports		Imports	
		1986	1996	1986	1996
ASEAN4	East Asia	43.36	54.30	51.56	60.02
	NIEs	26.78	32.72	13.65	22.30
	ASEAN	5.42	7.55	2.26	4.82
	China	2.01	1.46	1.19	1.91
	Japan	9.15	12.57	34.47	30.98
	United States	33.61	23.06	19.27	15.98
NIEs	East Asia	26.31	47.57	58.20	59.78
	NIEs	8.94	18.20	8.11	12.49
	ASEAN	7.65	15.65	4.01	10.30
	China	2.58	4.98	3.98	10.11
	Japan	7.14	8.74	42.09	26.88
	United States	44.05	22.66	18.78	18.67

Source: STARS: UN COMTRADE International Trade Data, October 1997, International Economic Databank, The Australian National University, Canberra.

Finally, structural changes in the East Asian economies are also reflected in their changing industrial structure (Table 14.4). The shares for manufacturing industry have been declining gradually in Japan and Singapore and sharply in Hong Kong. At the same time, the shares for the services industry have steadily increased over the past decade.

LESSONS AND POLICY IMPLICATIONS

The problem with the East Asian economy now is that shocks arise from both goods and capital markets. The former type of shock is mainly due to the reduction in export competitiveness, caused at least in part by the appreciation of their real exchange rates. The other shock largely results from countries' overborrowing, the misconduct of government policy which contributed to the 'bubble economy' and weak financial and banking systems.

A long-term strategy for resolving the crisis is industrial upgrading. This strategy requires further accumulation of a country's physical and human capital and secure external markets for its exports. Since the triangular trade and investment relationship between Japan, the United States and other East Asian economies will remain unchanged for some time to come, it is important for both Japan and the United States to stabilise exchange rates, stimulate economic growth (for Japan) and keep markets open to exports from the East Asian economies.

Even with some justification for imposing capital (or exchange) controls as an extraordinary measure adopted to deal with the crisis, countries in the region should try to continue to strive towards an open market for goods, services and capital in the ongoing process of liberalisation.

For China, the general consensus is that keeping the renminbi exchange rate unchanged throughout the financial crisis contributed to the stability of the regional economy by preventing regional economies from plunging into a new wave of competitive depreciation. But the government should not renounce exchange rate adjustments as a policy instrument for dealing with macroeconomic (external) imbalances.

The flexible exchange rate policy adopted by the government has contributed greatly to the remarkable achievements in external trade by China in the process of trade liberalisation. This is because, as Edwards (1995:10) points out, 'real exchange rate behaviour is a key element during a trade liberalisation transition'.

Competition from other crisis-hit economies in East Asia may intensify at later stages when liquidity problems in these economies are overcome and the elasticities of supply of exports rise.

Without devaluation, the only choice left for the government to maintain export competitiveness is to raise productivity, which arises through more efficient

Table 14.4 Changing industrial structure of Japan and NIEs, 1986 and 1994 (per cent)

Country	Agriculture		Industry		Manufacture		Service	
	1986	1994	1986	1994	1986	1994	1986	1994
Japan	3.0	2.1	40.3	38.2	28.6	24.5	56.7	59.6
Hong Kong	0.4	0.2	30.3	16.9	22.6	9.3	69.2	83.0
Singapore	0.6	0.2	37.4	35.3	26.4	26.1	61.9	64.6
Taiwan	5.5	3.6	47.1	37.4	39.4	29.0	47.3	59.1
Korea	11.2	7.0	42.1	42.8	30.8	26.8	46.8	50.1

Source: STARS: UN COMTRADE International Trade Data, October 1997, International Economic Databank, The Australian National University, Canberra.

allocation of productive resources. Of course, policy measures such as increasing the export tax rebate and provision of export credit, will certainly be helpful in boosting exports, but they are not long-term solutions to the problems facing China's external sector. As previous experience shows, the more efficient allocation and use of productive resources in the export sector of the economy follows from ongoing trade system reform and liberalisation. It is therefore in China's fundamental interests to continue its reform and liberalisation program.

A similar argument on the importance of an export-oriented development strategy for developing economies can be made from another angle. Attracting foreign capital has proved to be an effective means of acquiring much-needed new technology and skills, thereby upgrading industrial structure and raising productivity. China, with its big plans to attract and utilise more foreign capital in its economic transformation, is no exception in this regard. A firm commitment to reform and liberalisation will secure business confidence, thereby attracting more foreign capital into the economy.

CONCLUSIONS

Exports have contributed greatly to the economic growth and prosperity of the East Asian economies in the past, but a slowdown of export growth also helped trigger the financial crisis which wiped out so many of the gains from trade for these economies. They may have to reply with a strategy to 'export their way out' of the crisis. This strategy is not without its risks.

Uncertainties associated with this strategy include exchange rate volatility, capital outflows, export financing (liquidity problem), intensified competition (due to the wide spread depreciations), protectionism, and a slowdown of economic growth in other parts of the world economy, particularly North America and Europe.

The triangular relationship between the East Asian economies, Japan and the United States facilitated the rapid economic transformation in the East Asian economies in the past, but due to structural rigidities, also imposed some limits to the export-oriented development strategy of the East Asian economies. Resolving the current difficulties requires cooperation from all parties involved. In particular, the opening of markets is essential for the recovery of the regional economy and for the stability and security of the Asia Pacific region.

It is in this context that the continued global (WTO) as well as region-wide trade liberalisation (APEC) seems to hold the key to long-term solutions. It is particularly important for the East Asian economies, since they are heavily dependent on intra-regional trade. China has been less disrupted by the financial crisis and therefore may be able to play a more positive role in maintaining the momentum of region-wide trade liberalisation (APEC).

REFERENCES

Das, D.K., 1998. 'Changing comparative advantage and the changing composition of Asian exports', *The World Economy*, 21(1):121–40.

Dornbusch, R. and Leslie, F. and Helmers, H.C. (eds), 1988. *The Open Economy: Tools for Policymakers in Developing Countries*, Oxford University Press, New York and Oxford.

Edwards, S. (ed.), 1995. *Capital Controls, Exchange Rates and Monetary Policy in the World Economy*, Cambridge University Press, Cambridge.

Garnaut, R., 1998. 'The financial crisis', *Asian–Pacific Economic Literature*, 12(1):1–11.

Marston, R.C., 1991. 'Price behaviour in Japanese and US manufacturing' in P. Krugman (ed.), *Trade with Japan: Has the Door Opened Wider?*, University of Chicago Press, Chicago and London.

Noland, M., 1998. Statement before the House International Relations Committee Subcommittees on Asian and Pacific Affairs, and International Economic Policy and Trade, Washington, DC, 3 February.

Park, Y.C. and Park, W., 1991. 'Changing Japanese trade patterns and the East Asian NICs' in P. Krugman (ed.), *Trade with Japan: Has the Door Opened Wider?*, University of Chicago Press, Chicago and London.

Petri, P.A., 1991. 'Market structure, comparative advantage, and Japanese trade under the strong yen' in P. Krugman (ed.), *Trade with Japan: Has the Door Opened Wider?*, University of Chicago Press, Chicago and London.

Song, L., 1996. *Changing Global Comparative Advantage: Evidence from Asia and the Pacific*, Addison-Wesley, Melbourne.

NOTES

[1] As a result, Japan's share of exports of labour-intensive products in the US market fell dramatically in the early 1970s and the shares for Taiwan and Korea picked up (Figure 14.6).

[2] The most recent episode of a weak yen was during the period from 1995 to the present. This swing of the yen/dollar exchange rate has lasted more than three years and has been accompanied by a deterioration of the Japanese economy, and the financial crisis in East Asia.

[3] This was one of the reasons why a weakened yen against the US dollar towards mid-1998 was so worrisome for the regional economies.

[4] The computed F value (9.11) exceeds the critical F value (7.82) with (1, 24) degree of freedom at the 1 per cent level of significance, so that the null hypothesis is rejected.

15

CHINA'S TRADE EFFICIENCY: MEASUREMENT AND DETERMINANTS

PETER DRYSDALE, YIPING HUANG AND K.P. KALIRAJAN

China's open door policy has led to its increasingly deeper integration into the global economy during the reform period. Between 1978 and 1997, China's real GDP grew at an annual rate of 9.6 per cent. The average growth rate of trade was even higher, at 12.9 per cent, for the same period. According to the official statistics, China's export/GDP ratio increased from 9.1 per cent in 1978 to 25.6 per cent in 1997 (SSB 1997; APEG 1998). There is now consensus among economists that the official GDP data are under-estimated and that the per capita GNP in 1990 was about US$1,000 instead of US$370 (Garnaut and Ma 1993; Lardy 1994). According to these properly adjusted income data, China's current export-to-GDP ratio is slightly above 6 per cent. China still has great potential for export growth.

In what follows, the method used by Drysdale et al. (1998) to evaluate the efficiency of China's bilateral trade with individual countries will be applied. In a stochastic gravity model framework, trade efficiencies can be measured and their determinants identified. This will not only provide some idea about the efficiency performance of China's bilateral trade relative to other countries, but also suggest some policy measures to improve efficiency.

Bilateral trade flows have been the focus of an important part of the literature on international trade. In a comprehensive review of methodologies analysing bilateral trade flows in a many-country world, Drysdale and Garnaut (1982) identified two types of barriers (or resistances) to trade—objective and subjective resistances—and examined two analytical approaches—the gravity model and trade intensity analysis—which recur in this literature.

The gravity model, pioneered by Tinbergen (1962), offers a simple but useful framework for empirical studies identifying important factors influencing bilateral trade flows. In the studies by Tinbergen and many of his followers (such as

259

Linnemann 1966), trade flows between two countries are determined by their respective gross national products and population, and resistance variables such as distance. Estimation of these conventional gravity models provides a picture of the average of the sample countries (Krugman 1991; Frankel 1993).

Assume a gravity model $X + f(T)$, where X is China's bilateral trade flow and T is a vector of explanatory variables. On a vertical axis X and horizontal axis T, the conventionally estimated function can be expressed as a continuous curve $f(X)$ (Figure 15.1). Actual observations will be scattered around this curve. From estimation results, it can be predicted that if China's and the trade partner's explanatory variables are T_1, bilateral trade between China and that country is, on average, X_1.

The story at the average is important, but it does not reveal different performance across all observations. Even though the difference of a particular group of bilateral trade flows (such as trade among Asia Pacific economies) can be picked up by including additional dummy variables, comparison of individual performance is often impossible. In the real world, there are frequently observations with the same level of explanatory variables but vastly different trade flows (illustrated by points A and B in Figure 15.1).

The stochastic gravity model applied in this study generally follows the stochastic frontier approach that was first introduced by Aigner et al. (1977)

Figure 15.1　Conventional versus frontier gravity models

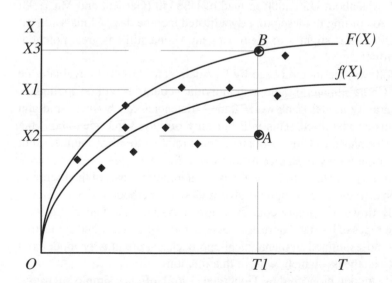

Notes: X is China's bilateral trade flow. T is a vector of explanatory variables.

and Meeusen and van den Broeck (1977).[1] Trade efficiency is defined as the ratio of actual to potential trade flow for each observation, following the popular idea of technical efficiency in production economics (Farrell 1957).

The Chinese case is examined in a broad data set for 57 countries for which data is available from the Australian National University's International Economic Databank.[2] Variable averages of the 1991–95 period are used to avoid problems with yearly fluctuations.

A STOCHASTIC GRAVITY MODEL

The gravity model first applied by Tinbergen (1962) has the form[3]

$$X_{ij} = \alpha_0 GNP_i^{\alpha 1} GNP_j^{\alpha 2} DIST_{ij}^{\alpha 3} DB^{\alpha 4} DP^{\alpha 5} \tag{1}$$

where X_{ij} is exports from country i to country j, GNP_i and GNP_j are the GNP of exporting and importing countries, respectively, $DIST_{ij}$ is the distance between country i and country j, DB is a dummy variable for adjacent countries and DP is a dummy variable for common membership of a preferential tariff area.

Later empirical models all followed the spirit of the Tinbergen model, although there were important variations in terms of the functional forms and variables included. Linnemann (1966), for instance, introduced a complementarity variable, measured by the scalar product of the two vectors representing the commodity composition of the exporting country's total exports and the commodity composition of the importing country's total imports. Wolf and Weinchrott (1973) further expanded the model, following Tinbergen's notation

$$X_{ij} = \alpha_0 GNP_i^{\alpha 1} GNP_j^{\alpha 2} DIST_{ij}^{\alpha 3} e^{\lambda C} + \phi S_1 + \delta S_2 + \rho S_3 + u \tag{2}$$

where C are dummy variables relating to socio-cultural 'distance', S_1 is proxy for economic structure, S_2 is the relative per capita income, and S_3 is the relative ratio of per cent labour force in agriculture between country i and country j.

An important feature of the conventional gravity model is its focus on the relationship at the average. In this study, we are more interested in determining the best performing frontier and the distance of individual observations from the frontier. Differing from Kalirajan (1999), the stochastic gravity model adopted here follows closely the model suggested by Aigner et al. (1977) and Meeusen and van den Broeck (1977) and draws on the procedures used to estimate stochastic frontier production functions in the literature (Coelli 1996). The major difference between the stochastic gravity model and the conventional gravity model described above is that the former has two error terms, one to account for trade inefficiency and the other to account for other factors such as measurement error in the trade variable.

The stochastic gravity model can be defined as

$$X_{ij} = f(T;\beta)\exp(v_{ij} - u_{ij}) \tag{3}$$

where $f(T;\beta)$ is a suitable function of a vector T (such as Cobb-Douglas functions in (1) and (2) above); β is a vector parameter to be estimated; v_{ij} is a random error having mean zero; and u_{ij} is a non-negative random variable associated with the efficiency of trade between countries i and j.

It is assumed that the random error, v_{ij}, is independently and identically distributed as a normal random variable with mean zero and variance σ_v^2. The random variable, u_{ij}, is assumed to have a half-normal distribution or exponential distribution.

In this model, the observed trade, X_{ij}, is bounded above by the stochastic quantity, $f(T;\beta) + v_{ij}$, where v_{ij} accounts for random variation of trade.

Given that the above stochastic gravity model is defined in terms of the logarithm of trade flows, the trade efficiency for export from country i to j is defined by

$$TRE_{ij} = \frac{\exp[X_{ij}]}{\exp[f(T;\beta) + v_{ij}]} \equiv \exp[-u_{ij}] \tag{4}$$

In empirical estimation, the computer package FRONTIER is used (Coelli 1996).

DATA SET AND EMPIRICAL ESTIMATION

The empirical study applies the following stochastic gravity model

$$\ln X_{ij} = \beta_0 + \beta_1 \ln GDP_i + \beta_2 \ln GDP_j + \beta_3 \ln POP_i + \beta_4 \ln POP_j$$
$$+ \beta_5 \ln DIST_{ij} + \beta_6 LANG_{ij} + \beta_7 COMP_{ij} + (v_{ij} - u_{ij}) \tag{5}$$

where X_{ij} is export from country i to country j; GDP_i and POP_i are exporting country's GDP and population, respectively; GDP_j and POP_j are importing country's GDP and population, respectively; $DIST_{ij}$ is the distance between exporting and importing countries; $LANG_{ij}$ is a language dummy; and $COMP_{ij}$ is an index of complementarity of resource endowment between the exporting and importing countries.

The data applied in this study is a cross-section data set containing 57 countries including China.

- Trade flows (X_{ij}) are averages of exports from country i to country j between 1991 and 1995, measured in thousands of US dollars at 1993 prices. Trade data are compiled from the International Monetary Fund's *Direction of Trade Statistics*.

- Gross domestic products (GDP_i, GDP_j) are averages of GDP between 1991 and 1995, measured in thousands of US dollars at 1993 prices. GDP data are compiled from the World Bank's *World Tables*. Note that, following Garnaut and Ma (1993), GDP for China in 1990 was adjusted upward by a factor 2.5 and for the following years derived using this adjusted income and the official growth rate.

- Population (POP_i, POP_j) are averages over the 1991–95 period, measured in persons. Population data are also compiled from the World Bank's *World Tables*.

- Distances ($DIST_{ij}$) are mostly geographical distances between the capital cities of the two countries, measured in kilometres. Distance data are taken from *The Times Atlas of the World*.

- The language variable ($LANG_{ij}$) is a dummy. It takes the value of 1 if the exporting and importing countries share the same language, and equals 0 otherwise.

- An index of complementarity of resources ($COMP_{ij}$) is constructed by the authors to reflect the role of relative factor endowments in encouraging or inhibiting trade flows between trading countries. A comprehensive study of factor endowments and trade patterns by Song (1996) reports quantities of various factors for individual countries. These are first aggregated into four types of resources: capital, labour, land and minerals. Next, taking world average of each factor as 100, indexes for each type of factor for each country are constructed. Finally, an index of complementarity of resource endowment is defined by

$$COMP_{ij} = \frac{1}{\sum_{k=1}^{4}\left[S_{ij}^k * \left(F_i^k \Big/ \sum_{m=1}^{4} F_i^m \right) * \left(F_j^k \Big/ \sum_{m=1}^{4} F_j^m \right) \right]}$$ (6)

where S_{ij}^k is the share of k-intensive products in total exports from country i to country j, F_i^k and F_j^k are indexes (relative to the world average, 100) of factor endowments in exporting and importing countries. It is obvious that if both countries are abundant in one type of resource, such as labour, and scarce in others, and if labour-intensive products are a dominant trade commodity, then a high number can be expected in the denominator. This implies a small overall number; that is, resource endowments in the two countries are not complementary with each other.

The estimation results using the above data set are presented in Table 15.1. The second column gives the results of the conventional gravity model applying the ordinary least squares (OLS) approach and the third column shows the stochastic gravity model applying the maximum likelihood estimation method.

In both models, parameter estimates are all significant (except $COMP_{ij}$ in the stochastic gravity model) with the expected signs.

TRADE EFFICIENCY AND ITS DETERMINANTS

Based on the estimation results and the definition of trade efficiency (4), we can derive trade efficiency (TRE_{ij}) for each bilateral trade flow (Table 15.2). There are two types of average for each country: one with the reporting country as an exporter and another with the reporting country as an importer. The average trade efficiency of the 57 countries was 0.34. In other words, the sample countries only achieved a third of the best performance observed in international trade in this period.

Table 15.1 Estimation of the gravity model

	Conventional gravity model (OLS[a])	Stochastic gravity model (MLE[b])
$\ln GDP_i$	1.279	1.200
	(68.8)	(61.1)
$\ln GDP_j$	0.961	0.935
	(51.8)	(52.6)
$\ln POP_i$	-0.104	-0.113
	(-4.9)	(-5.4)
$\ln POP_j$	-0.166	-0.172
	(-7.8)	(-8.3)
$\ln DIST_{ij}$	-1.014	-0.939
	(-27.9)	(-27.1)
$LANG_{ij}$	0.896	0.906
	(12.0)	(12.5)
$COMP_{ij}$	0.008	0.005
	(2.2)	(1.4)
Constant	-17.609	-14.463
	(-31.8)	(-26.1)
σ^2	2.587	5.075
		(23.3)
γ		0.781
		(36.7)
Log likelihood function	-5885	-5815
LR test of the one-sided error (degree of freedom 1)		139.6

Notes: [a] ordinary least squares (OLS).
   [b] maximum likelihood estimation (MLE). The dependent variable of the regression is $\ln X_{ij}$ (bilateral exports from i to j). Figures in brackets are t-ratios. Total number of observations is 3109.

It is interesting to note that Asian countries—such as China, Hong Kong, Indonesia, Korea, Malaysia, Singapore, Taiwan and Thailand—performed quite well in terms of trade efficiency. Some of the European countries also did well, including Belgium-Luxembourg, Finland, Ireland, Netherlands, Sweden and Switzerland. Surprisingly, trade efficiency for both Japan and the United States (except as an importer) were below the sample average. One explanation is that trade elasticity with respect to GDP is not constant, as large countries usually have lower trade dependency ratios.

Table 15.2 Average trade efficiency indexes for sample countries

Reporting country	As exporter	As importer	Reporting country	As exporter	As importer
Argentina	0.30	0.24	Jamaica	0.23	0.33
Australia	0.30	0.31	Japan	0.31	0.33
Austria	0.27	0.22	Korea, Rep. of	0.49	0.39
Belgium-Luxem.	0.43	0.46	Malaysia	0.54	0.40
Brazil	0.38	0.31	Malta	0.35	0.34
Canada	0.26	0.32	Mauritius	0.33	0.36
Chile	0.46	0.40	Mexico	0.23	0.30
China	0.28	0.27	Netherlands	0.41	0.49
Colombia	0.35	0.31	New Zealand	0.45	0.31
Costa Rica	0.40	0.35	Nicaragua	0.33	0.34
Cyprus	0.21	0.38	Norway	0.35	0.28
Denmark	0.38	0.29	Panama	0.20	0.47
Dominican Rep.	0.23	0.35	Paraguay	0.29	0.29
Ecuador	0.37	0.33	Peru	0.30	0.29
Egypt	0.22	0.39	Philippines	0.32	0.34
El Salvador	0.20	0.32	Portugal	0.30	0.37
Finland	0.42	0.31	Singapore	0.60	0.48
France	0.30	0.35	Spain	0.29	0.36
Germany	0.29	0.39	Sri Lanka	0.44	0.37
Ghana	0.31	0.32	Sweden	0.40	0.33
Greece	0.26	0.32	Switzerland	0.40	0.31
Honduras	0.29	0.37	Taiwan	0.52	0.41
Hong Kong	0.39	0.46	Thailand	0.47	0.41
Iceland	0.28	0.18	Turkey	0.26	0.29
India	0.29	0.27	United Kingdom	0.32	0.40
Indonesia	0.43	0.33	Uruguay	0.38	0.37
Ireland	0.45	0.29	USA	0.23	0.36
Israel	0.36	0.30	Venezuela	0.32	0.31
Italy	0.34	0.37	**Average**	**0.34**	**0.34**

Trade efficiency for China's bilateral trade with 56 countries in the sample was also determined (Table 15.3). The average efficiency index was 0.28 when China was the exporter and 0.27 when China was the importer, both substantially lower than the sample average.

It would be inappropriate to draw any direct implications from examination of individual indices, but it can be noted that, in general, China's efficiency was higher for trade with other APEC economies—especially Chile, Hong Kong, Indonesia, Malaysia, Singapore and Thailand. Taiwan was an exception with which China still did not have direct trade relations. On average, trade efficiency with the APEC economies (excluding Taiwan) was 0.35 for China as an exporter and 0.42 for China as an importer. It must be noted that this efficiency measure

Table 15.3   Bilateral trade efficiency indexes for China

Partner country	China as exporter	China as importer	Partner country	China as exporter	China as importer
Argentina	0.25	0.36	Jamaica	0.34	0.20
Australia	0.34	0.48	Japan	0.25	0.21
Austria	0.09	0.29	Korea, Rep. of	0.20	0.31
Belgium-Luxembourg	0.28	0.39	Malaysia	0.46	0.63
Brazil	0.23	0.42	Malta	0.24	0.06
Canada	0.29	0.43	Mauritius	0.37	0.04
Chile	0.44	0.55	Mexico	0.17	0.07
Colombia	0.15	0.16	Netherlands	0.37	0.26
Costa Rica	0.22	0.43	New Zealand	0.29	0.54
Cyprus	0.27	0.03	Nicaragua	0.18	0.01
Denmark	0.17	0.23	Norway	0.12	0.24
Dominican Rep.	0.33	0.00	Panama	0.66	0.01
Ecuador	0.31	0.30	Paraguay	0.45	0.14
Egypt	0.43	0.14	Peru	0.29	0.60
El Salvador	0.31	0.12	Philippines	0.36	0.36
Finland	0.13	0.40	Portugal	0.14	0.14
France	0.20	0.27	Singapore	0.43	0.53
Germany, Unified	0.30	0.35	Spain	0.21	0.26
Ghana	0.42	0.42	Sri Lanka	0.45	0.13
Greece	0.17	0.12	Sweden	0.18	0.38
Honduras	0.40	0.00	Switzerland	0.14	0.33
Hong Kong	0.59	0.54	Taiwan	0.14	0.03
Iceland	0.04	0.06	Thailand	0.39	0.46
India	0.19	0.17	Turkey	0.18	0.30
Indonesia	0.42	0.57	United Kingdom	0.28	0.23
Ireland	0.14	0.17	Uruguay	0.39	0.68
Israel	0.13	0.20	USA	0.32	0.23
Italy	0.22	0.31	Venezuela	0.21	0.06

has already controlled for impact of the common factors affecting bilateral trade including population, income and distances.

What are the factors determining trade efficiency? In this study, two types of policy variable are considered. The first is policies adopted by governments themselves and the second is regional agreements between governments. To identify the important policy factors influencing efficiency for the whole sample, the following linear function is adopted

$$TRE_{ij} = \lambda_0 + \lambda_1 TAX_i + \lambda_2 FD_i + \lambda_3 TAX_j + \lambda_4 FD_j + \pi_1 EU + \pi_2 APEC \quad (7)$$
$$+ \pi_3 CER + \pi_4 ASEAN + \pi_5 NAFTA + \pi_6 ANDEAN + \pi_7 MERCOSUR$$

where TAX_i and TAX_j are, respectively, the average tariff or tax rate on both imports and exports in the two countries for the 1990–95 period. The tax rates are drawn from the Fraser Institute in Vancouver and are expressed in percentage form (Gwartney and Lawson 1997). FD_i and FD_j are indexes of economic freedom in 1995 which range from 0 (no freedom) to 10 (complete freedom). The freedom indexes were constructed by the Fraser Institute and aggregated over more than a dozen freedom indicators covering macroeconomic stability, the role of government and corporate sector in business, price flexibility, legal system and policies regarding foreign investment and international trade (Gwartney and Lawson 1997). The rest of the variables included in (7) (*EU, APEC, CER, ASEAN, NAFTA, ANDEAN* and *MERCOSUR*) are dummies for common membership of regional agreements.

To see if determination of China's trade efficiency was different from the whole sample, equation (7) is re-estimated using only observations with China as one of the trade partners (a total of 112 observations) (Table 15. 4). All the dummy variables for regional blocs, except that for APEC, are omitted from the equation as China is not a member of any of them.

Equation (7) is first estimated using the OLS approach. However, both the Breusch-Pagan-Godfrey test and the Glejser test suggest that the equations using the OLS approach suffer from a heteroscedasticity problem.[4] The model is thus re-estimated applying the White-heteroscedasticity consistent estimation approach (White 1993). And these re-estimated results are the focus of interpretation (columns 2 and 4 of Table 15.4).

For the results using the whole sample (column 2), the trade tariff/taxes in both exporting and importing countries are found to be insignificant. However, the overall economic freedom index in both countries is very important in determining trade efficiency. The freer the overall economic system, the higher the efficiency in bilateral trade. The strange results on trade taxes may be due to the fact that the freedom indexes already incorporate trade taxes (Gwartney and Lawson 1997).

Table 15.4   Determinants of trade efficiency

	Whole sample		China's bilateral trade	
	OLS	White	OLS	White
Trade tax rate, exporter	-0.0030	0.0005	-0.0039	0.0089
	(-2.9)	(0.6)	(-0.6)	(1.7)
Economic freedom, exporter	0.0165	0.0156	0.0377	0.0405
	(5.8)	(6.7)	(2.3)	(3.2)
Trade tax rate, importer	-0.0031	-0.0011	0.0117	0.0141
	(-3.0)	(-1.3)	(1.8)	(1.5)
Economic freedom, importer	0.0108	0.0103	0.0365	0.0277
	(3.8)	(4.4)	(2.2)	(2.3)
Dummies for regional blocks				
APEC	0.0955	0.0552	0.0651	0.0368
	(6.8)	(4.0)	(1.7)	(1.1)
EU	-0.0333	-0.0416	n.a.	n.a.
	(-2.5)	(-4.2)		
CER	0.1212	0.0552	n.a.	n.a.
	(1.0)	(0.4)		
ASEAN	0.1364	0.0817	n.a.	n.a.
	(4.1)	(2.1)		
NAFTA	-0.1544	-0.1366	n.a.	n.a.
	(-2.2)	(-2.8)		
ANDEAN	0.1825	0.1062	n.a.	n.a.
	(3.8)	(2.2)		
MERCOSUR	0.0221	0.0285	n.a.	n.a.
	(1.0)	(1.4)		
Constant	0.1884	0.1836	-0.1490	-0.1515
	(7.0)	(8.4)	(-0.9)	(-1.3)
Variance equation, α		0.4873		0.5197
		(64.9)		(12.1)
Log of the likelihood function	1185.3	1155.9	59.5	60.1

Notes: OLS denotes estimation applying the Ordinary Least Square estimation approach while White denotes estimation applying the White heteroscedasticity-consistent estimation approach. Numbers of observations are 3109 for the whole sample (first two columns of the table) and 112 for the China bilateral trade sample (last two columns of the table). Figures in parentheses are t-ratios.

While *CER* and *MERCOSUR* did not seem to play any significant role independently of other determinants of bilateral trade efficiency, the impact of both *EU* and *NAFTA* are surprisingly negative. The formation of *APEC*, *ASEAN* and *ANDEAN* helped to improve trade efficiency among member countries.

The results using only the China sub-sample (column 4) reveal similar information. Coefficients for freedom variables in both exporting and importing countries are positive and significant, and trade taxes in both exporting and importing countries are insignificant in determining bilateral trade efficiency. The only exception is that the coefficient estimate for APEC is not significant in the China equation, suggesting that China's higher trade efficiency with APEC economies revealed earlier is mainly determined by the freedom variables in both China and its trade partner economies.

CONCLUSIONS

This chapter has focused on trade efficiency in China's bilateral trade and its determinants in the context of a multi-country world. The stochastic gravity model approach was applied to a cross-section bilateral trade data set containing 57 countries using the average trade flows and other variable values for the period 1991–95 (a total of 3109 observations). Trade efficiency indexes were calculated for each pair of trading countries. Finally, an effort was made to identify the policy determinants of trade efficiency. An equation was estimated separately to examine specifically the mechanism determining efficiency in China's bilateral trade.

Average trade efficiency for China was not only lower than that for the East Asian economies as a group but also below the average of the whole sample. Thus the potential for China to improve trade efficiency and further expand both exports and imports is huge.

The implication from the exercise of identifying efficiency determinants is that inefficiency may partly be removed through appropriate policy reform. For China, an increase in overall economic freedom—which includes a lower level of trade taxes—is helpful to improvement in trade efficiency. A freer economic environment in China's trade partners is also favourable for higher trade efficiency for China.

REFERENCES

Aigner, D.J., Lovell, C.A.K. and Schmidt, P., 1977. 'Formulation and estimation of stochastic frontier production function models', *Journal of Econometrics*, 6:21–37.

Asia Pacific Economics Group (APEG), 1998. *Asia Pacific Profiles*, Financial Times (Finance), Hong Kong.

Breusch, T.S. and Pagan, A.R., 1979. 'A simple test for heteroscedasticity and random coefficient variation', *Econometrica*, 47:1278–94.

Coelli, T., 1996. 'A Guide to FRONTIER version 4.1: a computer program for stochastic frontier production and cost function estimation', Working Paper 96/07, Centre for Efficiency and Productivity Analysis, University of New England, Armidale.

Drysdale, P. and Garnaut, R., 1982. 'Trade intensities and the analysis of bilateral trade flows in a many-country world: a survey', *Hitotsubashi Journal of Economics*, 22(2):62–84.

Drysdale, P., Huang, Y. and Kalirajan, K.P., 1998. 'Measuring and explaining trade efficiency', seminar paper presented at the Asia Pacific Economies Program seminar, Asia Pacific School of Economics and Management, The Australian National University, Canberra, August 1998.

Farrell, M.J., 1957. 'The measurement of productive efficiency', *Journal of the Royal Statistical Society*, Series A, 120:253–81.

Frankel, J.A., 1993. 'Is Japan creating a yen bloc in East Asia and the Pacific?', in J.A. Frankel and M. Kahler (eds), *Regionalism and Rivalry: Japan and the United States in Pacific Asia*, University of Chicago Press, Chicago.

Garnaut, R. and Ma, G., 1993. 'How rich is China: evidence from the food economy', *Australian Journal of Chinese Affairs*, (30):121–46.

Gwartney, J.D and Lawson, R.A., 1997. *Economic Freedom of the World: 1997 Annual Report*, The Fraser Institute, Vancouver.

Kalirajan, K., 1999. 'Stochastic varying coefficients gravity model: an application in trade analysis', *Journal of Applied Statistics*, 26(2):185–94.

Kalirajan, K.P. and Shand, R.T., 1994. *Economics in Disequilibrium: an approach from the frontier*, Macmillan, New Delhi.

Krugman, P., 1991. 'The move toward free trade zones', in Policy implication of trade and currency zones, *Federal Reserve Bank of Kansas*, Jackson Hole, Wyoming, August.

Lardy, N., 1994. *China and the World Economy*, The Institute of International Economics, Washington, DC.

Linnemann, H., 1966. *An Econometric Study of World Trade Flows*, North-Holland, Amsterdam.

Meeusen, W. and van den Broeck, J., 1977. 'Efficiency estimation from Cobb Douglas production function with composed error', *International Economic Review*, 18:435–44.

Polak, J.J., 1996. 'Is APEC a natural regional trading bloc? a critique of the Gravity Model of international trade', *World Economy*, 19(5):533–43.

Song, L., 1996. *Changing Global Comparative Advantage: evidence from Asia and the Pacific*, Addison-Wesley, Sydney.

Tinbergen, J., 1962. *Shaping the World Economy—suggestions for an international economic policy*, Twentieth Century Fund, New York.

White, J., 1993. *SHAZAM Econometric Computer Program: User's Reference Manual Version 7.0*, McGraw-Hill Book Company, New York.

Wolf, C. Jr. and Weinchrott, D., 1973. 'International transactions and regionalism: distinguishing 'insiders' from 'outsiders'', *American Economic Review,* 63(2):52–60.

Yun, S. and Sen, A., 1994. 'Computation of maximum likelihood estimates of Gravity Model parameters', *Journal of Regional Science*, 34(2):199–216.

NOTES

We are grateful for valuable comments and suggestions by Ray Trewin, William Griffiths, Ligang Song and participants of the 26th Conference of Economists of Australia, a seminar at the Australian National University and the workshop on APEC and China at the Chinese Academy of Social Sciences in Beijing. Special thanks are also due to Ligang Song and Xinpeng Xu for assistance on the data set.

[1] For a review of the literature on frontier production functions, see Kalirajan and Shand (1994).

[2] The sections on methodology and the econometric results for the whole sample were drawn from Drysdale et al. (1998).

[3] For a review of the literature on the gravity model, see Drysdale and Garnaut (1982).

[4] The B-P-G test statistic is 100.9 and the Glejser test statistic is 95.72, with 11 degrees of freedom. Both are far above the χ^2 critical value at 5 per cent significance level (19.68). The test results for the China sub-sample are basically the same.

INDEX